The Messiah's tweet and text messages

On

How to know yourself and God,

Worshiping God without politics or religion but in Spirit & Truth

∞ ∞ ∞ ∞ ∞ ∞ ∞ ∞ ∞ ∞ ∞ ∞

The Secrets of:

How to skip all middlemen and go straight to God

LIVING WITHOUT SINNING, WHILE WORSHIPING GOD, IN A SINFUL BODY

The true gospel of salvation

Breaking myths and lies taught on the inspired scriptures

The cultic churches, and why they attack

How to discover your real self, in you

Sodom and Gomorrah and the sins of the Church

(Then & Now)

And many more gems of truth

Donovan B. Harris

i

ISBN-978-1-7340755-0-2.

Dedication

I dedicate this book to the one eternal Father and his son, by their spirits vested in me.

Thanks

Thanks to my dear wife Diana of over seventeen years, for her patience, love, and support. To my sons: Ajani J, and Adael J. A. for their belief and trust in their dad. To my Mom and Dad, Jean and Fernando Harris, for all the good they have done for me. To my brothers Anthony, Ferron, and Leroy for their encouraging words. To my dear sister Blossom, who passed, for the tender care she gave. To all my real friends who have inspired me by their integrity, including John Whittingham and Elder Jackson, who passed. And lastly, and in all ways least, to my many enemies who press me to fight harder, what you plotted for **evil against** my family and me, **G**o**d** **n**ow ha**s** use**d** for good. The proof is before you, **a**nd in your hands. If God is God, turn from your wicked ways, get to know him, and serve **h**im. If position, greed, association, jealou**s**y, covetousness, lies, and money are you**r** gods, **c**ontinue serving **t**hem. "But as for me and my house, we shall serve the Lord." Josh. 24:15. All praise be to the highest God for his marvelous works in the affairs of men.

Another Title

THE TRUE WORSHIPERS and THE TRUE GODS

VS.

THE FALSE WORSHIPERS and THE FALSE gods

How to read this or any other religious or spiritual book

Remember, prayer and meditation are the keys. 1 Thes. 5:17.

The Alpha of prayer and meditation is always to pray and meditate before you open these books: "Thou, Most High Eternal Father, fill me with your spirit and open my heart to a greater understanding of you, Amen."

The Omega of prayer and meditation is always to close these books with prayer and meditation: "Thou Eternal Father, keeper of the spirits. Keep your spirit within me today as my guide as I go about my daily living, Amen." These are models of prayer.

This book is in a format of eternal truth, as the basis on which truth stands. The spirit of truth has presented the reality of truth in this book, which is in no way intended to offend but to allow the spirit of truth to do its work, as only the spirit of truth can, by leading us into all truth. John 16:13. Therefore this book is open for challenges from any source to question the facts presented here.

Text and Tweets

Text messages and tweets are combinations of scripts, both in a scripted or visual print, in a book or on an electronic platform.

Contents

Preface

Introduction

Part 1

Having a solid foundation on what is truthful, about truth, is essential to worship

Part 2

How fools make themselves many, in their self-deceptions and follies

Chapter 8

Chapter 9
A modern parable

Chapter 10

Chapter 11

Chapter 12

Chapter 13

The lust of the demons

Part 3

Slavery in the churches and other places of so-called worship

Part 4

Knowledge is the key

Part 5

Understanding your purpose

Chapter 28

His will is mine, how to know the real purpose of your life.

Chapter 29

Chapter 30

Part 6

Christian and his purpose

Part 7

The spirit, self, and God

Part 8

Here is the power

Having a solid foundation on what is the truth is the only way of *finding self and God, in a confused, modernized, religious, and politically polarized world.* Therefore, it is essential to have real knowledge in this world, to be able to survive and thrive both physically and spiritually.

A world where there are so many voices speaking at once. Many different religions, churches, synagogue, temples, and gods; Politicians, Pastors, Bishops, Priests, and Popes. Therefore, we are left to navigate a maze of theologies and religions, policies and politics, concepts and science, current events, and history, that our so-called leaders are not even sure of themselves.

Consequently, many books and movies containing fictitious histories have been taught over a significant period to keep us ignorant. However, while reading or watching, it is only sensible for us to read between the lines of tricks and, if possible, extract from these fictitious stories principles that will affect realities in real-time, and discard the lies at all cost. (One such story is about Santa Claus and his elves working in the wee hours of the night while all the boys and girls are asleep. I have extracted effective principles from that story that has helped me tremendously, though it is fictitious.) As a result, some basic questions should keep on rotating in our minds: Is my truth real? Is there a God? If so, who or what is this God? Am I the person I am supposed to be? Does a system govern me, or do I make my own decisions? Is the matrix real?

Well, these are some of the main questions we would be asking ourselves, occasionally, if we are able to think outside the box of many-tricks, even as members of the Christian Church, Synagogue, Mosque, non-denominational group, or are involved in any worship in, or outside of an organized cult, religion or political-ideological party. Remember, these are just human-made constructs.

"Is there a God?" "Am I worshiping God?" "am I saved, or a slave?" and "Am I, who I am supposed to be?" These are some of the questions in the hearts of those who can think for themselves. And not only those who are active with a religion, but more so those who are spiritually connected. Am I in tune with nature, the cosmos, with humanity and the source of life? Is there relevance for being, why am I here? However, if you have not thought of any such questions, you might be, in fact, a mentally enslaved entity.

I know, I wonder about those questions too.

For example, I love to sing, which is one of the talents I have. Each one of us has our abilities, skills, or gifts. However, sometimes when I am at a church in the services, or alone with nature, I would wonder, "Am I sending up praises to the source of life when I am singing, as I have been taught to believe?" And if what I am doing is going up to God, why does it feel so typical? Does God hear me when I am praying? Am I even worthy of being listened to when I am trying to "be holy"? And what does this be holy mean? 1 Peter 1:16. Am I doing anything worthy of any merit? Am I genuinely worshiping God? And, is there a source call God anyway?

I also believe that those who preach sometimes will be shouting and carrying on, thinking they are presenting the word, and they might be, I suppose. However, I also believe these preachers have similar questions if they can think outside the box of tricks, such as: "Am I just working up a sweat?", "Am I doing this just because of the money?", "Is it just another payday for me?" "Is this true worship?" "Is there a God?", if they are honest. So, I can't but wonder if all of this matter?

However, with that being said, we do know that the most consistent cooperate human social activity of all peoples, throughout every generation historically, outside of eating is "worship," whatever form it takes. Then, it would be sad to realize that it doesn't matter if it is an illusion that we "worship" or not! If there is

no one to worship.

So, is there a God? How do I know I am worshiping God or the source of life? These questions then become real questions when you can think outside the box. And, what is true worship, if there are so many different types of religions around us? How important is it to know the differences? And what form is this God, if there is one? These are indeed significant questions we have to be boldly honest enough to investigate because they are real questions that define our present and future destiny for good or ill, or do we just keep our head in the sand and keep on blindly hoping?

Introduction

No person living today is perfect, even our beautiful superstars will tell you this. Everyone you and I know, wants to change something about him or herself. As perfect as you think they are, and they think you are, there is something we all would like to change about ourselves. Therefore, nothing in our life is perfect unto itself; however, we can extract from the lives we live, the many books we read, and the movies we watch: lessons, principles, histories, and other essential truths, excluding the nonsense and lies, that can help an imperfect life improves its condition.

Similarly, not everything that is in all the books is necessarily right; however, there are coded principles in each that can enrichen one's life, if one can extract such treasures.

"All scripture given by inspiration is profitable for doctrine, for reproof………." (2 Timothy 3:16-17.) It follows then that those that are not given by inspiration, but by just the will of man, are not inspired. Luke 1:1-3, emphasis on verse three. (By-the-way the first word "is" in 2 Tim. 3:16 is a supplied word not in the original and changes the meaning of the text when used. To translate is human, to understand the right context is divine. Remember that throughout this book.) Therefore, those texts should be scrutinized carefully.

A word, if used wisely, is sufficient.

In other words, know how to pick sense out of nonsense.

Over many centuries the minds of men have been able to capture various concepts, theories, sciences, and stories and have written and created many works of literature, arts, plays, movies, histories, politics, and religions that have embodied the life and intents of the history of man and his imagination.

Many of these imaginary constructs have, over many centuries, morphed into hardcore pseudohistory that has been taught and sold as realities. Therefore, these historical illusions that are integrated with minuscule sprinklings of truth have metamorphosized into magnificent pseudo-realism. Consequently, these false realities have become the psychological framework on which the fabric of many new societies have been built to a great extent, and continue to be preserved without regard for total truth by these various orchestrators of governments. However, these constructs and teachings have been challenged in these last days by the facts. But these illusions that are not experienced by the self and are none realities that have been realized only by faith, which in itself is an illusion without action in truth, have captivated the minds of the masses. James 2:14-26. Examples: John 3:13 vs. 2 Kings 2:1, The Big Bang theory, discovery of a "new world" by Christopher Columbus. The first, second, and third world construct, the story of the Hollywood Christ (Jesus). These are just a few of the illusions that have been accepted as realities and fed to the masses by these orchestrators of deceptions and lies.

Religion, science, history, and politics are the usual instrumental tools that are used in these efforts, to captivate the minds of the masses. Hence, the theoretical theological-political illusions that control the world, with the intent of a one-world government by man.

Notwithstanding, the proposition here is that self is not who you think you are, by the lies you were taught, but you are who you are, by your reality. While faith is not who you are, but who you think you are. However, our faith can only become a reality when we live our experience, which then eliminates the need for hope. (To live your reality is to be truly conscious of the things around and in you) Therefore, we should realize that these are paradoxical forces of both illusions and realities: faith and truth. Consequently, the truth can only be real if experienced by the self and not by faith, as defined in some books. Now, by accepting these fictions as realities, psychologically, the result is to allow an illusion to be self while rejecting self as an illusion. Meaning you have to know who you are to live your reality. If you are living outside of your true self, you are just living as an illusionary identity and not a person. If what you just read went over your head, you really need not only to read but to study this book, and you will see the light of your true reality.

This book is intended to reveal the truth of self and our relationship to the source we call God, if there is such, by the spirit through the son, exposed in the gospel. It will show us how to identify our true self first, making the point that only then can we begin the journey to know the source of your existence. This knowledge then will enable us to worship in spirit and truth by using his coded text messages while living in a sinful world and body. Therefore, we will become true to ourselves and our sustainer when we know ourselves and live in our reality. Not in the illusions that are created by the opposing force of truth.

In our churches today, faith has taken the place of reality to the point where true worship has become an illusion. We are often engaged in so many different faith activities that we consider to be worshiping. These engagements are shown in lots of singing, preaching, reading of the scriptures, and other religious books, praying, testifying, and giving of monies. These activities or forms, when combined in a prescribed order, are looked on by most as worship, but is it so?

In these services, we are also engaged in lots of talking or discussions back and forth with each other. Sometimes even trying to be more verbose in prayer or a study over each other, or sit silently, thinking these activities are worshiping. But are we just entertaining ourselves when we are attempting to sing the right notes or say the right words while considering this to be worship? We even try to be eloquent and intellectual in our presentations, thinking this is worshiping. Yes, "Make a joyful noise unto the Lord, serve the Lord with gladness and come before his presence with singing," Psalm 100, thinking this is worship, but what does all of that mean? However, this is the kicker; what we do after leaving these places of "worship" will testify if what we just did was an illusion or not. If we live otherwise, what then is our reality?

In the "Bible times," we are taught, particularly in the Old Testament, that sacrificing was the essential activity associated with the initiation of worship. Without the shedding of blood, there was no remission of sin. Heb. 9:22. Therefore, a sinner was not allowed to approach God in 'worship' without first offering up sacrifices for his sins. That was the thought then. We also saw Abel offering up sacrifices for his sins. The first seed of Adam to do so. Gen. 4:4.

Then sometime later, people started taking their offerings to the priest. The priest would then take his first, and then the people's offerings to God. Leviticus 4, 9. Hebrews 9. These acts were to prepare them to come into the presence of God, still an initiation of worship. We must become aware that the offering of the sin sacrifice was not worshiping, but an act toward worship, asking for forgiveness first in the process towards worship.

In the New Testament, however, Love to God, love to man, doing Good for and to each other, were considered to be the most essentials of all the acts toward the initiation of worship. "If you love me, keep my commandments." "If you love one another, then they will know you are my disciples." (John 13: 34, 35.) An act always displayed this love towards each other and to God.

If we remember, the Good Samaritan who came to the aid of someone he knew needed help, showed he had a heart of worship. His act was a transition from the old ways of the initiation of 'worship,' as exemplified by the high priests and

Levites, in comparison to that of the new laws of worship: love to our fellow man first; the initiation, which shows we have love to God. 1 John 4:20.

In some places of 'worship' and churches today, there are similarities in these activities that are still encouraged and will not cease. However, the pertinent questions are: Are we called by God to engage in these activities to show that we are worshiping him? Did we make these things up? Do we do such because we know him, or is it just tradition? Some would argue these positions strongly; therefore, many churches are very ardent in these acts: giving offerings, being benevolent in giving, providing for the poor, and visiting the sick and those in prison, etc., however, while some of these acts are considered to be of the true fast. Isaiah 58: 6-7, were they the total actual worship experience by themselves?

And, what are the total essential elements of the authentic worship experience today? How does worship work? Were we given a blueprint for true worship? And can we engage in these present acts within the churches, without truly worshiping God? Questions, questions, questions. And this God. Who is he/she, if there is one?

These questions have been on my mind for over thirty years, and throughout that time, I have been asking the Christian religious leaders and Bible scholars in and outside the religion with which I am associated, for answers. Only to be given conflicting exegesis on these subjects with no end in sight. However, upon a spiritual journey of carefully dedicated personal prolong studies, prayers, and fasting, over these many years, I have gained exposure to many truths that I am now commissioned to present to you on these most pertinent issues.

Therefore, this book will give an introduction on these matters and attempt to initiate and encourage further discussions on these questions and more, with the intent to engage and bring clarity to the minds of those who are also interested in understanding and experiencing this true worship. (Also, for clarity, in this book, cults are religious organizations that have refused to take the truths given to us by the spirit, that has been proven by history and science. But would rather accept and maintain false religious teachings, based on their emotions, traditions, position, and the love of money and power.)

Notes:

Notes:

Notes:

Notes:

Part 1

"If you know the truth and act on it, you shall be free." (John 8:32, James 4: 17)

Therefore, having a solid foundation on what is right about truth is most imperative.

In today's world, truth is considered relative to one's belief system. But realities often correct our beliefs if our belief is not in harmony with the truth of our existence. It should be noted, however, that there is a fundamental difference between our spiritual realities and our physical realities. Our spiritual realities are always consistent with truth, even when we might not be aware of it. While our physical realities are not necessarily so but change accordingly, now, only a spiritual person can understand and know the differences, which is essential for both our mental and physical awareness of self. John 8:32, 16:13.

Chapter 1

The true worshipers

In the book of John, chapter 4, we see the messiah having a mentally stimulating and physically relaxing conversation with a Samaritan woman by Jacob's well. It is one of the most intriguing stories in all the scriptures for many reasons.

First of all, the Samaritans and the 'Jews' were cold war enemies at the time, and have been for many years as much as they were both Israelites. Many years before, back in the time of their forefathers, they had a significant falling out. One felt betrayed by the other on the question of worship; Idols or no Idols? (2 Kings 17.) And, there was no forgiveness up to that day at the well between these two people groups. (John 4:9.) However, here at the well, we now see these two groups being represented again by Christ and this woman. As they engaged in their dialogue, there were references made to the historical sites and traditions of their forefathers. One was trying to show the other which people group was more authentic of the two. One argued that their forefathers worshiped on that mountain, Gerizim. The other stating that worship is of the 'Jews' because it is in 'Jerusalem' that worship happens. Therefore, each argument was to convince the other that their people are the chosen ones who worship the true and living God: Mount Gerizim or Mount Zion?

Now, the Messiah (Christ) gained the upper hand in that conversation by getting very personal about the woman and her life. He had told her about her experience of having lived with five men, and the one she is now with was not hers. At this point, she realized that he was no ordinary man and asked: "are thou a prophet?"

I would like us to note that the messiah separated himself, initially from his disciples, to have this one on one personal interaction with this woman. He was not interested in the group or congregational setting at this time, but a one on one interaction for maximum effect. It is also good to note, that this was her reality; the story of her ancestors was not her reality, but a tradition of the past. Her present life was her reality, she owned it, and Christ was interested in her life, not her tradition, very important.

He had also mentioned earlier to her about this different water from the one she came to get. This water: the living water, he told her, when drank would result in no more emotional thirst for her. This opportunity to her, her future life, was even more attractive to talk about than the sordid details of her past and present life situations. (John 4: 1-43.)

She eventually left without her water pot but hurried back to her home town to share with her neighbors, including the men of her village, the good news of this living water by, which she received forgiveness and was refreshed.

It is important to note that she got the vision and started experiencing the changes right away. (Isaiah 1: 18.) Interestingly, she did not have to show any act or sign of change to Christ to prove she got the living water, and he did not mind. All she had to do was to reason with him honestly. (Isaiah 1:18, Rev 3:20.) This principle of change is also shown with the lepers as they went to the priest to confirm the healing power of the living God. As they proceeded to the priest, they were cleansed, being obedient to his words. (Luke 17: 11-19.) Remember, obedience is better than sacrifice. (1 Samuel 15:22.) Sacrifice, which was the initiation of worship in the old way of thinking. But now the truth (Christ) has come to present the new approach, or new covenant, through obedience.

So, she only had to believe genuinely, and she did. "Believe on the Lord, the Christ, and you shall be saved." (Acts 16:31.) The fact that she left her pot of water showed she was sold out to Christ's good news. That's all it took folks for her to find something more valuable than the temporary water she came seeking to fill her jar. She found Christ; have you? It is also important to note that she experienced a spiritual awakening with Christ: the refreshing spiritual presence, while not being in the designated place of worship: Jerusalem. Did you notice that? Are you stuck in a condition, or with what you came, looking? Or have you found something more valuable? Well, now that you have found the living water, have you done the exchange? (This book will expose you to this living water, that is most valuable than your religion, or whatever else you came with, and hopefully, you too will do the exchange, keep reading.)

Now in their very intense conversation is embedded some of the most profound expressions and teachings the messiah had ever made to anyone, explaining about the true worshiper as he spoke to her. But he chose a woman to tell. That in itself is huge, considering the social, religious, and political climate at the time and even now, towards women, especially "questionable" women.

Somewhere in their religious arguing back and forth, he said to her, "the time is coming, and now is, when the true worshiper will worship the Father in spirit and truth because the Father seeks such a one. God is a spirit, and they that worship him **must** worship him in spirit and truth." (John 4:23-24. This is my thesis text)

This encounter with Christ right here was precisely the changing moment of her brake through that she needed.

Knowing this, the messiah, therefore, moved away from the religious drama, away from the traditional teachings, and spoke of the realities that mattered most to her. It also strikes me as a very strategic move by The Highest God to use the messiah, to reveal such profound truth, to that side of the world, by not just a woman, but one who was on the outskirts of decency and morality. Not through a saint or a virgin. Not through his beloved disciples, as they were not ready. Not through the self-appointed religious leaders of the day, because they also were clueless. There is, therefore, a lesson or lessons somewhere here for us to learn. So, what did he taught here? Well, we see God can use just about anyone he chose to. Wow!! Did you get that? Yes, he can, and he sure does! If only we listen, and guess what? He can use you also.

These statements in John 4, have to be one of the top five, most significant comments the messiah has ever made. These teachings, however, have been misunderstood for a very long time. However, the correct understanding, meaning, and application off will transform many lives, revealing fresh truth about what is true worship, and how to be a true worshiper.

With that said, we must now investigate the meaning and implications of such a statement. So, let's dig in!

Now, first, we must analyze this statement he made.

He said in John 4:23-24. *"The time is coming and now is, when the true worshipers will worship the Father in spirit and truth, for the Father seeks such to worship him. For God is a spirit, and they that worship him must worship him in spirit and truth."*

There are three subjects mentioned here that are essential to a better understanding, and must be reviewed: **'The time,' 'The true worshiper,'** and **'The Father.'** We also have to look at the tenses: **"is coming"** and **"now is"** and then, we have the actions and descriptions, or verbal and adjectival expressions: **"will worship," "in Spirit and truth"** and **"seeks,"** also the characterization of **"God is spirit."** We need to know what that is?

24

Chapter 2

The Time

I would like us to jump right in and start with "**the time**" with your permission.

When the messiah said, "**the time is coming,**" we all would say he was referring to the future. Well, he said, "the time is coming," meaning it was not yet present while he was here. Yes, this "time" says that "sometime" in the future, there will be this "time" when such things will happen. This expression is in the future tense, which tells of a time when the world will witness the revelation of true worship. The questions, therefore, are: How will such things happen, seeing it was to be in the future? And How can we identify this presently, which is the future?

That statement he made also tells us that whatever was going on, either on the mountain top or in Jerusalem, were not considered by Christ to be the true worship. Therefore, they were not true worshipers in either of those places, not by his standard and evaluation at that time.

Now, to appreciate and answer the above questions, we will have to address a few more pressing matters of the past, to give us a reference point. So, remember we are digging, investigating, going through the rabbit hole, if you will. Therefore, we'll have to go back now a little further to see if there was true worship anywhere while Christ was here. Also, because Christ had said '**now is**' which tells us that presently while he was here, such thing was happening. That is, "worshiping in spirit and truth" was going on. So, the obvious question is, where was this "worshiping" happening at the time if he did not see it in those places of worship that had been set aside for worshiping that they both referred? Sounds very contradictorily interesting. In other words, there is a twist here, and we shall unearth it also.

Well, don't just stand there with your intellectual shovels in hand, let's continue digging.

Now, where were these true worshipers worshiping in spirit and truth? We were expecting to see these true worshipers, as we have stated, in those designated places of worship: Mount Gerizim or "Jerusalem," but remember they were not there, by his evaluation. Then how will we identify them if they were not there? Were they hiding? Were they a sect of mystery worshipers? Interesting! Many questions. Remember, we are still going through the rabbit hole, so stay on the path.

Well, to understand this, we have to unearth the first layer and see if there were ever a time when people worshiped the Father in spirit and truth before the messiah. This worship will allow us to identify what true religion was. Then compare that worship with what was happening at present with and around the messiah. We also have to find something tangible to show us, to know what the Messiah was referring to when he said: "**now is**." Is this a fair assessment? OK. This kind of worship will further help us to identify these people then and now. Then we can understand what worshiping in spirit and truth meant, was, and is by looking at this model so that we can answer all these questions.

Well, as we dig intently throughout the scriptures in the Old Testament. All we find that's associated with worship is the sacrificing of animals, as was mention before. In some cases, even of humans, as it relates not only to pagan worship. (Leviticus 18: 21, 20:1-2. Judges 11:30-40. Heb. 9:28.) However, we also find no such reference or evidence mentioned of a group of people worshiping the Father in spirit and truth, while engaging in those ritualistic acts of worship in the Old Testament. Therefore this 'worship in Spirit' is the main contention here that we do not see, which we need to find.

 We also have to remember that worshiping in truth, is relative to whatever you are told by God, at the time God instructs you. Therefore, if God asks you to offer sacrifices and you offer sacrifices. (Levi. 8:1-5, 16:1-34, 19:1-9. Num.15:8-12, 28:2. Ezek. 43:21.) Then you are adhering to the truth relative to that reality because of that commandment he had given at that time. Build me a sanctuary that I may dwell among you. (Ex. 25:8.) However, worshiping both in spirit and truth is what we need to find: the total package. Remember, this model of worship is what the Messiah said the Father seeks from his people. Therefore, true worship should be consistent with the revelation of the will of The Most, High God, at the time, with the elements of the 'in spirit' dimensions being present. In other words, you can't worship God without either the spirit and truth present, at the same time, being in the life of the worshiper. Having historical or intellectual truth alone will not work, that is just information. However, when you have the spirit, you will have the truth, because the spirit does not exist in the life of the believer outside of the truth. John 16:13. Therefore, this is what we need to find!

If we were to look at the timeline of man after he sinned, from Adam to Noah, Noah to Abraham, Abraham to Moses, Moses to David, and David to John, the forerunner of Christ, as close as all those men in the old testament were, after Adam to the true God, none is shown or is spoken off in the scriptures to have worshiped God in spirit and truth, except interestingly, for David. He was the only one who came the closest in doing so on principle. This way of worship is the reason why the Most, High God said of David, at that time, and of none else; 'He is a man after my own heart.' (Acts 13:22.) This form of worship indicates intimacy while David is considered to be one of the greatest sinners in the history of the scripture (2 Samuel 12: 7-13.), he is, however, recognized by the true and living God, to be one of the closest to himself, that revelation is fascinating information, which we will dig deeper into later.

I believe some would ask, what about Enoch or even Job, Elijah, or Moses? Well, although the scripture says that "Enoch walked with God...." (Gen. 5:22-24.), "Job was a righteous man." (Job 1:1, 8.) "Elijah was taken up in a chariot." (2Kings 2:2) and "Moses was a friend of God." (Ex. 33:11.) These statements would indicate that they also worshiped in spirit and truth. However, that type of intimate worship, we did not see and was not shown in the text messages relating to them. But what we know of them and all the others are recorded in Heb. 11: 5-40. These texts show that they all exercised a faith that pleased the Most, High God. However, we have to remember that "faith is the essence of things unseen, the substance of things hoped for," scripturally speaking. (Heb. 11:1.) Therefore, by Enoch, Job, Elijah, and Moses exercising this faith, it shows that they were also hoping for the promise that was to come. The promise, which was the Messiah, had not come in their days. Therefore, by faith, they were able to hold on to the promise, which was not a reality for them. (Heb.11:13.) Consequently, their worship could not reveal to us the missing elements, which we need to find, to identify what true worship is today. These men, though they had a relationship with God, their religion was an outward expression of sacrifices by each, which did not show the "intimacy" that result in true worship. Yes, we do not see that intimacy in those forms of religion, and we need to know these elements to understand what true worship is. This intimacy is what is required, without which there is no worshiping in spirit and truth. Therefore, their religion is not the model for the true worship that we are looking for to see. However, their efforts of obedience to God's commandments were accepted only on the merit of the one to come: the Christ.

So that we are not distracted by the last statements, let me explain further.

What we have to bear in mind is, without the redemption of man from a rebellious state, this worshiping in spirit and truth would not happen. Meaning, that if the Messiah had not come and redeemed man back to the place where the spirit of the Most, High God can come and dwell in man again. As in the case of Adam before sin, except in the particular case, as described by David, true worship will never happen, and the faith of Enoch, Job, Elijah, Moses, and many others would have been in vain. True faith, as defined by Christ, is the essence of things seen, and the evidence of things hoped for, experienced presently. (1 John 1:1-7) (Romans 8: 24-25.) In other words, those of us who are in Christ do not rely on hope and faith as defined by religion but live the sanctified life of the saints presently as a spiritual reality.

Therefore, nowhere in the Old Testament scriptures is there a description of any other worshiping the true and living God in spirit and truth, outside of Adam and David, this may come as a surprise to many. Yes, from Abel's worship to all those who were before the fulfillment of the life of Christ and the outpouring of the spirit on the day of Pentecost, none is described as having worshiped the Father in spirit and truth outside of David. Hebrews 11, summarizes the way those patriots and prophets worshiped. However, none of them is said to have worshiped in spirit and truth. These all exercise their worship externally by faith through their sacrifices offered. There is a difference in worshiping in spirit and truth and worshiping by faith, and this will be exposed to us further as we continue to dig in the word.

I am saying that their worships were accepted by the living God through faith in the Messiah to come. Working with the truth, they knew at the time. However, there was no merit in their worship. What gave them a pass was the faith they had in the one to come, which was symbolized by the sacrificial lambs that were offered by them. David's worship, God, also accepted at that particular time, was also on the merit of faith in the messiah: the son of God. (Heb. 11:32-33.) However, it does not show that they worshipped "in spirit and truth." Not the total package, as David also did. We will look at the revelation of his (David's) worship shortly. They were not able to do so because they relied totally on the sacrifices, they offered that pointed to the promised one, who had not yet come and was the only one that would allow this intimacy to occur again. (Heb. 11: 13.) "These all died in faith," except for Enoch, Elijah, and Moses, who were taken up by God. Those others "not having received the promises, but having seen them from afar off, and were persuaded of them, and embrace them, and confessed that they were strangers and pilgrims on the earth." Yet, they had not experienced the total worship package in spirit and truth.

So, why am I able to say that their worship had no merit in themselves? This pronouncement, to some, might sound blasphemous.

Well, because everyone who worshiped God after sin, in the old testament, worshiped externally by their offerings of sacrifices and gifts, because of sin. Those who worshiped in this way, with their sacrifices, did not please the true and living God. The true and living God did not find "pleasure," "intimacy," or "true worship" in these sacrifices. (Isaiah 1:11. Psalm 51:16.) It is telling us, therefore, that if you needed to offer a sacrifice in worship, you were not worshiping the true God in spirit and truth, and neither could you. (Heb.10.) Why? Because the sacrifices were a part of a temporary external exercise, in which the true and living God found no pleasure. (Psalms 40:6-10, 1 Samuel 15:22.) You see, these sacrifices and offerings were like buffers between God and man. And God does not find pleasure in buffers/customs. God wanted to be in man: the true temple, the same way it was when he created man, but the spirit of God could not enter man at that time because of man's sinful condition. Man would have died if God came into him again, in that condition, man being in his corrupt state; consequently, the buffers/customs. Therefore, to worship God in spirit and truth means God had to dwell in man again through his spirit. Just like he did with Adam before sin, and Christ after sin.

I think some may argue that God had asked them to offer these sacrifices, and God accepted these sacrifices. That is true in some cases, as is shown in the scriptures. (Heb. 11:4.) However, as much as these offerings were asked of by the true and living God, and given to him, this notwithstanding, was not the total package of worshiping in spirit and truth, that we are looking to see, this was far from what God was seeking from man. I know this might be a hard pill to swallow for some, however, keep on reading and it will become more apparent to you.

In Hebrews 10: 1-20, we prove that these sacrifices were temporary and without effect in regards to the cleansing of sin. Meaning, they, the sacrifices, did not take away the sins from the peoples. The sin of the peoples was still there. These acts of sacrifice were just symbolic. The blood that was sprinkled by the priest on the veil in the temple, and then was miraculously cleansed once a year, was an act by the living God to symbolize the forgiveness of sins. (Leviticus 16.) This act was done yearly to show it did not take away sin permanently. (Hebrews 10:4.) This temporary symbolic act is the reason why they could not worship in spirit and truth. To do so, and experience this intimacy, God has to be in you permanently, not around you, and God can't dwell in an unclean vessel. Whenever the true God dwells in you, intimacy will occur. Which is 'into- me- see' God, a reflection of the

Father. (John 14:7-11.) Then there will be no need for manmade temples or sacrifices. However, they had to offer sacrifices even though these sacrifices could not cleanse them for the true God to be in them but was symbolic, and this is the reason why their rituals of sacrifices were ongoing and only lost significance and ended at the sacrificing of the messiah: the real sacrifice of God. Mark 15:37-38.

Also, if these sacrifices took away sin and could have cleansed us, we would not have needed the messiah, the promised one to come. We would not have required a better promise. We would not have needed a new covenant, and they didn't get the promised reality, but those who came after did. Heb. 8,9.

Only the true sacrifice could have cleansed us, for the living God to dwell in us again so that we can experience true worship in spirit and truth. Therefore, this worship of sacrificing was of the old covenant that had no merit in its functions but was a shadow pointing to the true sacrifice to come: the man, the one they called Christ, the anointed one. Heb.10:1-4, Col. 2:17. He was the true sacrifice that would take away the sins of the world, permanently, and not just for a certain set of people, John 3:16, 17; "For God so love the world that he gave his only beloved son that whosoever believeth in him should not perish, but have everlasting life. God sent his Son into the world not to condemn the world, but that the world through him might be saved." Heb. 10:5-10, but for everyone: blacks, whites, and all the shades in between the human race.

These are true factual statements that we hold on to, not just by faith, but now by sight: experience, which means we do not only think of this but have experienced and still are experiencing this. We have not just historical, but actual present empirical proof of such worship in spirit and truth.

Again, in the old covenant, Because of their obedience and faith in the true God, God accepted their efforts. But the true God can't compromise his holy principles; he can't dwell in an unclean vessel, therefore worshiping in spirit and truth did not happen for those. However, now that we have spiritual proof of this transformation in our own lives, we now know the Most, High God has been able to dwell in us once again because of the work of his son. John 14: 10-21, 23.

Remember also, the messiah said, "worship in spirit," therefore we have to find **when** this "in spirit" worship occurred and **what** it was, to clarify the above arguments. Even though we know, we still need to find the tangibility of it.

So, we have a HUGE problem, if no one actually did worship in spirit and truth as a blueprint for us to see and follow, and the above argument would only be an assumptive one.

However, when there is a problem of such magnitude, you should always go back to the "drawing board."

So, what is or was the drawing board?

Answer: The beginning of the MAN, the making of man!! When everything was perfect. The beginning of man is the first place we should look to find the answer to this question.

Please don't be surprised by this if you were thinking well; if we cannot find such an event on earth, we should look to heaven. However, before we go to heaven, I would suggest we exhaust our resources here on earth that we have. Let's start at the beginning and see if there is any evidence there.

Chapter 3

The beginning: 'The Time' (cont.)

"And God said let us make man in our image after our likeness…." (Gen 1:26.)

"And God formed man of the dust of the ground, and breathe into his nostrils the breath of life, and man became a living soul." (Gen 2:7.)

"And God created man in his own image, in the image of God created he him; male and female created he them." (Gen. 1:27.)

"As it is written: eye hath not seen, nor ears heard, neither have entered into the heart of man, the things which God hath prepared for them that love him, But God has revealed them unto us by his Spirit: for the Spirit searches all things, yes, the deep things of God, for what man knows the things of man, except the spirit of man which is in him? Even so, the things of God know no man, but the spirit of God." (1 Cor.2:9-11.)

"The spirit itself bears witness with our spirit, that we are the children of God." (Romans 8:16.)

In the story of the creation of man, we see the composite of man; various elements and features were placed within and on man. First, we see that the man who was from the dust of the earth, an earthly vessel, physically: a head, eyes, nose, ears, mouth, neck, shoulder, chest, back, arms, torso, legs, feet, hands, fingers, and toes; a bodily form with physical features, this was man, having all these features or body parts but still could not do a thing. Why? Well, he, the man, was formed from the dust of the earth, but wait for it! He was lifeless even as a man, having these features; still dust, well-formed dust. (*Scientifically, all the elements within the body of man are within the earth.) Eccles.12:7.* Though we can't say, he was dead, because to be dead one had to have been living before, and then die, speaking of the body, but his state at this time was, however, lifeless. Therefore, the existence of physical man is a form that is lifeless. That is the beginning and end of man, but wait a minute, hold on!! Something else happened. Wait for it, wait for it, then "God blew 'his' breath into man's nostrils, and man became a live-in-soul." Wow!! Did you get that? (Gen. 2:7.) Meaning that now life was manifested in man, he was not only just a form or body anymore, but was now functional, yes, he could now think and move about; he now had life. However, we should note this life came from an outside source: the breath of God; this breath was lent to man by God. Job 33:4, Eccles. 12:7. We need to remember the significance of this. That man is lifeless in his complete physical state, without the breath of life coming from the Most, High God. Not only that! It clearly stated also that man became a live-in- soul, meaning something was now living-in man, that came from God to make this body, which is man functional beyond just mobility, this we often ignore and boast of how great we think we are as men, outside of God. which indicates a state of madness, or just plain dull ignorance. Therefore, we must be taught right and remember that we are merely dust, some say "star" dust, without the breath of the Most, High in us, and that includes all of us: The scientist, Agnostic, Atheist, communist, Socialist, Conservative, Liberal, Extravert, Introvert, Christian, Muslim, 'Jew,' Gentile and those in between, we are all just dust. Without the breath of the source of the universe, whatever name we ascribe to the source, we are not even "stardust," but just earth dust.

However, within the soul of man, body plus breath equal live-in- soul, God placed also the spirit of man. Hold on a minute, and God also placed within man his essence: the spirit of God. Most people are not taught this and do not know this truth of their real existence. Yes, this is what happened in the creation of man. 1 Cor. 2: 9-12, Romans 8:16, this is the reason man is described as a living soul in Gen. 2:7 after he started breathing. Now, this is a truth that many religious practitioners are still in ignorance; they do not have this knowledge. Yes, two spirits were placed in the form man, to make the man perfect with the life that was received, this is the reason the man was now described as a live-in-soul because now the spirit of God and the spirit of man dwelt inside this form, body or house, within the mind as stated in the above texts. The spirit of God and the spirit of man, not just the breath as we believe, taught, and have been teaching in the churches.

Now, the spirit of man is the essence of his spiritual existence, his cognitive self. His body or form is just a house for the spirit of God to dwell. The breath is the life source that enables this body to function physically. Therefore, the entire existence of man on earth is part flesh: dirt, part life: breath and part spirits. While the essence of God is the spirit, and he manifests himself through various elements.

So, God did a marvelous thing in the composition of man. He united himself with the man by dwelling in man through his spirit; after he made man from the dust, blew the breath of life in him, and placed man's spirit in that same body. Think about that for a minute; God dwelt in the original man through his own spirits. Thus, making the original man one with God; God manifesting himself through man. Meaning that the Most, High God was in man by his spirit, after giving the man a spirit of himself. Romans 8:16, this is the true image of God. Now, If God is a spirit and God made man in his image, then what else is the image of God in a man? This revelation means that this image can't be flesh, but spirit: the spirit of man. Therefore, the body of flesh is not the image of God, but a container that contains the image of God, which is the spirit; God giving the man a spirit like of himself. (SIDE NOTE: EVERY MAN NOW ALSO HAS EITHER THE SPIRIT OF GOD OR THE SPIRIT OF THE EVIL ONE IN HARMONY WITH HIS SPIRIT; THE HARMONIOUS OR THE REBELLIOUS SPIRIT. 1 SAMUEL 16: 14-15. PSALM 51. MAT: 12: 43-45.)

The principle here is simply that the Most, High God makes something: a body. Gave life to that body through his breath, then placed something more powerful; the spirit of man, within that thing he had made. Then he placed the most powerful of all; the spirit of himself, his spirit in harmony with the spirit of man that he had placed within that thing: the body, which God had made from the earth, that he gave life.

This knowledge is the fourfold creating principle of the Most, High God. Similarly, the matter that made earth also was formed by the Most, High God, from nothing but himself. Then the earth was formed from matter by The Most, High God, this matter formed, came from nothing, but himself. Then various things were created from the earth, and within the earth, which came from matter that was formed from nothing but himself and then placed within the earth by the Most, High God. After which life was lent to these things, from this eternal source God. (Gen.1: 1-25.)

In 1st Corinthian 2:9-16, it shows that only the spirit of the Most, High God knows the things of the Most, High, and only the Spirit of The Most, High God can reveal these things of The Most, High God to man. It also tells us that the same way The Most, High God has a spirit, man has a spirit. This composition of man is the ultimate likeness or image of the Highest God in man. Where did the man get his spirit? All things come from the Most, High God. (1Cor. 8:6.) Consequently, as shown in the scripture, the spirit of man knows everything about man, just as the spirit of the highest God knows everything about the true and living God. (1 Cor.2: 10-12.) Remember God; the creator was the one who made man, therefore whatever was in man, was placed there by the Most, High God, and came from the Most, High God, reflecting the Most, High God's image, thus the image of God in man.

Because of this arrangement, the man heard and understood the will of the true and living God before sin. And so, Adam had a very intimate relationship with the Most, High God before he sinned. So much so, that the very thoughts of The Most, High, were audible in Adam. The thoughts that the Highest wanted him to know. The man could hear the thoughts of God the eternal, because the spirit of the immortal God was in harmony with the spirit of man, being in man and coming from the eternal God. "The spirit of the Most, High God bears witness with our spirit, that we are children of the Most, High God." (Romans 8:16.) To bear witness here is to testify or speak truth to the recipient, not just by words but also by living that word in and through us. Notice that this text also verifies that there are two spirits within us.

The same way the spirit of the true God speaks to us today in our minds, the redeemed, was the same way Adam was spoken to by the spirit, but Adam was without sin. Imagine Adam had no distractions in a perfect environment, body, and thoughts. The thoughts of the Highest God were very audible to Adam then. Consequently, the worship Adam gave before sin, had to have been in Spirit and truth, because the spirit of the Most, High God was in him, being in harmony with the spirit of Adam.

Therefore, when the messiah said that the Father seeks such a one to worship him, this confirms to us that the restoration of man was essential for this experience to happen again. Consequently, the messiah had to bring man's spirit, back to the original place, that man was with the Father when the true and living God made and dwelt in him so that man can hear God again, and worship God in spirit and truth once more. This purpose was the main reason why Christ came and redeemed man back to his perfect state, which is himself. This state was the critical condition for man to be in; to be able to worship the Most, High in spirit and truth. Again, this pre-sin condition of Adam would indicate that the worship Adam gave to the Highest God was perfectly in spirit and truth. In Eccl.12:13. The scripture states that the whole duty of man is to fear and give glory to the Most, High God. That was the duty that God gave to Adam, and that's what Adam delighted to do. Now, we see no temples or sacrifices, or any of the rituals that followed in the worship that came after man sinned, in the way Adam worship before. Therefore, Adam worshiped in spirit and truth. This worship could only happen because of the spirit of the Most; High God in Adam. Which proves to us that those who worshiped after with their sacrifices were not worshiping in spirit and truth, and neither could they, because of their condition. They had to be redeemed back to the place of having the spirits of God and man being in harmony in them as Adam did before the fall for them to have that experience once again.

Therefore, this also shows that the true essence of man is the spirit that is within the flesh of man, which is God's choice.

As the essence of the true God is the spirit, however, the manifestation of the true God is both in spirit and in the flesh, because he is the maker of all.

Just imagine that you are a car designer and maker, and this is something you delight in doing. Every intricate detail that is placed in and on the car: the model, the specifications in and out are all done as your thoughts, and likeness dictate; what makes you feel good about yourself, what pleases you. This car is now your handy work. You do not belong to the vehicle, but the car belongs to you. This power of creating makes you master and owner over your finished product. If you are satisfied with your car design, construct, and performance, you then put your seal of approval, by adding your name or brand to it.

There is no difference here in the principle of God creating man, except God's creation of man is more intimate. This idea is the same general principle of the way the Highest God manifested himself by creating man, but he goes further than just putting his seal or brand on the car, which is the man. Instead, he puts a part of himself into man: his image, his spirit, along with giving the man a spirit of himself. It is not just his name or a mark, but his presence, his essence, which makes this relationship between creator and creation most intimate ever than any other. This placing of the spirits in man is God putting his stamp of approval not on man, but inside of man, by the indwelling presence of his spirits. Therefore, man belongs to the Most, High God, most intimately than every other living being. While the Most, High God belongs to no one but himself, however, he dwells in man by his spirits. This dwelling in man is the image that he spoke of when God said, "let us make man in our image." Now, to restore man to the image of God was the reason for God to become a man: the man Christ. And this God becoming a man will be explained in-depth as we go.

"In the beginning, was the word, the word was God, and the Word was with God. And the word became flesh and dwell among us. All things were created by him and through him." (John 1:3, Col. 1:16.) This life of Christ is the creation and recreation redemption story of man, as made by God through his son. This story was also the manifestation of the symbolic expression God gave Moses. When he told him to build him a sanctuary that he may dwell among them, God stated sometime after, that he would create a temple not made by human hands. This sanctuary was the body of Christ made by the Most, High God for the indwelling of his spirit again in man. This body of Christ was the co-operate body or temple, just as Adam was the cooperate body of man before the fall. (Hebrews 10:5, 2:9.) Here we now see Christ, the new model of man, the cooperate, man.

We also were, and have become temples of the living God, again, just as in the case of Adam and now as in the case of Christ, by the indwelling of his spirit. It is no more I, but Christ that lives in me. (1 Cor. 3:16, 2 Cor. 4:10, 11. Gal.2:20.) We are now lively stones in the temple of God, the cooperate, Christ. 1 Peter 2:5. This truth of Christ is in the scriptures regarding the true vine. (John 15:5.) Even the Gentiles have become a part of this body. (Romans 11:17-25.) God the eternal's choice. Big difference! This understanding is where many answers lie to the many other questions we have.

Therefore, we have a cooperate entity made by The Highest. The Highest God contains the Father and The Son. The Earth contains all living beings that were created by the Highest in this world, including man, and we as men contain the essence of the spirits, both of the Most, High God and of man. We also have the messiah, the son of the Most, High, who contained the redemptive power of the whole world. He restored man to his former state and better. Did you not hear that we shall be like him? (1 John 3:2.) Yes, he came to be like us so that we can be like him. (Romans 8:3, 8:16-17.)

 This actuality is the reason now the scripture states, the messiah speaking, "I stand at the door and knock, if anyone hears my voice, and open the door, I will come **into him** and **sup with him**, and he with me." (Rev. 3:20.) He is now able, through his spirit, to come inside again in harmony with the spirit of man, and fellowship as before, as he did in the garden when sin was not. This revelation speaks to the redemptive power and the true intimacy of worship that follows. The expression "sup with" talks about the breaking of bread together, having a holy convocation with the Father through his Son, by his spirit, as in worshiping with us, same as reasoning with God. The spirit of the Most, High coming inside of us and fellowshipping with us. This closeness is the real worship experience that is both in spirit and in truth. This truth is what we have found. This revelation is indeed the gospel of truth!!!

The Most; High God made these choices and arrangements because of the nature of himself. Therefore, the perfect relationship of God with the man had to be spiritual. So, God the eternal created a space inside of man where he can dwell therein and reveal himself, his image. This intimate revelation of God and man is never from the outside but is always an intimate internal experience. This inner experience is in a sacred space, a very private place. Where intimacy happens between the Most, High God, and the individual man, this is where true worship occurs. Not in a building made by human hands, but in the mind of man, the holiest place in the true temple, made by the Most, High God.

That is where the "In Spirit" worship took place: within man. If you noticed, he, Adam, did not need to give a sacrifice, not even an offering outside of himself. His worship was a constant communion with the Most, High God, in his spirit. As a result of this, his actions were worshipful to the true and living God. His only reason for existing was the fear of the Most, High God, and to reveal the glory (worship), of the Most, High, through his life choices, guided by the spirit of the Most, High God in him. This beautiful experience is the worship we are called to give today, just like Adam gave before the fall, and in the same way, the Messiah gave to the Most, High God after the fall. Christ was not just offered up as a sacrifice but offered first to live as a sacrifice in total obedience to the Father, just as Adam did before the fall: a living sacrifice. That is the worship experience we are redeemed to give.

Keeping the garden was man's physical function or work, and allowing the spirit to lead him, was his spiritual function of worship. It is essential to note also, that the body was made not just for the indwelling of the spirit of God and man, but the body was also made to work, to function. Hence, the reason for the breath. There is nowhere in the word of the Most; High that man should only be a vessel for the spirits to dwell in; no, the man was also designed to work. We should not just be spiritually minded but also physically functional. That is the essence of the existence of man; to work for and give worship, to the Most, High. The result was and is total obedience to the true and living God by the indwelling spirit of the Most, High God in us. **Hence worshiping in spirit and truth is a life, not a lifestyle or an occasion, just as the messiah demonstrated in the way he lived.** (by the way, Christ did not go to the temple to worship but to teach, however in teaching the truth, he was praising the Father, and the religious leaders hated him for it, no difference today. (Luke 2:46-49, 4: 14-32. 19:47.)

38

This life seems to be so simple to be true. However, this is what true worship is. First, there has to be an intimate connection within, with the Highest God, by his spirit. Then our actions reflect this arrangement that is within. The outward expressions will be consistent with what is inside. Just the same way, Adam; before sin, and the messiah did after sin. This life experience of Christ is the blueprint of which we seek. This life of Christ tells us that wherever we are, we should be worshiping the Most, High God in what we think, say, and do. **Worship is never a special event somewhere, where we have to dress up and act sanctified.** Then after leaving that space, go back to our 'normal' ways of living, which is not true worship. That is what is called variableness, having a form, formality to Godliness. Changing from one state to another and then back again: religion. If the Most, High God is in you, there is no variableness because there is no such thing in the true and living God. (James 1:17.)

Chapter 4

How does real worship start?

The initiation of real worship is never congregational, within the context of the New Testament and presently, but individually, within the mind of the believer. It could happen within a congregation, but this experience must happen first within the individual. The person has to have an encounter with the spirit of the Most, High God first, independent of everyone else. If those within the congregation or that physical space had an experience with the essence of the Most, High God before, then they also who are a part of this group would have been experiencing the power of the true and living God in their lives. The scripture in Phil. 2:12 tells us to work out our "own" salvation with fear and trembling. That's it, right there! Work it out! This term "own" means it is an individual experience. This working out occurs within the mind of the individual.

My experience of true worship is not dependent on another person's. Your knowledge of true worship does not depend on another's. (Phil.2:11-13. John 2:22.) Though the scripture state that we "should not forsake the assembling of ourselves together, and as one iron sharpens another, likewise the countenance of one brightens the other." (Heb. 10:25, Prov. 27:17.) However, these text messages should become more evident in the context of the entire word. In other words, the explanation or interpretation should harmonize with the spirit of truth, and these acts of coming together should be for obvious reasons for encouragement and strengthening.

However, having a personal, intimate worship experience every day, every hour, every minute, and every second takes precedence over everything else. Not only that, but only when the individuals live such a life, can a genuine assembly and encouragement of the brethren happen, instead of what we see happening in the churches today. With all the lousy living, the covetousness, the hate, the greed, lies being told on and towards God and his people, coming from the pulpit, etc. Coming together under these conditions will and continues to only result in discouragements, weakening, death, and the destruction of the ignorant people. This condition indicates that those experiencing that type of living has not been redeemed and are still outside of this experience of true worship. The worshiping of the devil will always be their portion, even though they think they are praising God. (Job 36:12, Proverbs 5:23, 10:21, Hosea 4:6.) "If you get down and quarrel every day, you're saying prayers to the devil I say." Bob Marley.

Now, anyone with just basic common sense will know that going to a field that has more tears than wheat will result in less reaping and more exhaustion. Therefore, from a spiritual perspective, we should be wise to go somewhere to assemble, where we are refreshed, replenished, strengthened, encouraged, and empowered. And this means most times; you might have to be by yourself with God, just like the messiah did, or with those of like minds. After having that refreshing, then you can refresh others. (Mark 1:35, Luke 5:16, Luke 6:12, Matt. 14:23.)

This refreshing is why each person needs to take time out every day to meditate and feed on the inspired words of the Most, High God, being intimate with God. Remember, I said the inspired word of God and the presence of his indwelling Spirit. This act, the Messiah did, as he lived on this earth. It was most important for him to remember that he could do nothing by himself. It was the presence of the spirit of the Father in him that did the work. We all have to understand and reach this place of awareness, not just intellectually, but also experientially. (John 5: 19, 30. 12:49-50.)

The Messiah was not only our savior and redeemer; he was and is also our real example. This truth means we can and must live the same way he did. (Romans 8: 8-10.) If not, we will not be able to worship the Most, High God in spirit and truth, as he did. However, the good news is, he has reestablished that connection between the Father and us. Therefore, the spirit of the Father and the son can now dwell in us again, as was the case with Adam before he sinned and the messiah after Adam sinned, and you do not need to be in a church for that to happen, because you are the living temple. This indwelling of the spirit proves that there is no excuse for us not to live a sinless life, even though we are sinful by nature. (Romans 8:1-17.) This living by the spirit, too, shall be proven in this book; *how to live above sinning while in a sinful body.*

Remember, on the day of Pentecost, each disciple had to have had an individual experience with the spirit moving on each heart separately as they waited, first. When they all had that encounter, then the spirit of the Most; High God was able to be poured out or manifested in a fuller measure on all those who were present. (Acts 1:13-14, 2:1-4.)

The mind of the person has to become aware of the presence of the spirit of the Most, High God. The person has to acknowledge that the spirit is ready and waiting to come and dwell inside, where the spirit belongs. This experience is called the conviction of the spirit. (John 16:7-8.) This experience of conviction is within the mind of man, not the body, as some people believe, as the spirit of God is not subject to the fallen nature of man. When the spirit of the most, High God comes in, the scripture says: he the spirit of truth will not only convict but will also guide you into all truth. (John 16:13.) This guiding and conviction are never about your feelings or emotions, but your consciousness. You are only guided in your mind by the spirit because it is in your mind where the spirit dwells, and not by your emotions or feelings as many are falsely led to believe. (my people perish through lack of knowledge, meaning, they do not have the spirit of God, because when you have the spirit of God, you also are knowledgeable.) (Hosea 4:6.)

One of the first sets of truth that is revealed by the spirit of the Most; High God is; you will become aware of who you are as a created being, by the true and living God. What you are composed of will be revealed to you by the spirit of the Most, High God, in you. Many are confused about who they are and, as such, are confused about who God is. Therefore, they are not able to worship the Most, High God, in spirit and truth, because they do not know who they are; Consequently, they can't understand who God is. (Romans 11:33.) Therefore, it is imperatively essential for you to know who you are, to initiate the journey to having the right knowledge of God, and that knowledge comes only from the spirit of God in you.

There are many steps, though, that will need to be taken for this to be realized, this knowing of 'self.'

What the spirit will reveal to you first is who "self' is. The spirit of the Most, High God does that first, because you will not begin to know who the Most, High God is until you know your true 'self' first. You can't be taught the deep things of God until you know yourself. (Phil. 2:8. Heb. 5:7-8.) Also, to understand and appreciate this truth, we have to become humble; otherwise, we will become arrogant and prideful as Adam and Lucifer did, and lose our second estate.

Now, think for a moment, if you are the image of God and you do not know what you are constituted off, how can you begin to know God, who is far beyond finding out? Wouldn't you think that God has revealed reflections of himself in you, you being his image? This knowledge, which is giving to us, is an introduction to the realities of God. Remember, an image is the reflection of the original. We will pick this up later.

If you are within a religion or group that does not teach the true constitution of man and his true identity and functions, that religion or group has not had an encounter with the spirit of the true God as yet, at this level and is possibly a cult. Remember now, being emotional is not being spiritual. Many Christian are very emotional and make the mistake of thinking being sensitive is being spiritual. The difference is, decisions should never be made on our feelings or emotions, but on spiritual principles: consciousness. In other words, *a person who makes decisions because of the way he or she feels, and not on principles of thoughts, being inspired by the spirit of God, is not spiritual.*

Therefore, the more ignorant you are, the more emotional you become in making decisions. This ignorance of self is the reason the scripture says: "My people perish through lack of knowledge" Hosea 4:6. Where emotions and feelings are abundant, awareness is absent. With the right knowledge and consciousness of self, from the spirit, our sensitivity is restricted to its rightful place. Those who are ignorant are usually very emotional on spiritual issues, and all Christian leaders who are deceivers, do like to have these types of unaware sensitive ignorant people in their congregations. This way, they can manipulate the ignorant flock by exploiting their emotions. We will not condemn them, but pray that they too will soon have this spiritual experience of true worship.

Let's recap some of what we have learned so far: (Gen. 2:7. Job 32:8. 1 Cor.2:11. Psalm 51:11. Romans 8.)

The Most, High God created man: the lifeless form, or body.

The Most, High God then gave life to this lifeless form: Breath.

The Most; High God placed the spirit of a man inside with the breath of man.

The Most; High God also has a spirit of himself.

The Most; High God also placed his spirit inside of man; the spirit of the true and living God.

The spirits of the Most, High God, and the spirit of man were in total harmony within man before sin.

The true worship "In spirit and truth" takes place inside the mind of a man.

The man was in total obedience to The Most; High God because of this arrangement.

Man is the possession of the Most, High God.

Man doesn't own himself; however, he can only function at his highest level by 'self'; self-being the image of God, which is his spirit.

Man is stamped or sealed on the inside by God through his spirits. The spirit of man is the cognitive self of man, which is also a part of the image of God.

Man has both the spirit of himself and the spirit of God in him, while in a physical space or body.

That constitutes the constitution of man.

Chapter 5

The choice of Adam

Adam, who had all these attributes mentioned above, was now able to choose to worship the true and living God. We have to remember that the Most, High God Made Adam and Eve also with the freedom of making their own choices. In Gen. 2:15-17, we see that the true and living God gave man the freedom of choice. However, this freedom was a tremendous responsibility which carried with it both irreparable ill consequences, or greater blessings even in man's capacity. Man's decision would prove his outcome. This principle remains with us today; however, this is one thing that we have total dominance over. The omnipotent God had made us and has given us this power of choice. Even after sin, we still have the freedom of choice to determine our destinations.

It is interesting that after Adam had made his choice to sin, the omniscient God had to come looking for him. Why would the omnipresent God, whose presence is everywhere, need to look for Adam? (Gen. 3: 8-13.) Have you ever thought of that?

Well, before Adam had sinned, the spirit of the omniscient God was always within Adam, as we have learned. So, the Highest did not need to go looking for Adam as they were still in communion: in oneness, intimacy. Remember, Adam would worship the Father in one way and one way only; that was **in spirit and truth**. The Father was in Him both in spirit and in truth. The spirit of the omnipotent God was the essential element of Adam's consciousness and worship. However, that had changed. Immediately upon Adam's choice to sin, the spirit of God left him. The worship was no more in spirit, as the spirit of the omnipotent God cannot dwell in an unclean vessel: a rebellious mind because Adam had chosen to rebel against the eternal God. This rebellious state of mind was the reason God had to come now and look for Adam, showing that there was no intimacy anymore because the Agape relationship changed because of Adam's rebellious choice. God had to now communicate with Adam from the outside. Gen. 3: 8-11.

45

Now, how was it possible for a perfect human, made by a perfect God to ever sin? This question has left many baffled, confused, and suspicious of God. However, there is no need to be wary of God. Why? Well, we have to remember that the image of God was in man. Meaning he, the man had all the qualities of God through the spirit of God at a lower level while he had the freedom of choice to make his own decisions. Being perfect does not mean you have no choice, as we have seen, and having options does not mean you will choose to do one thing and not the other. Well, the man had a choice, and he chose evil rather than good. Choosing evil here meant that man interfered with what was forbidden by God. I have to emphasize here that God will not restrict the gift of choice that was given by him to man.

In the Garden of Eden, the choice was clear. We see Good, and we see Evil. Two elements of creation by God. Yes, God created both good and evil for his purpose and glory. Isaiah 45:7 confirms that God created evil, Surprise!!

This creation of evil by God is misunderstood by many, hence the confusion of how a perfect man could sin. We have to acknowledge first that everything that was made by God was perfect and for his glory and his alone. (Col. 1:16-17.) Therefore, that being said and understood meant that evil was also made for his glory, too, just as good was for his glory. Everything made was "perfect," this included evil. Yes, you read that right. (Gen. 1:12, 31, 2:9, 16-17.) The "perfection of evil" is what is known as God's purpose. This truth of the scripture must become clearer within the proper context, of course. Anything and all that God made was for his purpose and his alone. Somethings are for our good, and others are not, but all are for his glory and his alone without being all scientific and complex about it.

I will give simple illustrations, if possible, by just stating that God made good and evil for balance in his creation. Similarly, as night and day, why would you run in the dark when you can't see, then blame God for your injuries? Up and down; why would you try to go up to get down, then blame God? Left and right; why would you teach that right is left and left is right, which confuses, then blame God? How does this balance work? Well, God has given us a mind to think, along with natural laws, applying common sense and nature. To caution you, the context here tells that evil is not sinning, but disobedience to God's will is. Also, evil existed before man did, hence the ability to choose, and everything was perfect.

The workings of evil in this formula is only for the Omniscient one to know. It could be like an element to a secret recipe or sauce that is not to be shared, which, if taken alone, will kill you. However, his will must be in whatever way God desires; we will not know everything; therefore, all we need to do is trust and obey in this regard.

This trust was the problem Adam had; he had a choice to trust God but did not, which resulted in the fall of man. Therefore, with the absence of the spirit of God in Adam because of his rebelliousness, the man began to die. This separation from God is the death that Gen. 2:17, speaks off. The man started dying the second death; that second, the spirit of the Omnipresent God left him, instantaneously. Therefore, the perfect man became imperfect because of the presence of death in his life, a result of his disobedience.

It is vital also to know that with all the attributes within man, the eternal God gave man the freedom of choice, to choose anytime, anything he desires, whether good or evil, while the spirit of the Omnipresent God was in him. Remember, the "tree" was of the knowledge of good and evil. The spirit of the true and living God in man does not prevent man from making his choices, even today, this truth is fundamental in our relationship with God, and should be remembered at all times. We can also say that now that man has had knowledge and experience of evil, he can now decide to choose good rather than evil, because of this knowledge, love, and obedience to God.

The 'tree' here in the garden is a symbol of knowledge of evil, good, kingdom, prosperity, dominance, etc. The word garden is also a term used to refer to the home.

The "tree" in the garden was placed there for man to exercise his power of choice. This tree was also a test for man. However, upon that choice, if it is wrong, the spirit of the Omnipotent God will no more dwell in man and will leave man immediately upon his decision, as we saw with Adam. If the choice is according to the leading of the spirit, which is the best choice, the spirit will stay. Now, if the decision is right, the spirit will still be with the man and will work with the man to make the best choice. However, Adam decided to make a wrong choice, and the spirit of the eternal God left him immediately upon his decision. We should not believe, however, for a moment that Adam had only two ways of choosing. No, he had many options. There were good, there were better, and there was best. He also could have waited. He even could have rebuked the woman, his wife, for good. He did not have to think he only had to choose between good and evil; he had better and best options also. You can use your imaginations to figure out further what these other choices could have been if you were in that position, yes, but we are placed in this position daily, even now, as you read. Ok-ok-ok, so he could have chosen better by standing his ground and not participate with Eve. And best would be, having Eve by him, working together and taking brakes together. That way, he could have prevented her from straying from his side. It is still a proven fact that when both spouses work together, there are successes in many ways. Any couple that can't work together should not be together in the first place, as disaster is inevitable.

However, God had made them compatible to work together, and they were doing so. Is it a possibility that Adam might have been working and was too preoccupied with something else? Two issues that still affect relationships today. You have to remember also that while they were both perfect, there were some differences, including; the man likes to see things while the woman wants to hear words. Therefore, they would have responded to some things differently. If that were true, however, they were to have complemented each other with those differences. Their differences the devil observed and used to his advantage. He knew that Eve was very curious, like to explore and learn as much as she could. As is the case today, while Adam likes to be focused and do his work. Though there was nothing wrong here, this state caused an opportunity for the devil, not in the perfect creation of Adam and Eve, but their relationship with each other. She was supposed to have been a helper, not a distractor. He was supposed to be a supporter and a nurturer, not a loner. It was their responsibility to understand each other, not God's. Is it possible also that there was no courting before marriage between the two? I know this sounds strange, but this could have been the reason why their communication was not perfect, though they were perfect, even with us, communication is still a big problem today. This issue was how the devil was able to get in and always does, by communicating with his victims. Miscommunication with each other, on the other hand, was the reason in the way they explained what happened after God confronted them for disobeying his words.

Adam blamed Eve as if he did not have a brain of his own. He gave his power over to Eve; it seemed, right then and there. It also shows that he did not act responsibly. This response by Adam shows that the irresponsibility of the man started way back from the first home: the Gordon of Eden. Eve blamed the serpent that deceived her. This response made more sense to a certain extent when you look at the case objectively because it stated that the deceiver did beguile her. I'm not trying to make any excuse for Eve; however, Adam had no reason either. (Gen. 3.)

To make this clearer, remember the serpent spoke to her. This interaction was a spirit being manifesting in this physical form to mislead the woman. He is Lucifer, the one who was in heaven. He became known as the devil who revealed himself as a serpent being, not a snake. (Isaiah 14:12, Rev.12:12.) This operation was all spiritual science. The problem is this is too much for some scientists and theologians to handle. We will look at this in a different book.

So, the Omnipotent God had to come looking for Adam, meaning that the spirit of the Omnipresent God was outside of Adam because the spirit of God had left Adam. We need to remember that this proves that **the Omnipresent God can not dwell in a place or person if his spirit is not there**.

Therefore, we now see man beginning to "worship" externally by the offering up of sacrifices to the Most, High God, after he had sinned. This, the true and living God had told him to do. The starting point of this offering of sacrifices was after God made them coats of skin and clothed them. (Gen. 3:21.) The coats of skin came from an animal; the animal's blood was also a symbolic payment for sin. There was no merit or holiness presence in the blood of the animal. The coats that covered them both symbolized the righteousness of the one to come. There was no righteousness in the coats either. These were all symbolic. "Without the shedding of blood, there is no remission for sin." (Heb.9:22.)

Thus, started the offering of sacrifices until Cain killed Abel, and put a temporary end to this form of worship. Subsequently, Seth arrived and got a son named Enos. (Gen. 4:3-16, 4: 25,26.) And the man started calling on God again through these rituals of sacrifices once more. This mode of "worship" was to continue over many centuries before someone would worship again **in spirit and truth**. This place is where the messiah comes back into the narrative.

This killing of Abel by Cain showed the result of a man losing his first love and him coming under the influence of evil by the effect of sin. We can safely say probably, within a short time, Adam messed things up. Therefore, he had to leave from his first home after the spirit of the Most; High God left him. (Gen.3:22-24.) We can also see that man started digging his own grave, the minute he found himself outside of the Gordon of Eden, from whence he was living, showing that he No more was in an intimate relationship with God.

Now we need to go back to the question of what was the messiah saying? when he said: "now is" **We have just established that true worship was, that is worshiping in spirit and truth. This worship is the fellowship of the Omnipotent God in an intimate communion inside the mind of man.** The presence of the spirit of God has to be in harmony with the presence of the spirit of man. No one had or has been able to show how to worship the Father in spirit and truth as Adam did after he had sinned up to the time of Christ, except for David giving us a peek into such worship. He asked for and showed us the way, which is in the son of the Most, High God, and how to obtain such worship. (Psalm 51.) But worship was now outside of man because the spirit was not able to dwell in this unclean vessel: man. **He was now defiled and doomed to eternal death**. (Romans 6:23.)

However, in Psalm 51, we see a perfect model of the first initiation of moving toward true worship after sin. This worship was a 'special' experience by David. I use the word 'special' to indicate a uniqueness that I can't explain entirely. In verse 1-3, David's acknowledgment of the presence, and the mercy of the Most, High God, and his sins simultaneously, proves he was connected to the truth by the spirit. Then he asked the true and living God to wash and cleanse him from his sins. This initiation was a faith request because the messiah had not come and died as yet. In verse 4-7, he reveals that sinning with his body and mind is sinning against the Most, High God. Though he was conceived, and formed in sin and iniquity, by his parent, he now realized that the Most, High God desires truth in him and has given him the truth to know wisdom. Not because he was sinful by nature, excuses him to sin.

Now he asked the eternal God to purge him and wash him so that he can be clean. In verse 8-10, he asked for joy even after the correction of the Father; and the Father to forgive and forget his sins and iniquities. In verse 10, he gets to the meat of the matter. Now David asked the Father to create in him a new heart, or mind; righteous ways of thinking, and this will renew the spirit of the man in him: his spirit. In verse 11-12, he acknowledges that the spirit of the Most, High God is also in him and asked the Father not to leave him by withdrawing his spirit from him: the spirit of God. It is only through the knowledge of the spirit of the Most, High God in him, David, which gives him the joy to know of his salvation. In verse 13-15, he testified of the truth of the result of these acts by the Most, High God. He will then teach the ways of the Most, High God, and sinners will be converted to the true and living God, by his teachings. He will continually sing forth the praises of the Most, High God, for his wonderful works within him. In verse 16-19, David testifies to the true knowledge of the Most, High God, that the true and living God does not desire sacrifices or burnt offerings, but the sacrifice of a broken spirit; a broken and contrite heart, and mind. This true knowledge could have only come to David through the spirit. To acknowledge that God did not seek the sacrifice of animals when that was the only way that was taught to go to God, this was thinking outside the box, at that early stage. This experience also shows that when the mind is in tune with the spirit of the Most, High God, then and only then will our lives as offerings be acceptable to the Most, High God. Then as David did, we can worship the true and living God in spirit and truth also. This worship became a reality for David, and faith was replaced by him experiencing this reality of true worship. Likewise, with us more so, having been redeemed by the messiah back to God. We now live this reality. Not by faith, but by evidence of his spirit being alive in us. (John 16:13-15.) As much as these expressions of David were prophetic, they were also a reality for David as proven by the statement of the Most; High towards David and Christ. (Acts 13:22-23. Matt. 12:18, 17:5, 2 Peter 1:17.) The word "Beloved" is consistent with the expression "of my own heart," therefore, both expressions are in the same vein of the thought of "intimacy." Speaking of this love between the Father and his sons.

Let us recap a little of what we have learned so far.

The true and living God made man.

The Omniscient God put his spirit in man, who also has a spirit of man that was placed in him by the Omnipresent God at creation.

Both the spirit of the Most, High God, and the spirit of man were in harmony, resulting in an intimate relationship between the true and living God and Man before sin, which resulted in worshiping in spirit and truth.

The man Adam was given the freedom of choice but chose to rebel against God, while the spirit of the Most; High God was in him, which resulted in the spirit of God leaving man immediately, because of his rebellious heart: mind, telling us that God does not force his will on man.

After the separation, the true and living God comes looking for the man.

All interactions and worship were now done outside of man, through symbols and rituals, not inside in the spirit, as we saw with Adam before he fell. Because man now lived with a rebellious spirit towards God, he had to take an outside gift or offering of sacrifices to God. (Gen. 4:3, 4. Heb. 11:4.)

Therefore, man could not worship anymore in spirit and truth; just an outward ritual of the sacrificing of animals was now his portion. **The worship in spirit and**

truth is a consciousness internal spiritual experience that only happens when the spirit of God is within man, being in harmony with the spirit of man. It was not the will of God towards the man that his spirit should leave him. The Most; High God did not find pleasure or intimacy in those sacrificial offerings. He could not, as this was not the original plan God had for man, in the way God had made him. (Isaiah 1:11-17, Psalms 51:16, 17.)

However, God allowed the man to engage in these external practices to teach man of his dependence on the true and living God, from an external perspective. Even though the people chose to rebel against God, he granted mercy to the participants in these external rituals of sacrifices.

In Psalms 51:17, David speaks specifically to the spirit of sinful man after brokenness. This brokenness will then be able to be restored and fill by the spirit of God, through his son. Then the true and living God will be able to come and fellowship within man once again, which will result in worshiping in Spirit and truth. This David tasted, whose linage the messiah came through. (Rom.1:3.) Therefore, David's experience was a prophetic experiential taste of what was to come. Praise be to the Most; High God for his merciful acts in the affairs of man.

This revelation is a fascinating truth that has evaded many religious practitioners for thousands of years.

Chapter 6

The Living and the spiritual Dead

The visual aid of the constitution of man:

Spirit gives Life; John 6: 63

Perfect man constitutes Body + Breath of life + Spirit of man + spirit of the living God.

The body contains all the physical components in one form.

Breath of life makes the body functional.

Body = dust (None functional material man)

Body + breath of life = living man. (Carnal Man, not sure who he is)

Body + breath of life + spirit of man = existing soul (conscious man, being aware of his existence)

Body + Breath of life + spirit of man + spirit of God = living Soul (Spiritual Man, being aware of his total dependence on God)

The living soul is composed of the body and the breath of life. Within the breath of life are the spirits of God, and the spirit of man. Within the spirit of man lies the spiritual consciousness, which is in harmony with the spirit of God within the mind.

Let's look at the car again. The frame is the body. The brain is the engine. The spirit of God and the rebellious spirit of man, I would liken unto premium sustainable and cheap un-sustainable gasses inside the engine. Both will not occupy the same space at the same time for optimal functions. The ignition switch is consciousness. And the spark is the knowledge that starts the engine. The knowledge is the connectors within the consciousness of the mind. The mind is the computer in the car.

By-the-way **a living dead is a person who does not have the spirit of God in him**. He is just an existing soul. Adam became a 'living dead' after the spirit of God left him. He was like an expensive car having cheap gas in the engine. This car would be putt-putting, blowing out smoke, and not running on all cylinders, then comes to a halt in very short order.

It eventually becomes a car that looks very good on the outside and has all the modern features that you would want but has to be driven by a tow truck, going wherever the tow truck driver wants.

The tow truck is the fallen nature, and the driver is the spirit of the Devil because there is no presence in the vehicle of the spirit of God. Now there is no consciousness of the true state of its condition; therefore, it will just go with the flow of things, wherever the wind blows as they say.

This unconscious condition is the reason we associate sleep with death; because there is no spiritual consciousness or awareness during sleep, even though you are breathing. Yes, you are alive: breathing, but you are dead, as in not conscious. Some people are not aware of who they are, and they are just existing but not living. These kinds of people repeat the same mistakes generations after generations because they are not spiritually conscious. They assume others' views of who they are supposed to be and are in an unconscious spiritual and social state of being, not knowing who they are for themselves. They are like zombies, living dead who are destroyed daily by a socio-economic-political system that is established to consume them. Then some think they know who they are by assuming other people's identity for themselves. They believe that the devious act now favors them, but they also are spiritually dead zombies walking around with a false identity.

 Many who call themselves Christians are also just existing. They are just alive; functional, yes, but lack the indwelling spirit of the true and living God, not living. Those Christians who are not aware of the truth because of the absence of the spirit of the true and living God in them are also like zombies, living dead. They are destroyed daily by a socio-religious political system that is established to consume them too. All of these systems are control by the same power: the power of what some people call the devil. This condition is one of the many reasons there is no difference between the religious churches and the political world today.

It is essential to note, at this time, the differences between the body of Christ: the true church, and the assembly of the devil: the false church. Revelation 17 and 18, describe this false church. In the bible, the false church is a symbol of a woman, and the true church is a symbol of a woman in the text messages. The woman in verse 1 of Revelation, chapter 17, is described as a whore who rides a red dragon and sits on waters, which is the religions of the world. These waters are the symbolism of peoples, multitudes, nations and tongues, verses; 3 and 15. Verse 2 tells us that the leaders of the earth commit fornication with her, and the people of the earth are made mentally inept by her teachings. She is blasphemous, powerful, filthy, mysterious, mother of harlots, the abomination of the earth, drunken with the blood of the saints, and the martyrs of Christ. This woman or church that rules over the kings of the world is no other than the fourth beast world Political Church that still rules today. No one can dispute the actions of this evil empire historically.

On the other side, Revelation 12 speaks of the woman clothed with the sun and the moon under her feet, and upon her head a crown of twelve stars. The red dragon who the whore rides, attacked the woman who was given birth to destroy her child; the body of Christ, the true church of the living God; those who keep the commandments of God and have the testimony of the Christ. (By the way, the evidence of Christ is living like Christ lived, not walking around with or having a library of books called "testimonies.")

 Also, the daughters of the whore are those who pay allegiance to this demonic religious and political institution of the devil.

Therefore, all governments presently are influenced in many ways by this demonic institution, as we are still living in such time: the feet of iron and clay. Also, America has become the right arm of this institution, consequently the physical, economic, and spiritual lynching of the jewels of God, here in America and around the world.

However, the main point I would also like to note here is, there is a big difference here between the physically functional and the spiritually living. A physically functional person or church will accomplish his/its strategic goals, but will not be satisfied within. An example is one of the great minds we had, the founder not of the apple on the tree. On the other hand, a spiritually living person or church will know all is well, even if he just had the dream of a promised land. Both had life, both have impacted the world, both were functional, but only one started living while alive. While one had acquired a great wealth of this world, he was existing and not living. The other, however, had had mainly struggles in his life while he lived for, and promoted equal rights, and justice for all. He not only existed but was also living because he had the spirit within.

 The primary understanding is that man is characterized into three different essential parts. (1) The Form. (2) The Life. (3) The Consciousness. The body that came from Adam and Eve is referred to in Gen. 1:27-28. This body, we know, is the only thing we get through our parents: the physical properties. (Gen. 5:1-2.) This physical expression is the gene pool of our physical existence. But life comes only from the Most, High, the eternal spiritual properties. The consciousness also involves a process of mental maturity, intellectual exercises, and experiences: the intellectual properties. The parents influence these different aspects of our lives we have, the teaching we received, the books we read, the places and culture we imbibe, the people we meet, and the spirits that are within us. All these others are outside influences, unlike the spiritual consciousness that comes from the spirit without and within. The spirit of God and the spirit of man when in harmony, produced eternal life that comes from the Most, High God, through his son.

If we should look at these two different persons or churches mentioned above. One was in harmony with the spirit of God, and one was not. Both were ambitious, and both had good relationships, a family and friends: the intellectual and physical properties. However, both were not satisfied with their lives. Both went to work, and they felt like they were living the dream at some point. Both loved every minute of the day, at some point. Both had twinkles in their eyes through the day, at some points. They both appeared to enjoy their lives and the lives around them. They both loved the places and the people they work along. (well we hope)

One thought he was totally in control of his life. He owned the home: temporal properties. He was making all the money he wanted, and more: temporal properties. He was then expanding, taking on new projects and was looking toward an even brighter financial future: temporal properties. What else was there to achieve? However, he felt like something was missing. The other might not have had those extras: temporal properties; but was in harmony with the spirit of the Most, High God: the eternal property. (Ephesian 1:13-14.)

Of these two, one was only functional while the other was living, just as the functional church versus the living church, the religious church versus the spiritual church.

The significant difference in both was their conscious spiritual state. Both persons were given the same amount of time in the day. Both had loving friends and family around them. Both had the basic amenities of life that should make one relatively comfortable. Both were physically functional. However, one felt like a living dead, Rev. 18:2, while the other knew he was on top of the world, because of the spirits in him. (Rev. 19: 6-8.) This comparison illustrates the parallel opposite of the spiritual dimensions in our lives and churches.

If we have the life source in us, we are on top of the world, though the world may not agree. If not, we are just a living dead, Christian or not. The world will admire us because of the worldly prosperities they see, but those admirations are as temporal at these physical prosperities we possess.

Being on top of the world spiritually does not mean there will not be issues and problems in our lives. Remember, we have to take up our crosses and follow daily. (Luke 9:23.) However, we will know the solutions to these issues and problems, because the spirit of God is in us, and we will have peace and liberty. Besides, these problems are spiritual exercises for us. (2 Cor.3:17.) Our real prosperities, therefore, are spiritual and eternal. And we have proof of this by the manifestations in our lives. Our problems are just spiritual exercises, to make us stronger both spiritually and mentally, as we will grow up to the fuller measure of our redeemer and king. Praise be to the Most, High God!!

Remember, Christ learned obedience through suffering. (Heb. 5:8)

Chapter 7

Conscious or not?

Biblically: consciousness = thoughts + choices (actions).

There is spiritual consciousness, and there is also a Physical consciousness. These consciousnesses are from two different perspectives. Spiritual awareness is within the spirit, and spiritual things are understood only spiritually. (1 Cor. 2:11-15.) This spiritual essence is within the mind: knowing. (1Cor. 2:16.) Man possesses both the spirit of God and the spirit of the self or the spirit of a man. Without this understanding, the individuals will not appreciate spiritual truth.

While material things around us are appreciated on a physical level, outside the mind, in and around, the body, you are consciously aware of your body and your surroundings: material things. This consciousness of the physical body is where the physical senses come alive. The touching, tasting, smelling, hearing, and seeing are outside stimuli that affect the thoughts.

This principle in scripture is illustrated by the text message, that says "yield not to temptation for yielding is sin" Meaning you will see (outside physical stimuli) or become aware of (internal spiritual stimulus) something you should or shouldn't do, but is present in thought, as in awareness. That in itself is not sinning. However, when we add our inside stimuli: thoughts, with our outside stimuli: temptations, this results in actions. We are then engaged in conscious decisions. This process then results in a sinful and disobedient act in both body and mind.

The messiah gave the teaching of this principle in the example of **looking** on a woman **to lust**. (Matt. 5:27-28.) This principle of discipline also applies to women looking at men with the same intent. The thought to look on the person with the intent to lust is different than just looking on the person casually without such intention. Remember, he did not say looking at a woman and stop there. There is nothing wrong to look at a woman, even to admire her, let's be practical. We sometimes have to look at each other to communicate when we are in each other's presence. However, lusting is taking it to a place we are forbidden to go to, and in today's world, it goes both ways.

The action comes in after an intent, even when there is no action present, the intention still is affected in mind. Meaning when you look at someone, what is your purpose? No one can read your heart, except your spirit and the spirit of God that is within you. You can look at someone with a desire to help the person in many different ways. Therefore, you will know why you did what you did. So, was the intent good, or was it evil? You determine the outcome by the sentiments of your intent, or heart. This conviction also tells that no other knows the plan of your heart except the spirit of God and you.

This decision was what Adam retorted to doing. You see, Adam had already decided in his heart after he heard from Eve. His decision to rebel was final. He did not have to lust after anything, but by looking at his wife and thinking, he was going to lose her. He went ahead, I believe, and decided to rebel. Thus, the intent of the heart. Immediately the spirit of God left him. Had Adam remain obedient to the true and living God, we know that God would have worked it out perfectly for him. The understanding of obedience is a lesson we should take note of and always apply its principles. Many of us have experienced this kind of exposure to evil influences. There is something you knew you should not get involved with, and there was a struggle going on within the mind, however, the moment you decided to go against your conscience or the spirit, you became weak. When you look back after all these experiences, you realized you had the strength to resist until you decided in your heart: the mind, to disobey. This failure is what happened to Adam, and continues to happen to us today. We have become enslaved by our fallen nature and think we are what our senses tell us. However, as truthful as that might seem, we are not to believe that God had left us alone to perish in that fallen state.

The good news is that the Messiah came and reestablished the moral-spiritual code of living within the mind. This place is where the spirit of God dwells in your 'heart,' the seat of consciousness: your mind. Your state of consciousness is where it all takes place. If the spirit of the true and living God is not there, then a rebellious spirit is there as we saw with David. No one can be neutral; it is either the true and living God or mammon and Satan. (Matt. 6:24.) What this means is that though the carnal flesh is bent towards sinning, and we are condemned to die the second death, however, because the messiah came and redeemed us back to the Father by subduing this corporate carnal flesh. The spirit now infuses our minds. The indwelling spirit is the antidote within the sinful nature. Therefore, there is a war within. The good news, thus, continues, and that is; we now have the power to bring this carnal nature under subjection by the spirits within us. We see this in the exemplary life of the messiah. (1 Peter 4: 1,2.) He had the fallen

59

nature within his body, Romans 8:3; however, he was not of that fallen nature in his mind. (Phil. 2: 5-8, 13.) Likewise, we are now redeemed back to that state. "Be ye transformed by the renewing of your mind. Having the mind of Christ." (Romans 12:2, 1 Cor. 2:16.) This mind condition is where the power of the redeemed resides; in the redeemed mind, just like the messiah. Yes, we are to live without sinning, while in this sinful body. Praise be to the Most, High God. But this is a choice we have to make either way, as Paul also speaks to this power. (1 Cor. 9:27.)

Now the rebellious spirit is activated by our own choices and desires, which allow the evil influence of the devil to come in when we choose to disobey the Most, High God. (James 1.) Emphasis on verse 14 and 15.

When we conceive a thought that is contrary to the will of the living God, we will be aware of it. If we are not objectively aware of such contradictions of thoughts, this would be an indication that the presence of an evil spirit already controls the person. Hence the conscience is already seared as with a hot iron. (1 Timothy 4:1-2.) For those of us who are aware, we will have to choose to accept or reject this notion, this influence, because we have the spirit of the Highest God in us. We have the option of coming into agreement with the spirit and allowing the spirit of the Highest God to lead us or not, allowing the antidote of its essence to work. We must remember, though, that we are the ones who have the intellectual right to decide which way to go with this thought, not the spirit. Which is very important, and can't be overemphasized, that we are the ones who make the choices. That is the importance of us understanding that we have to make a decision personally, every day. The spirit of God does not force us to do anything. However, we should not allow any other to influence that decision except the spirit of the Most, High God. And by coming into agreement with the spirit of God in us, we become one in our expressions. Consequently, our lives will reflect the will of God, as an individual, not a group.

Part 2

How fools make themselves many in their self-deceptions and follies.

"When I was a child, I spoke as a child and understood as a child, but now as a man, I put away that childish babbling nonsense and misunderstandings." (1 Cor.13:11.)

It is a sad sight to see, when intelligent people, allow themselves to become stupid for the sake of money, position, and association. In the religious world, being associated with a particular cult, religious order, or political party, has become the main reason for existing for many. To the point of sacrificing any sense of individual integrity and intelligence, to gain temporary trappings and acceptance, in these worldly economies of churches cults, and states. Because of this, willful ignorance, many will go as far as becoming fools to be accepted by others, even when they know the truth, be it an individual, a church organization, or government.

(Proverbs 18:13.)

Chapter 8

The sinful projected thoughts of others

 Within this self-deception, some assume projected thoughts of themselves on to others. This state of mind is a common assault on how the devil has plagued the churches and the world today. More so in the cultic churches than the world. *This self-deception is when someone looks at you and assumes what you are thinking base on their sensuality and interest. When you are not considering the thoughts, they are thinking, that you are supposed to be thinking that they believe you are thinking while you are not feeling those thoughts, that they are feeling because you are not thinking like them.* They see you, but they assume your thoughts, or they would like you to think like them. ***There is a saying, "action speaks louder than words." However, I would put it to you this way; "intent trumps presume action."*** Only you and God can know your thoughts and the intents of your heart towards those around you. Therefore, do not be influenced by these things' others (Cult) say about you that you know are not true of yourself.

In the real world, the act of misrepresenting someone's character is shown by law as an illegal offense and is defamation of one's personality. This act is further broken down into two forms: libel or slander. Libel is a written or published defamatory statement. Slander is defamation that is spoken by the offender. However, if someone is described accurately by others, then this becomes a testimony of the facts.

Unfortunately, the church (Cults) is corrupted and clueless in dealing with such maladies in its body, unlike the world which has instituted the court system to deal with such ills. Therefore, the members within the cult churches, unfortunately, have often resorted to the same court system of the world. Some members will trust totally in the Highest, to resolve such issues within the churches because the spirit of God does not qualify the leaders, but they are qualified with human degrees and, as such, are afraid of and cannot handle the evidence of truth. Therefore, these issues are becoming more prevalent in these churches, and are sometimes encouraged by some of these leaders, for manipulative and control purposes. Consequently, the court system of the world has become more righteous in dealing with such ills than these cult churches.

62

The example of the Pharisee and the sinner comes to mind. (Luke 18:9-14)

So, two men went up to 'pray.' One a Pharisee. He was very sure of himself and compared himself to the other, a Publican sinner, who was truthful to God about his condition and pleaded for mercy in his spirit. Both eventually left. Only the sinner left with the influence of the spirit of the Most, High God on him.

Interestingly, the Pharisee was a man of religious fervor and discipline in his work and life. However, he thought by his acts, he would justify himself, and by his speech, he could condemn. He also compared himself to someone he thought was sinful, for good measure, but he came away empty. **He was indeed right about the sinner being a sinner but wrong about himself being a saint.** Often time devious religious minds look on others through their sensuality tinted lenses and project their sinful state of being on them. Thinking that others are like them, and trying to be comfortable in themselves, they project their distorted image on their targets, even further, by imagining that the ones they hate are worse than themselves. When a church applies that asinine approach to any situation or case, coming from the leaders to the followers, the result will always be a people with a broken cistern.

The Publican also a man of zeal and discipline in his work and career, knew he was a sinner, but approached God with a humble heart. Therefore, He asked for forgiveness and came away filled with the blessings of God. **Those who are assumed to be in the kingdom, because of status, are not, but those whom they presumed as not, because of position, are**. Many are called, but few are (have) chosen. (Matt. 22:14.) The Most; high God makes the choices in these affairs. "We should work out our own salvation with fear and trembling." (Phil. 2:12.) But not trying to do this work, by condemning others.

It is interesting, however, that the Pharisee, though he saw himself better than the other, it did not say he when around judging the publican to others. Unlike the modern-day Pharisees, who need an audience not just to judge others, but also to promote self.

Chapter 9

A Modern Parable of the man who helped his enemies in real-time

(How one fool makes many in a cult church)

Another example is this modern parable of the man who helped his church enemies.

 A man was asked for help from a single mother of a particular cult church. She had come to this great America from her country in search of a better life, like many others. However, she needed to establish her residence. Therefore, she had to make one of the most critical decisions in her life for herself and her family back home. Now that she was in that condition, she found a church where she could find some comfort and peace of mind. She also had to find someone to sponsor her being there, preferably a man, so she set out to work.

She had had many problems with men before, who had tried to use her over an extended period back in her own country. The one she finally met and married was also from her homeland, who also abused her. He hated her and would neglect her every chance he got. She, at times, became sick because of her working so hard to pay him for her stay and to take care of her bills. In fact, on one occasion, she was so sick at home and unable to do anything for herself, she decided to call the man who helps his enemies.

 She had met him at the same church she attended, and they had become acquaintances. He was aware that she had a husband who she was living with at the time; however, he did not know her situation. So, upon her calling him and asking him for help, he asked her, "why don't you ask your husband to help you?" Her reply was a rather frightful and pathetic one. She stated that her husband did not care for her, and was in the basement doing whatever he thought was more important at the time.

With compassion, the man that help suggested to his wife, who was traveling with him from the same church the woman attended, at the time she called, that they should help her. They were on their way home, which was one hour away. The time was approximately 10 pm on a Saturday. And his wife, who as an RN, had to be at work the following morning for 7 am. They thought about it for a moment and decided to help her. The journey took them another 40 minutes to get to the woman's house. They were only 20 minutes away from their own home when they started back to her house. They got to the house and found that the woman was sick and in lots of pain. Right away, they begin to administer help to her. They made her hot tea, and the wife of the man gave her back massages that helped to release the gasses. They both had medical backgrounds, so it was not difficult to figure the issue base on the symptoms present. They stayed with her and administered more help until she recovered enough to take care of herself. During the entire time there, the woman's husband remained in the basement and did not show his face once. They eventually left and were able to be home by approximately 2:20 am that morning.

The woman stayed with that abusive man for some time after, then separated from him eventually.

Throughout the years, this woman would call on the man that help, many times to assist her. Whether she was tired from overworking and was trying to stay awake while driving home from work. During many stormy nights, he would be on the phone with her to keep her company, or if she got lost, he would be there on the phone to help her find her way home, sometimes at very late hours of the night in the winter, and he would inform his wife of such. If she were relocating, he would be there to help her. Often, she would be in financial constraint, and he would also help her. On several occasions, she would ask for his advice on purchasing big-ticket items such as her cars. He would give her reliable information, but she would off time, not follow, and would then suffer significant losses. Often, she would lose her jobs or have no Job; she would call him crying. He would encourage her not to despair, but to pray, and believe she would find another. He would tell her that within one week or sometimes two weeks, she would get a Job. His words always came through because he believed that the Highest God will always provide and encouraged her to have confidence in the promises also.

She also mentioned that she had a son in the Island, and he and his grandmother needed help, which the man assisted her financially. The text message states:

"whatsoever you have done to the least of the brethren you have done it unto me." (Matt.25: 40-45.)

So, in this parable, why should this man be so kind and generous to this woman? You might be asking. You see, the man in the parable had lost a sister of his, whom he loved dearly, some years before. This woman had, in some ways, reminded him of her. Also, it was the 'Christian' thing to do.

She eventually, after some years, told the man that she wanted to file for her son, but she did not know how to and did not have a lawyer, or any money to do so. She also needed him to help her with her son when he gets to America. This request the man agreed to, as by this time, he took her as the sister he had lost. He was able to advise her on some of the basic procedures to accomplishing her goal of filing for her son. First, he would always start with prayer and encouraged her to exercise real faith every step of the way. Then he would help her to do first things first, a little at a time. She was able to achieve her goal by following his advice. But she was afraid of taking her son to her church for fear the members would be indifferent towards him, being a "special need." However, the man encouraged her not to worry, because he believed the people would accept him there.

Prior to her filing for her son, on one occasion, she called the man asking him if he could buy her airline tickets to go home to visit her family. To this, he agreed, with the understanding of her repaying the loan. She was able to do so, and it was a joy for the man who helps his enemies to know that he could have been a part of reuniting a family. Sometime after, she asked again for the same favor, only this time for her and her son, as she had to go back to the country to consult with the immigration officials in the pursuit of completing the filing for him. This loan request was granted again for her after they both agreed that she would repay the loan. It happened that by the end of the trip, the loan amounted to over $1000.00 US.

Many months after coming back from her trip, the man inquired of her if she had forgotten about her obligation in starting repayment. She eventually called the man one day and informed him that she was advised by her mother not to repay everything because he had purchased the tickets that would put her son on another plane going to the same destination. However, this problem was rectified by her buying another ticket for both to fly on the same flight while at the airport, which resulted in a significant increase in the cost of the tickets. This increased cost was also from the same man resulting in the price mentioned above.

However, she was able to get to her destination and accomplished her intended goals.

Something strange, though, started happening shortly after. The man who has been helping the woman would now hear her make some questionable comments. Like "you are a rich man," "you have money," "You and your wife are working, but I am not." (lesson: be careful how you help others when you do)

These comments over the years started to have the man thinking whether she was pretending to need a friend or use a friend. The man was also told by another person (Bro. P), who has had some experience with her, that this woman was very vindictive if she did not have her way. However, rather than judging her on others' encounters and merits, he decided to give her a chance to reveal her true self. Over the following years, he would, as usual, help her in many different ways within reason.

One of her main problems was her son, who has Down syndrome, was susceptible to becoming sick, and her being fearful of him being overweight, with other issues. So, she asked this son of God to "keep an eye on her and on her son," (her exact words) to help them from getting more obese or sickly. She had asked the man who helps his enemies to help her, in this regard, along with another fellow who lived in a southern state: a naturopathic doctor, as she claimed to have no other person to help. These statements and requests she made to him even though she had families around, of which he did not know at the time. However, the man had compassion on them and continued to help in whatever ways he could because he loved them like his son and sister.

 She also knew the man and his wife have always tried to be of help to those around them. From time to time, she would ask the man what he thought of her physical appearance, presence, and how to improve the physical conditions of both her and her son. As they both were close to being more obese, and he would try to help them manage their weight issue. He would give his honest opinion. This son of God, tells the mother that they both could also develop diabetes because they both were suffering from being overweight, and their diet was in question. Therefore, they need to have a health program suited for them and to follow it religiously. (**Most people within some religious community would boast about being associated with a group of people who are known to be healthy; however, they 'themselves' are not.**)

 They would, at times, watch the program "The Doctor" together when he visited them and would have discussions on their health issues. He would also encourage her to engage in regular exercises as often as she could along with her son. And adjust her diet to a healthier one. For many years the man would help them financially, with spiritual counsel, moving, repairs, financial counsel, their health issues, and always praying for them. The man was like a brother to her and a father to her son. He would even at times leave his work just to bring money and food to them when they were in desperate need; while she would not receive any help from her church within those years. Sometimes she would call him crying on the phone because of that neglect. Unfortunately, the church she attended did not care enough to have a program for such members, but would rather condemn them if they did not return a tithe or offering, and would tell them they would not go to heaven if they did not pay a tithe. (cult) This type of brainwashing was her saying; she would, at times, say she does not understand why the church fails to help people like her, who are members of the church. His response to her was: "this church is more interested in your money than your soul." (cult)

However, because of the various questionable comments and behavior of this woman, the man decided that the relationship could not continue as is, and started to wane himself from her. After telling her his decision, she responded with ill feelings towards the man because it seemed, she thought he would be a crutch for her many needs. She thought he had money to give to her whenever she needed, emotionally, when there is a need for someone to understand her cries or an ear to listen to her when she needed a friend. He, however, realized she just wanted to use him and refused to be used by her for her conveniences.

She had also invited the man to her house on Oakton Boulevard where she had lived for a time, where she plotted with another of her female friends, (Sis. D) another 'mother in Zion' member from the same church, to seduce the man in having sex with them both. They went as far as competing in modeling their bodies to entice the man in her house, while he visited her, however, he refused them both. Not because he was a perfect man, but for three basic reasons. (1) The spirit of God was "upon" him. (2) He was a married man. (3) They were not attractive, as they had an unrefined presence. In other words, they were not his type, besides he took her for his sister.

One day at her church, he eventually told her that their friendship would not be the same, and he would not be talking to her as he used to or visiting her as before. Not that the association was over, he just thought it best to be sure as to what was happening without judging her. However, after telling her this, she became paranoid and obsessive and started calling the man's phone at various times of the days and nights. So much so that he would not answer his phone. She became very angry with him, to the point of not being able to sleep, by her confession. It also appeared that, because she had to repay the loan to the man but wanted a part to be a gift; Upon which he refused, also him refusing to have sex with her and her friend. She then proceeded to tell others in the church that he was looking at her son in a sick way, which was encouraged by the leadership of this cult church. As the administration hated the man and have been attacking him every chance they got because he also refused to be made a member slave of their cult church as many are. But he insisted on presenting the truth and being an independent thinker. One brother (Bro. F), told the man of God, that he heard that he likes boys, which was very interesting because the man of God has two boys (sons) of his own, whom he loves dearly. However, what he saw was, the young men had no real role model to look up to in this church and tried to help by showing what a real male is, always advocating for authentic practical mentoring for the boys, which was a challenge to the weak leadership there at that church. However, he did not realize how wimpy the leadership was, that he, as an alpha male, would be a threat to these wimpy men in this cult, including the pastors, except for a very few. The positive role model was too strong for them to handle because it exposed them for being wimps; when an alpha male came into their presence. He would challenge their lies and deceptions, their immaturity and childish ways, their cowardly and foolish hearts, and show what a real man looks like in action, 'not just a bag a mouth.' So, the women who are intelligent and mature would find these qualities extremely attractive, which they did not see in these wimpy men of theirs. So much so that many of these women would express this to this man in various ways and even offer themselves to him. His confidence was another reason why these wimps hated the man of God because the women could see real confidence in this man. So, these wimps conspired together with this confused and desperate woman to attack this real man, to feel like real men themselves.

He approached this confused woman at the church one day and told her he knew what she was trying to do. However, he was still concern that she and her son would be sick because of being overweight and would not get the help they needed from her church. Something they had talked about before when she had asked him for help. The nonsensical attitude by her and her sidekicks would have made it worse for her if her son were to become sick, meaning that while he wanted the friendship between himself and her to cease, he was still true to his word in helping her and her son stay healthy. (*An alpha male never gives up on his commitment, even with a million wimps is attacking. Only if the person he is helping begins to be a fool, and she sure has*) He, at the time, was also in the pursuit of creating a new kind of exercise program, which would also help such types of people to exercise safely and effectively, which would have helped this woman and her son immensely in improving their health. However, because of her clouded judgment of the facts, and obsession with cheap friendship, and evil counsel from these wimpy church cult leaders who hated him. She refused to acknowledge what the man did for her to prevent her adverse living conditions up to that point when the church refused to help her, and now she has lost out in a more significant way even. She especially refused to listen to good counsel again, now that he told her their friendship was over but proceeded to join with those in the same church who hated the man because of his independence, gift of knowledge, ambition, talents, and even his presence; being an alpha male, and his attire, just like they hated Joseph. (Gen. 37:3-5, 11.) Many a time even the preachers, including pastors, elders and visiting speakers would attack the man because of the manifold blessings he receives from the Most, High God in their presence; and his refusal as a real man, to be controlled by, or support their evil church theologies and policies. (Psalm 23.) They would preach negatively about his abilities, gifts, his looks, and his attire, etc., anything they could talk about because of their desperate jealous, envious, and hateful cultic hearts towards him.

Not long after her initial attack, she came back to the man again, asking for financial help to make a third trip to her home. This time he gave her some money instead of loaning her, even though he knew she had plotted with the others to attack him. Why, do you ask? Well, the word of God says to do good to those who hate you and despise you. The action by you will be like coals of fire on their heads; their conscience will judge them if they have any left. (Prov.25:21-22, Rom.12: 19-20.) (*Besides, he doesn't give a hoot about what the cults say or think about him*)

 In this case, the woman had personal issues that she did not know how to manage. But judge the man because of the internal issues that she had, and many still have to address today. However, she wanted him to be a scapegoat for her sick carnal mind, that she had admitted to, having told him of her sick desires about the woman at her work. Also, the so-called leadership within that church and the pastors hated the man for many years and had plotted many times for his demise, and now they: the woman, and the church leadership, with other cult members, thought it great to join together to attack this man of God, who help them; his enemies.

These types of attacks are not unique only to the servants of God today. Remembering Potiphar's wife and Jezebel? (Gen. 39, 1 Kings 21:1-11.) The weird thing about this woman and her conspirers, is they pride themselves as being remnant Christians. But even her wimpy Pastors and Elders and other members on the church board within her cult, as in the story of Jezebel; all these religious subjects, got in on the action, to plot, condemn, and make derogatory comments against the man, who was helping her and her family members when she was ignored by them, even during the time of their initial attacks. Those are the same church people who ignored to help her and did not know that the man was helping her and her son, at that time. As he believes in the council: "not to let your left hand know what your right hand is doing." (Matt. 6:3,4.) However, they were anxiously waiting to attack the man of God, out of desperation. What's more interesting is, many of these same cult attackers have asked for and received help from the same person they were attacking. Also, some were being helped by this son of God while they were attacking him, including a number of these wimpy elders. A few examples are as follow:

One fellow was asked to be an elder by the board. (Bro. E) He accepted, however, the mothers on the committee objected to him being an elder because something suspicious was said to them, that he was usually in the pastor's (Bro. H) vestry with the young ladies. They suspected something was going on and decided he was not fit to be an elder. However, the man who helps his enemies was also a member of the same board at the time and was present at that same meeting. Thought that this approach was presumptive of them, and question the validity of their assumption. He proceeded to ask these so-called "mothers of Zion" to present proof of their allegations towards this young man; this they could not do. Therefore, he questioned and opposed their apparent accusations because of the lack of evidence. Consequently, with the allegation dismissed, the young man was accepted as an elder and had been serving for many years since.

Some years later, this same young man, who had now been an elder for many years, had family issues. His wife was having major problems with him because he was ignoring his family while following a wayward pastor (Bro. R) of the church at the time. This pastor was a wimpy divorcee, who had no moral scruples. He was leading this poor fellow away from his first obligation: his family, not the church. However, the man who helped his enemies, being the "Family Life Director" at the time, sensed what was happening and spoke to his wife about the situation. This man and his wife then approached this elder and his wife and expressed their concerns for them. They eventually were able to convince this couple of their need for counsel, after much resistance. They also went ahead and paid for the elder and his wife, out of their own pocket, with their permission to get the needed therapy for their family life. This family life retreat session that they attended helped the elder and his wife to restore their marriage relationship, which alleviated him from further, unknowingly, or knowingly, abusing his wife and children.

Now, because of the young man's addiction to a position and association, over truth. He also has joined in the attack by refusing to tell the truth on several occasions. One such is the man who helps his enemies, helping to secure equipment for the church. This man who they hate, staying an entire night outside in the cold at a local "Black Friday" store on Howard St. in Evanston, Illinois, with this elder. The man of God, putting his life in danger to secure order among the rowdy crowd so that the equipment could have been purchased for the church. However, upon reporting to the church body the man that helped was not mention by this wimpy elder at all because he was instructed by the pastor at the time, who also threatened the man who helps his enemies that he could have him killed, not to mention this vital service rendered to the church by this man. However, there was great recognition made to the elder for doing such an excellent job for the church, and he said nothing about the man who helped to secure the equipment. (cult) That was many years ago (07); however, he has also, in recent times, stolen and refused to return SanDisk that belongs to the man of God. That disk that was bought and paid for by the man of God has copies of taped sermons that clearly reveal the wimpy resident pastor of 2014-2019, at the time, had consistently attacked and falsely accused the man who help his enemies, in his sermons, of imaginative immorality that is cherished by himself and his pastoral sidekicks, because of the lies of the woman that the man of God had helped. These so-called sermons will also prove of attacks coming from a number of these other incompetent cult pastors and elders. He had also lied and covered up in the past for previous pastors and continues to do so, even when he knows the truth. It's just Sick remembering 'Black Friday.' It is more sickening that upon asking for the disk, this elder, rather than giving back the SanDisk, he took other SanDisk that he knew were not the right disks, and asked if any of those were the one, knowing full well they are not. The type of wickedness that these types of wimpy deceptive minds do in the cult churches as leaders today is sickening. (sick)

Another incompetent elder, (Bro. C) was found guilty of adultery, by his confession to the church, and of course, the members hated his guts as a result. However, the same man who helped his enemies came alongside him, even though he knew this elder hated him but encouraged him. Explaining to him that if he sincerely repented, God has forgiven him already, and he can stop walking with his shoulders slump and head down, but now walk with the confidence of a child of the king. He eventually was promoted to be the first elder, some years after, mainly because of his financial support. (cult) He has hated the man of God for many years and is consistent in his attacks while pretending not to be. One of the most hypocritical persons in that cult church.

Also, a couple and their children were living in a property belonging to the church (Sis. P); however, they were unable to pay their rent consistently. During a board meeting, which was at the church, a decision was about to be made to evict this couple with their young children. We have to remember that these people in that family were members of the same church (cult). The man who helped his enemies was at this meeting and objected to such a cruel and insensitive act by the board, and had to fight with those who wanted to throw these people out of their home. He believed that if he was in the same position, they would do the same or worst to him, and would not go along with them. Understanding that the pastor at the time had Post-Traumatic Stress Disorder issues, and was not in a frame of mind to be leading a church anyway, but the members present had no excuse, other than being of callus hearts. However, the Highest God was able to use the man who helps his enemies once again to thwart another diabolical scheme and save this family, unknowing to them. Notwithstanding, the woman of this family has also collaborated with the woman who hates the man because he refused her, too, and with the same incompetent pastors and elders and others to attack the man who helped her and her family.

A woman who presents herself as a mother in "Zion" (Sis. B); along with her husband who is the chief financial contributor to the church, presented her case to the board one day with great disappointment, that her husband was sick, and no one came to visit them at their home. The son of God thought of the truth in her concern and decided to stop by her house after the meeting, to see how her husband was doing. However, upon greeting him, everything took a weird turn for the worst. They, the husband and wife, both started to vent their true feelings toward a particular person with offensive expressions. They stated how they hate the person and how both of them had helped the person when they had nothing. It was only after an earful of complaints from them both that the wife realized who they were talking to when she hurriedly stated that her husband was on medication for altered mental illness. At this juncture, the visitor prayed with them and left. This woman has also conspired with the first elder and others to attack this son of God. One reason being, that he corrected her in a Sabbath class that the spirit of God is not flesh, and that there is nowhere in the scriptures that state such nonsense. This kind of unbiblical teaching is the type of rubbish that's taught in that church. (cult) This couple is probably in their late seventies; if not older, however, they also showed how clueless they are.

Also, another couple who have been fighting back and forth with themselves for many years, (Bro. H, and Sis. F) and had gone to the same man for advice on several occasions. This couple also has been encouraged by this same man to seek family life counsel. By directing funds to defray the cost for their session, as the man who helps his enemies and his wife were the family life directors at the time. They were also able to help them get to the session. However, this couple's problem could not be remedied by these sessions because of the presence of impotence and immaturity in their relationship, something that still exists today, as there are no signs to say otherwise. The husband of this couple has been the type that would always be in another person's business, but never able to manage his own. So much so, that his only young daughter had to leave his house, prematurely, to live with her partner for peace of mind. The wife has also started to express her devious traits after being employed by the local institution that manipulates these slave ships call churches. After employment, she began to attack the man to show her employers that she was employable, not having the qualifications for the real job, as stated by the president of that business entity, at the time he visited the church. (cult) This woman has gone as far as sending offensive video, to attack the man of God, to show that she deserves the job. These demonic attacks also prove how occultic their environment is and how corrupt these people are.

These are just a few of the local church leaders and members who have been helped by this son of God; however, they have chosen to attack this son of God, because of their devious state of mind. The scriptures state: whatever you have done to the least of my brethren, you have done it unto me. Matt. 25:40.

"Great spirits have always encounter violent opposition from mediocre minds" Albert Einstein.

Now the (2014-2019) pastor/s at the time and his associates have used this issue of the Jezebel-like woman as a tool for mind control and intimidation tactics towards the ignorant members, a tactic of a cultic church. But the man who helped his enemies "saw him from a mile," and knew of his agenda before he exposed himself. You see, this is the trend within a manipulative cultic organization whenever someone presents the truth to the people. As we see in the cases of the messiah, John the Baptist, Martin Luther the reformer, etc., whenever our enemies can't refute these truths, we will always experience the same attacks. These so-call leaders had tried to shut them down and will use any method necessary, as they are trained and brainwashed in doing so. However, those who are entrusted to present the truth without fear or favor must do the work they are sent to do with the power that comes from the Most, High God.

These examples are just scratching the surface of the many cases of the enemies in that one particular cult church, toward the man of God. All of those characters mentioned in the parable, along with many others, have conspired to attack the man that helped most of them, and the leadership of that church. It is interesting that one of the previous pastors, who often boast off having a Ph.D., in biblical studies, who stated "my brain is bigger than all you church members brain combined," had threatened the man who helped his enemies; that he can have him killed because he questioned and opposed the lies, he presented to the people. Then this Jezebel-like woman who the man also helped, in February of 2017, told the man that she could destroy him, because of her deluded mind, and him refusing to be used by her for sex and money. Coincidental? No!! There is a devious thread there that connects them all; this thread is the manifestation of being possessed by the evil one. The main reasons for their attacks have many factors, such as hatred, envy, jealousy, the greed of money, covetousness, insecurity, failure to control, incompetence, stupidity, employment, association, and not being able to brainwash the man of God.

Another being also the 'trump' Pastor, who is into the type of psychology, which the bible describes as an act of sorcery. Acts 8:9-24. He was able to bewitch most of the people. Both young and old, to believe this lie by using witchcraft along with his wife. In our modern time, this sorcery is called Neuro-linguistic Programming (NLP), using words to convey a message to distort the minds of the weak. He was able to hypnotize most of these ignorant souls in a very short time by making specific comments and using certain music, along with his side-kick elders. One such method was to complement the Jezebel type woman every chance he got in the services so that the members will believe her because of his approval of her. Possibly not caring to know that she had attacked the man of God because of his refusal to be used by her for sex and money. But doesn't care because he thinks he can use this lie to attack this man of God's character to accomplish his agenda, and the possibility of getting a bigger church with a bigger paycheck, which was what happened in this parable. He was moved to a bigger church in 2019 and is now receiving a bigger paycheck. What you need to understand is, within a cult church, the pyramid structure of favor and grace has customized favors to the pastors because of their total obedience and submission to the manipulated and manipulative boss above them, to accomplish their devious endeavors. If they don't play by their rule of deception, their bosses will not put in a "good" word or recommendation for them to their bosses; for them to be transferred to another church and receive a bigger paycheck and more of the benefits. But will instruct others to make their lives miserable until they accept the way they see fit to accomplish their desired goals; this is similar to complementing Jezebel and Ahab for their acts toward Naboth and the prophets of God, and Potiphar's wife toward Joseph, (1 Kings 21:1-9, Gen.39.) so, they can receive more of the spoils.

This pastor and his wife, along with others, would make certain derogatory inference statements towards the man of God. However, other members within that church would not question the validity of such inferences, not only because they hate the man of God, but also because they are afraid and ignorant of the truth. They think they might lose the association, employment, favor, and grace from the leadership of that organization and be blotted out from the book of life. As corrupt as the institution is, they rather comply with them, than be targeted by them also. These acts are characteristics of a cultic environment, organization, and church.

What this devious pastor had also done, as mentioned, was having other speakers to come and say the things he wanted to speak from the pulpit in some instances, attacking the son of the Most, High God. (1 John 3:2.) He has done this to circumvent the law, as he was made aware by his institutional lawyers that as an employee, his organization can be legally responsible for defamation of character, as they have made comments of such between the years of 2016-2019.

The man who helped his enemies had asked on many occasions to have an open meeting with the church to bring the truth distorted by his accuser to light; however, the incompetent first elder, (Bro. C) this incapable pastor (Bro. M) and other incompetent board members have plotted against such meeting because of the embarrassment the truth will present to them. (Cult.) They would rather have secret meetings, then come to the church subtly and give a twisted version of the truth in the meeting session. (Cult.) These types of deceptive maneuver they call psychology. However, the truth is they are just boldface liars, doing the will of their father, the devil.

For example, the first elder opposed having a public members' meeting with the man of God and the church but agreed to have a meeting with the man of God who helped his enemies, along with the other elders. However, upon arriving at the meeting place: the church. The man of God found that there were no other elders there, this surprised him as he had asked for and was expecting the other elders to be there, per the request for such. However, only to be told by the first elder, (Bro. C) in his own words: "I made this decision, not to include them, because I think I am more intelligent than all the other elders, and do not think they were needed, because of their lack of intelligence." At that meeting, the elder was made aware by the man of God, what the Jezebel type woman had inferred about him, the man of God. That also was told to him, the elder, to give him another chance to prove who he was: an elder or a wimp. In his typical fashion, he acted as though he was surprised, and it was the first time he had ever heard such. However, at another meeting, subsequent to this in 2016, this time with pastor (Bro. M), a witness (Bro. K), and this same elder (Bro. C), still pretending not to be a part of the plot, said it was best for the man of God not to tell his wife of the false accusation. So, they at the meeting could keep this allegation to themselves. The group would include the first elder, the pastor, a witness, and the man of God. However, the man of God had asked the witness to be at the meeting and had told his wife before of their plots and the false accusation. Also, the pastor and elder were both shocked to see the witness (Bro. K) at the meeting, so much so that the pastor commented "you don't trust us," because of the presence of the witness, which the man of God agreed to. The man of God, knowing that both the elders and the pastors have been plotting against him and would continue, understandably, they were his enemies and would stop at nothing to accomplish their goal with Jezebel. The fewer people they though knew the truth, the more credibility and control those sorcerers thought they had. This approach is another method they use to control the masses. (Cult.) This attitude was also expressed by the other pastor (Bro. R) without morals, some years before, who threatened to have this son of God killed. (Matt. 23:15.) This first elder who pretended to be surprised, however, was using the lies of the Jezebel woman, and the other accusers as he was with the previous pastors to attack the man of God. They had been promoting different plots with the pastoral office and its sidekicks for many years against the man of God. This hatred and attacks on the man of God came because of his stance against their false teaching and stealing of the peoples' resources in the name of their false gods, which started back in 2005.

Not long after that meeting, on June 10 of that year 2016, a program was orchestrated and presented on the elements of the subject discussed in the previous meeting. The young woman who chaired the meeting was ignorant of the facts but very eager to impress these devious leaders. Now in this program, only the first elder, elders, and pastors were allowed to speak from a panel that manipulated the meeting by telling the congregation that no one else is allowed to speak from the floor except the moderator, along with the members of the panel, as stated by the pastor. This way, they could make inferences by twisting the truth to give an impression. Knowing that the people are ignorant and afraid, they use this lack of knowledge as a tool to lie and deceive just like their daddy. (John 8:44-47.) That also proved they had something to hide, as the son of God was there to reveal the truth, but they threatened him that if he speaks, they will close the meeting. (Cult.) {*Similar to the session in 2005 at the regional conference meeting.}* No different from those who accused Christ. It is interesting that when a question was asked by one member, on what was the "mission statement'" of the church, to the panel at that meeting. Not one of those so-called wimpy leaders, who sat on the committee could answer that simple question, including the pastor, as they did not know, but was so focused on attacking the man of God. And most embarrassingly, the one they were attacking had to remind them that the mission statement was right there on the Sabbath program they had in their hands. The response they gave to the question was an accurate and definite picture of world-class incompetence at its highest level, even at this local cult church. These are the types of morons we find as leaders in these pathetic cultic churches today.

All cult pastors and elders, like the above mentioned, are insecure, incompetent, and impotent because their theologies have no merit in the Holy Word, and they have no relationship with the true and living God, only with a cult institution. The truthfulness of their actual condition, they are just finding out, if ever, but rather than confessing the truth and seek the true and living God, they believe they have to lie and manipulate the ignorant to be paid, and feel important while being jigaboo cults, which makes them into little angry, demented puppets, who do not have minds of their own. However, we know the truth must stand as illustrated in Ezekiel 2, 3, at all costs.

Therefore, beware of wolves in sheep cloning. Once the spirit of the Most; High God is within you, even though you might be in this cultic environment, you will not fall to the schemes of the devil and his little angry jigaboo puppet cult workers. Remember, they will hate anyone who stands up for truth and righteousness. (Gal.4:16, John 8:44.)

Now you know that a pastor of virtue and integrity is not a fool and would investigate the issue or issues by listening to both sides before jumping to a conclusion and making references and giving inferences, without which he will ultimately make a fool of himself as the cults always do. (1 Kings 3: 16-28. Proverbs 18:13.) However, this deviant, impotent, incompetent imbecile cult pastor had his own premeditated personal agenda to attack, as directed by his cult bosses; however, he made a fool of himself and his cult institution in the process, because he thought this Jezebel type woman was the perfect opportunity to fit into his plan to try and gain his selfish objectives, as did Ahab. You see, the son of the Most, High God, who helped his enemies had been objecting to the incompetence he sees in this cult organization at the highest level, and have been teaching the bible truths, for many years, on various subject matters that these intellectual cult dwarfs can't refute. Even after having studied at their prestigious religious cult institutions of so-called higher learning, with their many PHDs, they are still unable to count. "They are always learning, but never coming to the knowledge of the truth." (2 Tim. 3:7.) Consequently, the truth that was taught by the son of God was a rebuke to the lies told by these incompetent cult pastors, and they could not have the people becoming aware of these lies they were spilling, this happened to them because of their cross-eyed exegetical cult thinking, mixing truth with error, just to be employed, they have lost their marbles and their way. So, this incompetent cult pastor was sent, specifically to attack this son of God, just as his previous colleagues have. Therefore, he had to include and plot among their local cult leaders, elders, members, and their wives, to attack anyone who presented truth without fear or favor, or they will lose support from their cult employer. (1 Kings 19:1-2.) However, we who stand with truth will not fear these puppets and their cult institutions, but baptize them into the truth.

So, these bible truths that are taught by this son of God can't be refuted by them, which made them very angry and mad to the point of threatening to kill and destroy him who speaks the truth. Therefore, whenever this son of God comes into their presence, they become very uncomfortable and feel inadequate to their task, to teach their lies. They are aware of this son of God's knowledge of the truth from the lies that are spilling from their lips and will question them publicly on it. They, therefore, opted to attack his character using the words of a woman who hates him, because he refused to be used by her for sex and money. Him, refusing to have sex with her and her friend, who are both considered to be righteous mothers of this cult Zion by these pastors and elders of that particular cult church. Also, him demanding that she paid back her loan and refusing her request for friendship on three different occasions, are sins to them and her. So, they took her twisted story and conspired with her to attack. However, another problem they don't know they have also is, all of this was allowed by the son of God, who inverted their psychology to expose them for what they are. Now the world will see how one cult fool reveals many in a cult institute. Surprise!!! This mystery will be explained further in the next books to follow.

Now because of the love that was expressed to these enemies by the princely king ruler, applying the principle of loving your enemies. These sorry souls could not believe the reality of such love and considered it an illusion, so much so that they hate the man of God for loving them, and showing compassion on them when others would not, this state of being can only be, when the mind is out of touch with reality, but rather accept an illusion as reality, and truth as an illusion, which is an effect of false religion and theology: brainwashed, which is the wine of Babylon.

Others are trying and will continue to work and build a case to satisfy their thirst for proving their distorted view of the man who helps his enemies. Just as Christ knew who these were, he also knows who these are. Some believe that they are trained with the most exceptional intellectual maneuvering skills to achieve their goals; however, they are exposed even before starting, this is called in the holy scripture the spirit of discernment, which trumps intelligence. (1 Cor.12.) A word should be sufficient for the wise.

Chapter 10

Discipline is Love or Stupidity

In the parable, the man who helped his enemies also believes in the disciplining of our young men in the churches, as he has done with his own. Without discipline, our young men coming out of these cultic churches would make this world an eviler place to live. Interestingly, this corrupt church leadership had attacked the man who helped his enemies for even disciplining his son. How can these sons of ours be the real men of tomorrow if discipline is not a part of their growth? So, he was threatened by them, because he believes in teaching his boys to be men by disciplining them when it is needed. The bonding of his family is another reason why these enemies of the Most, High hate, and thirst for control because of jealousy, envy, and just plain stupidity. However, when they get this control, they do not know how to effect positive changes in their own families. The breakdown of their family structure will tell.

Consequently, the lack of leadership and discipline in that particular cult church has caused many of these young men to have gone astray. Some to prison and even cause of death in other cases. The condition of this particular church concerned this son of God, who tried to help these blinded people to see the light. Unfortunately, they rather darkness rather than light. (John 3:19. Proverbs 26:3.)

One such case is one family that had one of its sons ended up in prison as a result of the lack of real leadership and discipline in this church. The same reason for him ending up in prison started at the church at an early age, by the leaders' refusal to address those early signs with discipline. They thought that by ignoring these problems that would make them disappear, which only made them worse. The result was in the daily news. The lack of discipline was the cause of one boy going to prison, and the boy's mother's heart to be broken, which contributed to her death as a result of the lack of structure and discipline in this cult church. (Proverb 17:22.) Our people are destroyed only because of weak, incompetent, spineless leaders, that are more interested in being seen and heard while stealing from the poor than being real men with real knowledge to impart. They are like little toy figures for window dressings, or what some people call wimps and 'Fig-a-r-e-e-s.'

The boy's father was an elder, a first elder who ignored his primary obligation to his family because of the evil influence of the pastors that led him, and as a result, has lost his family. Most of these incompetent religious leaders are taught to ignore their family for the sake of the work of the cultic churches and end up losing all that is meaningful and true in their lives if there were no early spiritual interventions made. Leaders without real knowledge are like the blind leading the blind, as we see in our political and religious leaders today. However, sad to say, some politicians are more righteous than many of these leaders that have come through these particular cult churches. Of all the pastors that have been in this specific church, over seventy percent are clueless, spineless, and need to grow up.

Chapter 11

O, Really! Nicodemus?

In the case of the messiah's encounter with Nicodemus, also a ruler, or a pastor in today's economy. The messiah was disappointed in him claiming a position of leadership before the people, while not having the necessary knowledge in regards to the subject discussed. The issue was the second birth by the spirit. (John 3:1-12.) In verse 12, the messiah concludes that it was useless trying to tell him heavenly things if he is clueless about earthly things. It would be interesting to ask today's Nicodemus' the same question. How are we born of the spirit?

There is no difference for these incompetent present-day-so-called-leaders, who are puffed up with their air of degrees, blindsided by their associations, and stupefied because of positions. As a result, these, too, will not understand this fundamental truth. How then will they be able to appreciate heavenly honesty, if they can't manage simple issues, that are none-issues, just by telling the truth? They will never be able to handle real-life problems because they lack the spirit of the Highest in their own lives. (John 16:13. Luke 12:1.) No wonder their family life is such a mess.

An example is this preacher (Bro. M) telling his church members they do not have to tell the truth all the time. As a result, one of the members came to the son of God and told him he does not need to tell the truth all the time. The "truth," the son of God, understood her to be referring to is her deceptive, seductive plot, being the other woman, who plotted with her Jezebel friend to sexually seduce this son of God, who refused them both. The scheme by her and her friend is the truth she is referring not to tell because she heard this incompetent, impotent spineless wimp of a jigaboo cult pastor, present this lie from the pulpit, which shows how well these sorcerers can bewitch their subjects.

However, in all of this, we have to remember that God looks at the heart, your intent. And sometimes, when you help others, the devil will try to attack you because he knows that you helping that person or persons will deliver them from his clutches. Also, remember this earth is balance by good and evil. Therefore, wherever good is, evil always presents itself. However, by their works, you shall know them. Matt. 7:15-20.

In like manner, the messiah was attacked by the religious devils for healing and teaching so many people. (John 8: 40-44. Luke 11:45-53.) Therefore, we should not be surprised when we are too. (John 15: 20, Matt. 10:22.) We also have to remember that "we wrestle not against flesh and blood, but against principalities and power, and wickedness in high places." (Ephesian 6:12.) Meaning that, if you find yourself in a similar situation like the man who helps his enemies, and the messiah. The people in the circumstances are not your main enemies but have allowed themselves to be used by the enemy of the Most, High God: the devil, their daddy. Just like they: the Pharisees, the priests, and the religious leaders were used to attack the messiah and the men of God. (John 8:44-45.) Therefore, it is a spiritual war, so let them bring it on!!

The man who helped his enemies, remember, he too has had many pastors, and their wives, many elders, and many members alike plotted and expressed their desire to kill and, or destroy him, and have attacked him, as the pastors, elders, members and religious mothers in the above parable did within these years of threats to the man who helped these people. His truck, car, and house were also mysteriously set on fire in February 2014. Only to hear from his mother-in-law, that the pastor who threatened to have him killed, called her to find out if he was doing ok. Interestingly, he has never called before the fire to inquire of the man's health, let alone called the man of God. However, in 2016, he called this son of God to have some upholstery work done for him without asking about his welfare, who refused his work. Remember, this was the same pastor who had told the man of God; he could have him killed. It was the same pastor who called this son of God an assassin, and it was the same pastor who said this son of God was his nemesis. All because he opposed the lies that were spewing from his mouth. It is also interesting that one of the women who conspired with this Mr. Ph.D. Pastor, against this man of God, had said to the man of God, she heard that his house was in a fire. What's interesting is, the fire had not occurred yet. Unfortunately, she had died and can't speak on the matter. However, it would have been revealing to know how she got that information, seeing that the fire did not happen until after she said so. Which tells she had prior knowledge of the plot before it happened.

It is also interesting that one of the primary accusers, Jezebel, in the above mention parable came back to this son of God and apologize for lying, and asked for forgiveness, but at the same time saying she does not know what she did, implying that she was not in control of her mind but indicate that others manipulated her. The "trump" pastor has also stated in a sermon that the people at that church were mentally ill. Also, the same pastor, who told the people he has the biggest brain because he has a Ph.D., came to the man and tried to change his attack story, by saying he did not mean that he would kill him personally, but others would after he had been saying he did not say this to the man. But then he also had asked if they could be friends. Just like the woman who also came to the man and asked not only for forgiveness but also to be friends again. She also wrote a letter stating how much having that friendship was a blessing, and even writing a check, for a portion of the money she still owes, giving evidence to this son of God's credibility. The letter and check were shown to the devious "trump" pastor and elder at the meeting in 2016, by the man of God. However, they continued plotting against the man of God, even after the evidence. Their response would indeed indicate they were and are manipulated by the same deviant spirit, just like Potiphar's wife, Jezebel, Ahab, and the elders in that experience. (Gen. 39, 1 Kings 21.) Yes, she did ask the man in a remorseful tone; a crying voice, which is her "M.O.," (witness by sis. S) She is one who likes to shed tears at the drop of a hat, to appeal to the emotions. Therefore, she asked with tears in her eyes and voice if they can be friends again like before as she can't sleep well at nights and having headaches, her confession to this son of God.

The forgiveness was granted by this son of God, after he prayed with her, in the same cult church foyer, with the youth pastor (Bro. D) looking on. However, she was told by this son of God whom she attacked with the pastors and his associates, that being friends again was considered a spiritual issue that only the spirit of The Most; High God would allow. "Two can't walk unless they agree." (Amos 3:3) And they certainly are not in agreement. He also is a man of his words, had decided to discontinue the relationship with this cult church, and had told her this before she started her attacks, knowing that she would attack him with the others. He being a man of his words can't change to please the emotions of a person, a church, or even a country.

However, because of her being giving a position, which he had encouraged her to take some time before, and having an association and fake support from those kinds, like those people who attacked the messiah, the same types behind her, attacking the man who helped her. She has refused to confess the truth publicly for fear of embarrassing the entire pastoral staff, members of the church, and auxiliary staff of the cult organization for that church, and herself. Therefore, until they have confessed the truth publicly, they all have condemned themselves. (John 8:32. James 5:16. 1 John 1:9.) Remember, you shall not only know the truth to be set free, but you should also speak and live the truth to be free;

consequently, if they do not speak and live the truth, they are in bondage. Their prophet had said an entire conference would perish; this could be one such conference if they do not repent of their corrupt cult ways.

Why should you write these things in this book? You might ask. Well, the same reason God allowed the stories of the messiah's and his followers' experiences with the same types of people to be recorded. (Matt 12:14, Mark 3:6, John 11:53.) The experiences spoke of in this book also proves that the bible is not just a book of fictitious stories of make-belief or imaginary people and circumstances, but has real historical contents and implications. These scriptures and testimonies are not only to be read but more so for our learning. "There is nothing new under the sun." (Eccl.1:9) Some are righteous and holy, and some are unjust and filthy. They will do what they do continually while being religious because that's in their hearts to do. (Rev. 22:11.) What nature are you? Remember, religion is like a politician or prostitute in a white robe with a halo over her head, nothing else.

 The story is also a modern story of the story of Jezebel, Ahab, and Naboth. (1 King 21.) Potiphar's wife and Joseph. (Gen. 39.) These bible stories are not just stories on pages, but become alive by living people like us today, all over the world in various places and circumstances daily. The text messages in the scriptures are like dry bones on the pages, but become alive when we live these truths through our own experiences. Our day to day struggles and achievements are confirmation of those who have gone on before us. Imagine you are what you are reading because you are experiencing these same text messages in your life. They become not just words on pages in the bible anymore, but your present reality. Like Joseph, this son of God also is hated in the cultic churches, not only by his brothers, but also by his sisters and mothers, because of their ignorance, and the truth he tells, without compromising with such a religious cultic system of false worship, and traditional religious Mumbo-Jumbo theologies. Remember! Only those who stand with truth will stand forever! Amen. To the Most, High be all the Glory, honor, and praise.

Chapter 12

Judging self without knowing

The fact that Eve was looking at the tree does not mean she desired at that time to eat of its fruits. The serpent noticed her posture and presented a projected thought to deceive her. He said to her, 'did God said you should not eat of this tree?' Indirectly, by including all the trees in his question. He being the great psychologist, with many of his students in the cult churches today as pastors and elders, said to her in response, "you shall not surely die, but God knows that if you eat of this tree, you shall be like him; your eyes shall be open and you shall be like him." In other words, you are allowed to partake of all the other trees, and that is cool, however, limited, but did you know that if you partake of this one, you will be even closer to God? Yes, you will be so close that you will be like him, having your eyes open to knowledge. (Gen. 3:1-7.)

The devil at this time used his delusional mind as a catalyst to deceive Eve, in believing in his lies.

 In the cult churches today, many often make this same delusion of using their sinful nature, for discernment. Anyone who presumes something negative about someone else, because of their own sensuality, must be careful of the work they are doing. Oops! Sorry, they can't because they have already been deceived. They then make a further mistake by judging, not knowing that they are sinning and judging themselves. The scripture says: "judge not, as will be judged in the same way you do judge others. The same measure you gave will be given to you." (Matt.7:1-3.) If you judge others, you are not doing the work of God, but the work of the other spirit that is within you, the devils. (Mark 5:6-9. Luke 23:18-23.)

In the above parable and bible accounts, the stories are factual, and not judgmental in any way, but are reflecting the truth that is presented from the Holy Scriptures and experiences with these demonic spirits that were and are still manifested within the cultic church congregations today. The challenge is there for anyone of these types of persons to refute these truths. Knowing that they can't, they, therefore, need to confess the truth publicly, and ask for forgiveness and repent of their wicked cultic ways. (Acts 3:19, 1 John 1:9.)

So, the action is physical, while the intent is mental. Therefore, evil thoughts with actions are physically sinning, while evil thoughts alone with bad intentions are mentally sinning. All sins are confirmed within the mind first, which then results in physical expressions most of the time. That was what Adam did; he first conceived in his heart: mind, then the spirit of the Most, High left him, then he acted on the sentiments of his heart. Remember, however; he did not just one day choose to do so out of the blue. There was another influence present, the devil who instigated and prompted him under cover of his wife. She had already been infected with the sin germ and was now used as an agent to inject Adam. Therefore, be careful of those around you, especially the ones closest to you. You are always influenced by those you come in contact with if you are not the one doing the influencing. Be wise in choosing your company and church.

However, ironically, as it is, many of these men who are so-called leaders, including many pastors, are the ones influencing their wives to commit devious acts with them because of their positions in the cult churches and or organizations.

The devil had already planned to destroy the Most, High God's precious jewels. Remember, the text message states in 1 Peter. 5:8 "be sober be vigilant; because your adversary the devil, as a roaring lion, prowls about, seeking whom he might devour." That means that whenever anyone in or outside the church tells you that they want to destroy or kill you, they are doing the work of the devil, like Jezebel, Pastor R, and Sis. V did. They have already allowed themselves to be filled by the spirit of the evil one through the manifestations of envy, jealousy, hate, greed, etc. However, Adam ultimately chose for himself. You can't blame someone else for making your own choices. The devil does not have that power over you; you have volunteered to be used by him. You have allowed the evil one to use you because of your wicked intent towards your brothers or sisters, just like Cain, to gain some temporary relief. (Gen. 4:5-8.) However, we who are attacked daily by evil forces both physically and spiritually, our response to these threats, should be seasoned with grace for these poor confused demonic souls: pastors and members alike. Knowing they are weak by their selfish desires, evil plotting, scheming, and wicked intent. They need help that can only come from an experience with the true and living God that they do not know, regardless of how long they have been in the church, or their positions. They will profess to know the Most, High God, but they don't. (Matt.15:8.) We now have an opportunity to show them who the true and living God is by being an example to them, the same way the Messiah was to his enemies.

 We represent light; they darkness. (John 3:19.) We represent life; they represent death. Proverbs 18:21. We represent freedom; they slavery. John 8:32. We represent consciousness; they ignorance. John 1:5. We represent goodness; they evil. Romans 12:21. We present the spirit; they the flesh. 2 Cor.3:17, Romans 8:1-8. We offer the truth; they give lies. John 14:6, John 8:44. Therefore, we stand firm in what we represent and present to The Most, High God, all the honor, glory, power, and praise, both now and forever. Rev. 5:13.

Chapter 13

The Lust of the Demons at Simon's and the head elder's Houses

Another example that can shed more light on this subject is the lust of the demons that have plagued the cult church and homes. There was an invitation the messiah got to a significant person's house: a church leader. (These examples are essential because they expose the working of the spirit that is within. Which tells if we are of the true and living God or the devil. We are counseled to test the spirit to see which it is.) (1 John 4:1.)

Luke 7:36-50.

Within the culture of the messiah's day, a guest would be offered water to wash before being entertained. That should not be any different from the messiah as a guest, being served by this very important host, towards this most important guest. However, this common courtesy, the messiah, was not shown. Was this a deliberate insult on the part of the host to show his friends that the messiah did not mean much to him, though he was the one who invited him? However, a certain woman of the 'day' that the messiah had met before was at the feast and preceded to wash his feet, then opened an expensive Alabaster Jar of exotic rear perfume and began to anoint the Messiah. This act from a woman of the "night" might have been looked on as very emotionally engaging, by those who knew who the woman was, and might have even had some encounters themselves with her. However, her intentions were clean, and the messiah's mind was pure. She wanted to show how much she appreciated what the messiah had done for her. The problem was not with the messiah or the woman, but those who were looking on with lustful minds themselves. They tried to project their evil-mindedness, sentiments toward the messiah and the woman. However, it was the spirit of the Most; High God that moved in the heart of the woman to do an act that the high priests should have done but were clueless in this regard. They knew at the birth of Christ that he was to come, Matt.2:1-5, but because of their lack of belief, after they saw and heard him, they rejected him. (John 1:11. Matt.22:15.) Because of their doubt, many were left to their reprobate minds, even at this house.

If they had the spirit of the living God, they would have not only known of him but accepted the Master and be a part of this critical spiritual act. Instead, those who were possessed by demons tried to condemn the messiah and the woman with their corrupt minds. (Luke 7:36-50.)

In other words, do not jump to conclusions on things that you do not know and do not understand. Instead, go and pray, asking God to show you what is going on, and allow the spirit of God to lead.

The carnal man is only interested in what stimulates his desire and will react to that feeling to please his sensual self. Consequently, he will project his ways of thinking on to someone else who he targets as an enemy. While in his religious mind, he believes he is doing the will of God, but rather is steep in the work of the devil, pleasing his sensuality.

In the parable of "the man who helped his enemies," He also was invited to a party to honor the head elder's wife at their house. Or so they said. However, it was used as a plot or to set-up an attack and to condemn the man of God.

 At the party, there were members of the board and this particular member, the same impotent jigaboo who always has people business on his mind, but never his own. While the man who help these enemies was sitting there talking to his wife. This perverted jigaboo came into the room and bent overexposing his posterior, so much so that the wife of the man who helped these enemies had to rebuke him and told him to cover himself. What was most interesting was that both pastors, the head elder, as it was his home, and other board members were there looking on, as though they all had plotted and schemed this act of this jigaboo to condemn the man that helped if he would respond the way of their perverted scheming demented demonic jigaboo cultic minds because they had discussed the deviousness of the woman 'Jezebel' and decided to use her false allegation to attack this son of God, again, because he refused her and her friends, sanctified sisters, and mothers of Zion's sexual attacks, and efforts to be used by her and their organization for money.

 Well, not long after, the man who helps these foolish enemies left this demonic jigaboo environment with his wife.

 It is also interesting that the demonic jigaboo wife (Sis. F) of this demon possess fellow (Bro. H) send a message to the 'man who helped his enemies' phone. This message exposes and confirms their wicked thoughts, as it speaks on the question of projected homosexuality. However, the question is: why would a man expose

91

his posterior to another man, unless he is expressing what he is? I am Just asking. Maybe 'him' or his demon-possessed wife can answer. Especially if he has a wife and has not engaged sexually with her for so many years, but rather calling her an 'old gate.' As we know by now, even these people need the gospel and the glove. Or was this a part of the demonic jigaboo plot, as mentioned by this pastoral staff and its board member sidekicks?

We have to remember that many who call themselves Christians, who pride themselves as being "remnant," are indeed remnant, but no other than demons possess 'remnant' people, their jigaboo act towards each other proves this. These acts are a result of their state of mind. However, they need to know that being branded as "Remnant" or "Christian" does not help them. You can't be righteous by association or brand names. Also, within their own company; they think they are children of God, but none in that group or company wants to correct the other, because all want to be accepted so eagerly by each other at whatever cost, cult; only to be acting as children of their father the devil. (John 8: 44. 16:2.) These types also show how devious and demonic they all are, who were a part of that plot, just like those who plotted against the messiah. However, the Most; High reveals to his servants all the secrets. (1Cor. 2: 12 -15.) These acts show the characteristics of a cult organization, where the pastor (Bro. M), as the representative of the organization, was involved in steering these attacks with the first elder (Bro. C).

This occult behavior was revealed many years before to this son of God, who helped these enemies, in a vision. The same first 'head' elder (Bro. C) was seen leading the scheme in the vision. He, being one who is more interested in being approved of men rather than knowing the Most, High God. He who would rather be diplomatic than being truthful, staying on the surface rather than going deep. Lying to the people to be accepted by his superior, rather than searching diligently for the truth, and when finding it, teach it. This attitude is the character of a wimpy jigaboo slave. Therefore, he will do just about anything for the attention, Sad. Interestingly, this son of God had gone to this same elder's house and ministered on several occasions to him and his wife, (Sis. A) even though he knew this 'head' jigaboo hated his guts and was jealous of him. (Matt. 5:44.) Most of these attackers have been ministered to by this man and his wife in many different ways over the years. However, they hate the man of God because of their greed, jealousy, covetousness, incompetence, and ignorance. Symptoms of demon possession. (2 Timothy 3: 1-7.) And the man's refusal to be used as a slave to support these lazy lying deluded pastors and a corrupt system is also reasons for their hatred and attacks against him.

It is rather interesting that this elder was so upset with the man of God, so much so that he refused to pray for success in his trip to Malaysia in 2015 because he believes that he was traveling too much; spending all that money on his music ministry, and thought that the money should go to the church instead. His only response, when asked to pray for journeying mercies, was "AGAIN!!!?" You see, this son of God had gone to Australia a few years before on his music ministry. However, he only started to be a part of that music ministry at a different church because the men at this church showed signs of stagnation, incompetence, and immaturity. This same elder's wife had also mentioned that he was upset with the many traveling of this son of God, back to Jamaica, his country of origin; this is what I call humongous jealousy at its best.

I used those examples to show how man is attacked psychologically, because of his dark hatred desires, before he is physically drawn by the devil, through the very nature of his own covetous and hateful heart. (James 1:12-15.) Also, to show it is never about the next person. It is always about "you" and "me," the "individuals" and their relationship with the Most, High God. Whatever they: your enemies do, should not affect your relationship with the true and living God in a negative way, but should be used to draw you closer to him, your only true constant friend. The only way this can happen is to know that your priority is never with a government, church, organization, persons, or person, but only with The Most, High God.

Unfortunately, the church's objective today is to keep their members in slavery, by hiding the truth from them, so the financial support they think they need continues. However, we see these text messages: "you shall know the truth, and the truth shall set you free." (John 8:32.) "When he the spirit of truth comes, he will guide you into all truth." (John 16:13.) These counsels are given to prevent us from becoming like those jigaboos slaves we see and know.

Consequently, to be able to worship in spirit and truth, the mind has to be made right by knowing the truth. We cannot allow any distractions to come into the mind from anyone or anywhere because this is where the spirits dwell. The spirit of the individual man and the spirit of the Most; High God has to be in constant harmony. Not an external relationship of going to church, but an internal integral one of intimacy with the Father, through the indwelling of his spirit daily. Nothing or no one is allowed in this sacred space between you and the Most, High God. But the enemy of our souls will use his attacks to distract us from what is most important in our lives; our relationship with the Most, High God. Therefore, this truth exposes the fact that those who do devious things, as mentioned above, can't be of The Most, High God, because to plot and scheme evil has to be within evil minds. Those of us who have the mind of Christ, do not plot evil but do good even to our enemies as the man of God did to those, who attacked and continues to attack him. (Phil.2:5. Matt. 9:36.) None of those nuts (crazies) cult members can say they did not know and got tricked by the lie of the woman. They were only responding the way they do because of the evil spirit in them.

As a result of not having true knowledge, most members of the cult churches are ignorant jigaboo slaves. Caught up into various infighting for position, association, money, and favors that result in a continued cycle of slavery, to the destruction of their very own souls.

Conclusion: As a man, especially a black intelligent, independent thinking man in an institution of slaves call church. If you are intelligent, independent, have knowledge, wisdom, and understanding, and objects to false theologies, you will be targeted, just as Christ was. They will try to offer you bribes first, for you to compromise, and if you should refuse them, they will attack. If those member slaves are unable to attack you to your face, because of their stupidity, they will conspire and make up stories about you with their leaders. If you refuse to lay with these conspiring Jezebels in these cultic churches, they will try to call you names. If you refuse to support these lazy cult pastors, who have spent so many years learning and obtaining many degrees, but are unable to teach things that are spiritual, sensible, true, or presents any solution of any kind worthwhile, but has become like a plague of parasites on the poor, they will hate your guts. If you try to teach these brainwashed cult slaves to be independent and how to have a real knowledge of self, these same slaves will attack you because of fear of thinking for themselves. However, we pray that all these types will have an encounter with the spirit of the true gospel so that a change can be made in them also.

Part 3

Slavery in the world and churches

Slavery, unfortunately, is not just a thing of the past but is every present with us today. However, today's form of slavery, in many parts of the developed world, is most subtle than ever. This subtlety allows the slave to think he is free because the illusions of his apparent physical needs are satisfied. He is also given a particular position of notoriety, without an accurate knowledge of his self, power, and responsibilities, or lack thereof. (Romans 1:18-32, John 8:33.)

Unfortunately, having knowledge, understanding, and wisdom in a given field of endeavor does not exempt one from being a slave, if those gifts are not used to the progress of knowing the truth of oneself and others.

Remember, knowledge is information gathered, understanding is information applied appropriately, and wisdom is the awareness of the results gathered by the experiences in the progression of one's life and the lives of those who employ such knowledge and information.

Chapter 14

Props and Puppets

 As was stated in the previous chapter. Likewise, many today may have the same distorted mindset of you. However, rather than accepting their sick conditions, and asking the Most, High God to help them. They would try to give the impression that someone else is guilty of their carnal maladies. They are often seen in groups, within these cult churches, with others having the same deluded mentality against the truth, so to get the support system they need. Many of these types are working for a corrupt organization or any other corrupt institutions that align themselves with religious cult Babylon.

They have to attack those that stand for the truth, to keep their association, employment, or to be employable. There is an idiom, 'when you go to Rome, you do as the Romans do.' Also, it is true, when you take Rome into your house and drink the wine of Rome, you become what the Romans taught, which is just a logical result. Look in their lesson study books. This brainwashing includes auxiliary staff members and pastors, departmental leaders and presidents, local elders, and members. Those employed with or without a portfolio are all used now as props in different ways for Babylon. Therefore, in this way, what I call 'projected sin' can be assumed by others, about you, if you do not comply with their dictates. This attack is natural for them to do because of the brainwashed organizational teaching that they have received through systematic false theology, especially if they hate you because you refused to be used by them while they are desperate for a job, position, association, or money.

Now the difference between a "prop" and a "puppet" is, a prop is someone who is a fill-in for just about any common task; no significant resource is used for the training of such a person. Similar to an accessory on a stage, or a TV set. These props are purchases that are made from the 'petty cash' and not usually a budget item. These persons (props) have no portfolio and can lose their petty cash job at any given time. Therefore, they'll do just about anything to keep that low, level job, and whatever benefits that come with that, while puppets are those who are trained systematically to be used as props in a recognized position. They are given a portfolio, just for them to feel good about themselves, while they have no backbone. Most pastors in an organized cult religion are puppets. Either way, they are both used as enemies of the truth. Another name for these is Jigaboos: a slave term for both blacks and whites in such a condition and or position. In the big geopolitical religious scheme of things, these institutions and people are known as "pawns."

Remember, the Messiah, who was the truth, was hated by many of these props, puppets, and pawn types Jigaboos. (John 8:32-55.) And they were trying their hardest to smear him while sneering at him, to keep their positions. However, he had the spirit of the Most, High God within, and that was all that mattered. The same is true of us today. (Luke 21:12-19.)

Chapter 15

Slavery then and Now

During the industrialization days of slavery, when slavery was king for the white and Arab racist bigots. One of the most effective methods that were used by the slave demonic masters to keep the slaves in slavery continually was keeping the slaves ignorant. They took away the languages of the slaves so the slaves could not understand what was being said or written about them even if they heard or saw it. This way, the slave jigaboo masters could maintain their authority over their subjects. They were, in effect, able to direct the lives of the slaves the same as one manipulates a puppet. As long as they kept the slaves ignorant or gave the slaves the basic distorted knowledge, brainwash; this they though as necessary to have them, the slave jigaboo masters accomplished their own goals. This way, they would always be in control, so they could and have worked the slaves to death, to gain all the wealth and power they had then and today. Their main objective was to live off the slaves as liken to a parasite and continue to live off the legacy of slavery as compare to a saprophyte for many years to come. Today, a jigaboo parasite saprophytic society, living off the living and the dead.

Now, if you do not know who you are, then you are a jigaboo living dead. There is no way different than how the churches operate today. Except, that its emphasis is on the intellectual or mental aspects of jigaboo slavery, with not just the same materialistic greed, but a further deliberate spiritual exploitation a cycle of slaves enslaving themselves and others using what they call psychology, and false theology. This structure is where black pastors and other "minorities" are recruited on a mass scale as puppet slave masters of the auto slavery religious system. The main objective is to exploit the spiritual and physical wealth of the mentally weak masses, through their deliberate teaching of false theologies and the manipulation of misguided emotions using psychology.

Chapter 16

How do they do this?

In the organized religious churches today, most ministers are trained as subordinate slave jigaboo masters to manage their jigaboo subjects. Not as shepherds caring for their flocks, but as subordinate slave managers, or indentured servants, controlling other slaves. We know this because, whenever real practical questions are asked of them, that affect our present and future existence as a people, these slave managers/pastors are unable to answer appropriately or take appropriate action, but become very angry and defensive of their organization's position, and are always eager and ready to show control, but are unable to give proper insight and leadership, however, will be anxious **to tell you, your reward is in heaven.**

Now, to be an effective jigaboo slave manager, he or she has to be taught slave management skills, on the same principles as in the controlling of a literal slave, but without the abusive physical components in some cases. Today it is known as psychology, speaking in other languages such as Greek, Latin, etc., and having credentials or papers from the slavery jigaboo's headquarters or institutions call conferences, seminaries, colleges, universities, etc., that most slaves do not have. These are the types of tools that are needed to be a religious slave master, having a slave master's degree, in the established jigaboo churches today. These types of structures are looked on as necessary in any progressive organization or democratic society of slaves. However, the slaves do not understand that these institutions exist for the continuation of their enslavement, in real-time, in this their very own slavery empire.

The genius in this is, these institutions teach their subordinates how to accept being slaves with benefits, while keeping the subjects or slaves, as slaves, in a way that they, the slaves, are deceived or brainwashed into thinking they are not slaves, but "feel free." (John 8: 32- 47.)

"I freed a thousand slaves I could have freed more if only they knew they were slaves." Harriet Tubman

However, these modern-day slaveholders are more sophisticated in their sophistry, in that their psychological abuses are not considered abusive at all by these slaves, but as "keeping of the flock." One of the most deceptive illusions of this structure is that these subordinate slave masters look, and sometimes live precisely like the slaves they are managing. Most of the time, they are from the same communities of slaves. This way, they can keep those in slavery to continue this auto-slavery system. They are also of all different skin tones, faces, and races in the broader community, which is another way they can quickly blend in and be a part of the population of slaves they are managing without easily drawing suspicion unto themselves from the other slaves.

The fundamental way this work is limited information is given to the subjects, not enough to enable the slaves to think independently and to come into his or her consciousness of self and be able to make intelligent decisions, which is truly more than rounded education. Most choices that these subjects make are influenced heavily by the control of these modern slaveholders or pastors, who are also in control by their superiors. Their structure is a hierarchical tree, a pyramid scheme, or a system. With this structure in place, they are now able to use the herd mentality psychology to control. They give the members slaves the impression that they have control by giving them certain statuses such as elders, deacons, church secretaries, clerks, etc. We know this because most of these slaves are given position, not because of their giftedness, but their willingness to obey their slave masters. This way, these members have the feeling that they are doing great, with the understanding that they respect and follow only the decisions that are given to them by their slaveholders.

They are also able to have a board of leaders, or elders and board members meeting, where they oversee the business of the local church. There is nothing wrong with that in itself. However, they have been brainwashed to comply with the dictates of their slave masters on making decisions to keep themselves in line. Their lives as a whole are no more the better for it physically or spiritually. As no plans are coming out of those meetings that would initiate an improvement in the lives of the people, they represent over all the many years. A few might be doing good materially, in their own eyes, and those few will fight "tooth and nail" for things to stay the way they are, entrapping the others below themselves, just for their status quo. There is no actual program implemented that is towards helping the local members in general significantly, other than for those slave masters to continue to keep them as slaves bringing in those tithes and offerings. No equal opportunity here for the masses; however, some would rather pride themselves as the top church in sending their resources to their slave masters, while their local members suffer in silent apathy for their basic spiritual and physical needs to be met. Most necessary financial resources are stripped from the local churches and communities and are used elsewhere for others to benefit, while they are told to send more and more, and they will be blessed. This act of giving away your resources for your needs, then praying for your needs to be met, is an act that only an enslaved jigaboo brainwashed mind will do. This trading of reality for an illusion, then praying for the illusion to be a reality, is a distinct characteristic of an enslaved jigaboo mind.

Another ingenious act by these jigaboo devils is initiated if the members are becoming awaken, and are starting to ask specific questions of importance, yes, a very devious and sinister manipulative act is implemented: they will begin to employ individual jigaboo member slaves, who they can control from within that congregation to work within the administrative body of the institutions they call local conferences. This way, they can use these positioned jigaboos to appease the others that are coming into the truth. This manipulation is how wonderful a work these institutions do to continue to captivate the minds of these slave subordinates called pastors, Elders and members alike, to continue to do this fantastic work of brainwashing of self and the masses in the name of their pagan religions and gods.

These leaders are like the slave that has the keys for his slave master's property, but can't benefit anything from it significantly; other than stealing, or been given papers, that's called credentials, or the feeling of symbolic accomplishment, if he or she keeps the other slaves in their positions as slaves.

Similar to Obama winning the presidency, of 2008. It sure felt good and symbolize progress to the ignorant, but did nothing for the people in general and the "blacks" in particular, only a few interest groups. Because he was presented as another "black" president, Bill as the first (hah!), but was he just another wolf in sheep cloning or a jigaboo puppeteer? They accepted him as one of them, only to be screwed. He said 'change' must come, but the change that came under his presidency, was not for the better of the people, but the worst. Check the changes in the constitution under his administration, especially for him to have claimed to be a constitutional lawyer at the time, very sad.

They also do not look the part as slaveholders, because they look just like the other subjects around them; but they think of themselves as different from the other. They refer to themselves as being learned and more intelligent than the brainwashed ones, while some have voluntarily brainwashed themselves, just for money and status. Others will even express how brain-drain they are by going as far as telling their congregants that they have bigger brains than all the members combine, and have to wear many hats. They are so boastful of the temporary positions they occupy that they will do anything to keep it. These new slave jigaboo handlers are wolves in sheep cloning, they pose as ministers of the gospel in various positions within the churches, but do not have a clue of what the gospel is.

Chapter 17

How to Identify, your status

There are ways to identify if you are an enslaved jigaboo or a slaveholder jigaboo, in a slaveholding institute or church. While this might be very hard for you to accept about yourself, if you are in your right mind when you read this, you will not be able to deny the truth. Here are a few common signs.

One is, being opposed by the leaders when you ask questions that are important to you, and you accept without resistance. (2) New information is given to you for you to follow without discussion with you first, even if it is not in your best interest, and you follow without question. (3) Decisions are made that affect you, and you are not a part of the decision process at any level, but your leaders tell you they have made those decisions already; you have nothing to worry about, and you have no problem with that and do nothing. (4) If your ministers act or speak, thinking they own you, by ignoring what is important to you, but requires your support for them, and you support them. (5) If your elders think they are in charge of you but are not responsible to you when you are in need, and you accept that condition. (6) If the members hate each other because of the different understanding of the various interpretations of the text messages in the scriptures, and the leaders take side with those who can give more money, and is unable to provide a clear, unbiased explanation, and you continue to support them. (7) If the pulpit and, or office is used by the ministers as his platform to promote his own, or the organization's agenda while ignoring what is good and right for the members, as instructed by the biblical text messages, and you think that is ok. (8) If the elders or visiting preachers preach to promote the resident pastor's agenda and not the word of the Most, High God without fear or favor, and you applaud them regardless. (9) If the members call the pastors wife the first lady, which makes them second class members with or without knowing it. (10) If the members sign cards and give extra money to the pastor for appreciation, even though they know the pastor is a liar and is ungodly in his administration. (11) If the women are call mothers of Zion, by the leaders, pastors, and their affiliates, however, these women make Jezebel looks like an angelic choir girl, but the leaders promote them regardless because of these Jezebels attack those who oppose these lying leaders. And my favorite; sending your money as tithes and offerings to these thieves, and think it is ok for them to do whatever they feel with your money without being responsible to you, by not giving an accurate account; however, you believe that God will take care of them for your stupidity. To mention, a few jigaboo facts act.

 If you are on the receiving end of these atrocities, but stay on this slave ship of Zion and support such, you are indeed an enslave jigaboo, in a slave institution call church. If you are a part of the administration, administrating these injustices to the people, you are a subordinate jigaboo slave who has been enslaved to be used to enslave your people voluntarily or otherwise. These behaviors are not just slavery, but the most accurate definition or description of mental illness, which is so prevalent in the jigaboo churches and jigaboo governments of the world today.

Chapter 18

How to get out of slavery from your black or white jigaboo church

First and foremost, you have to know and understand the inspired text messages for yourself. Do not depend on the institutionalize brainwashed pastors or elders to tell you the truth. They have an ego and position that have to be fueled and kept, and they will say and do just about anything to get that high and hold that position. They are no different from those drug head Zombies. Remember, the text message states, "My people perish through lack of knowledge." (Hosea 4:6.) How is it that these leaders are so educated and intellectual, but their followers are so distraught and ignorant? It's rather a simple answer; you have to have the spirit of the Most, High God for yourselves, that they don't have.

Remember the text message says again: the messiah speaking, "I will send you the spirit, and when he the spirit of truth comes, he will guide you into all truth" (John 16: 13.) This promise was not just for the disciples, but for each and everyone that believes, then and now. The spirit of the Most; High God is our teacher. Not the pastors or elders or any leader in the organizations in which you are a member. They should also be students of the spirit. Why should you listen to another student when the teacher is there to teach you the truth? (John 16:13.) The student will tell you what he thinks, not what he knows to be the truth; this is second-hand information for his gain, just for him to look good or impress others. How can you know what he is saying is true, if you do not understand the truth yourselves? You would be a very dense student to listen to another student when the teacher is there teaching. Of course, you would have failed the exam before taking it. Well, if the teacher is not there, which is the spirit of God, as in most cases, you should go where you can find the teacher, and the spirit will teach you.

You should also find out what spirit is speaking to you through these speakers. The text message says we should try or test the spirits to see if they are of the Most, High God. (1 John 4:1-6.) Now, how do we test the spirits? Well, we test the spirits by comparing what is said by these speakers with the truth. Anyone who stands before you and speaks lies is of the devil and has the spirit of their father, the devil. (John 8:44.) If you are not clear about what they are saying, ask them to explain clearly, if they are unable to do so, they have no business standing before you, and are not of God. Therefore, you should rebuke them. (Matt.16:23.)

Understanding also, that those who speak in "other tongues" do not necessarily mean they have the spirit of God, it could be another evil spirit. Their lives will tell. Being able to love your neighbors as you love yourselves, also being able to love your enemies both inside and outside the cult churches, tells a different story. Because you are not the one doing the loving, but the spirit of the Most, High in you. Your natural will is to get back at these wicked ones, but you find that you love (AGAPE) them regardless of their acts. (Luke 6:26-28., Matt. 5:43-48.) (*Most of these types of Christian speak a lot about Agape, Philia, Eros, Ludus, Pragma, or Philautic but do not understand the true meaning of Agape when shown. For example, they talk about the concept of Agape excessively in these types of cult churches; however, it is not seen or demonstrated by these talkers. Therefore, when Agape, is reflected through others, it is not understood by the cults, and an attacked by these same types of church folks who attacked Christ will ensue*). However, do not trust them though you love them; only a fool would do such a thing as mixing oil with water, thinking oil and water will blend into one. (Psalm 146:3, 118:8, 9.) Therefore, anyone who hates, plots evil schemes, speaks lies as truth, deceives the people, is covetous and jealous of others, etc. 2Tim. 3:1-11, have not the spirit of the Most, High in him or her, but is a child of their father the devil. (John 8:44.) Stay away from those, but love (Agape) them from afar.

Chapter 19

A carrot here, and there

Remember now these slaveholders, also use the membership carrot stick card, to enslave the ignorant members. The illusion is that most members within the church think that having a membership is liken to having a golden membership card to club heaven, or a boarding pass for the ship of Zion. They will do almost anything to keep such flight cards or boarding passes. However, knowing that having a membership in a church does not mean you are a member of the family of God, and one with God, even on earth, should take you back to your senses. Knowing that paying a tithe also is similar to paying a membership fee to any exclusive church club of your choice.

With that fee payment, some benefits will be granted to you, but not to those who do not pay. Also, members who pay these fees are exempted from individual scrutiny, even if they break the laws or by-laws of these clubs, even by corrupt pastors or managers. These members also are promoted to positions they are not qualified for but are made eligible by their donations and membership fees. Think of a person who is not educated or able to reason intelligently, being made education director in an organization because of their money bag. However, the poor, even if they are gifted, are marginalized and sometimes totally disregarded. (One woman who was a retired educator after many years, was told she couldn't be used in the church unless she returns a tithe from her welfare check by a devious pastor) These are some of the many ways in which members are being manipulated and enslaved in these jigaboo corrupt church club institutions. Any church where the money is used to gain favor, advantage, and in exchange for certain positions and privileges, is nothing, but a corrupt market place that is practicing religion, politics, and business. It doesn't matter if they call themselves the remnant. (Matt. 21:13, Luke 19: 45-47.) An apple doesn't fall far from the tree. Well, there is only one way to say it: "Welcome to the daughters of Babylon." (Rev.14:8.) The real cults.

A church that teaches that you have to pay a tithe to get into heaven is a deceiving and demonic corrupt slavery organization that is trying to sell salvation. They point their fingers at the catholic church for selling indulgences and other favors, to increase their coffers, while they too sell salvation through tithing, to increase their coffers. They deliberately mistranslate Malachi 3, to keep the people ignorant of the truth for temporary personal gains. Also, the misplacement of the book of Nehemiah, especially chapter 13, to further disguise the facts. You would think those who boast of being the "remnant" and have the "truth" would tell the truth, but money has become their God, so they lie for their God, sick. A word to the wise is sufficient.

Part 4

Intelligence is useful, Knowledge is better, but wisdom is the key. As we all should know that being intelligent is not just having the ability, but applying that ability to acquire knowledge and skills. While knowledge is information gathered, wisdom is understood through the appropriate application of such knowledge with intelligence, resulting in positive engagement and effects from our actions in our present and for our future lives.

Proverbs 8.

Chapter 20

"Now is," the truth about evolution in a nutshell

So how was it possible for the messiah to say "now is" at that time? How did he know?

If we look carefully at who was speaking, we will have a better understanding.

Now, to understand who the messiah was, and why he was able to say "now is," we have to go back to another beginning.

The book of John 1:1, 14, tells us: "In the beginning was the word, and the word was with God, and the Word was God, and the Word became flesh." Remember this word that was **with** God and **was** God **became** flesh! Very important to remember that.

Anyone who believes in the big bang, should not have a problem accepting that the Word became flesh. Why? Well, it takes less faith to believe that something else can come from something than something coming from practically nothing. Besides, science is experimental. You need something to be used to experiment with to get a result. If there were practically nothing, the result is conclusive. Nothing from nothing equals, NOTHING!!! That is why the creation account is scientific, and the Big Bang is a theory.

Therefore, we are here in the flesh, an undeniable fact of our existence. In other words, we can engage reverse intelligent reasoning to get back to intelligent beings of the flesh that presently exist: us. But the big bang theorists need to show a speck of "blob" by reverse biological engineering from what, man? Then this blob is then reversed further into nothing, which proves that this theory of evolution is nothing but a figment of the imagination of man's brilliant (crazy) mind. Now, being brilliant in thought does not make something that does not exist into something unless it came from an intelligence outside of created man, which is the creative spiritual force and the source of all intelligence, which is also what we call God, or you can say the 'source' if you are more comfortable saying that.

There is no question that the earth is possibly millions of years old. However, man's existence in the flesh presently lends itself closer to an intelligent creation account than nothing can. As funny as it might sound. The big bang theory is closer to the first sexual encounter the first man had with the first woman. This Big ban is reflected in the process of sexual initiation, copulation, ejaculation, or swimming like a fish, and impregnation or the fertilization of an egg. Development and delivery come after; then, we have walking on all four: or crawling. Standing up on two, or walking upright. That is your evolution or development of the physical man in a nutshell, and we are still evolving, but mentally! The true cycle of the physical evolution of man has not changed since the creation of man. The Imaginary science, with interesting names, cannot replace reality.

Also, the different stages of the appearances of human development in man, socially and environmentally, purported by the evolutionist, can be explained simply by the increase of knowledge to invent new and better ways to survive. The reverse, therefore, is true; if you should take away all the modern amenities consistently over some time not similar to the period used to acquire them, we will ultimately revert to the condition we were in before these amenities existed. Knowing, however, for that to happen, our minds, not our bodies, will have to revert to a lower evolved state for each phase. And guess what! It would not return ultimately into a slime particle, but into a crazy state of being. (Daniel 4:25-33.) Therefore, the difference of a man with a stone, a man with a spear, a man with a wheel, a man with a bicycle, a man with a car, a man with a plane, a man with a space ship, and a man, is not the man, but the stone, spear, the wheel, the bicycle, the car, the plane, and the space ship. We see here that the mind or intelligence of the man is what has evolved because of the advancement in technology, but not the body. The physical or biological man is constant, which speaks to further evolution in the mind of the man and not the body. His appearance will change in regards to how he dresses and functions with the new tools acquired. So, the only part of the man that evolves is that which is in liquid. An act of the sperm and egg coming together to initiate the first stage of evolution in the body of the first mother, who was created by God or the source. Here is the answer to the question: what comes first, the chicken or the egg? The chicken came with the egg. The second stage of evolution continues in water also, but this time it is the mind within the brain. Yes, the physical man is constant; however, the things he makes changes base on his needs and mental awareness, which lends itself to his increased mental development or the evolution of his mind. The English proverb that states: "Necessity is the mother of invention" is not just a proverb, but a statement of reality which challenges destroy, and proves the big bang theory is a myth of a "brilliant" (crazy) mind.

How do we know the Messiah was the word?

Well, we saw the messiah in praying to his Father, making a fascinating statement. In John 17:1-5, he said, "……. glorify me in your presence with the glory I had with you before the world began." Now, why was it so important for him to pray for glorification? There is a significant amount of revelation that is within that statement.

He is here referring to an experience he had, in the spirit, before the world began. How revealing it is that he would ask for an attribute that he had with the Father before the world began. In asking for something that can only be in a different realm and state of being, tells us that he knew of his prior existence with the Father. He was the spirit that moved upon the face of the deep in Genesis 1 and John 1:1-3.

His preexistence shows and confirms that he was the word that was with the Father before the world began. He was the one with the Father, who was also God, who made the world together. They are the 'us' in Geneses 1:26. And God said, "Come, let us make man…" Therefore, he knew that glorification is the one authentic experience that only the true and living God can have, and as a man, he was limited. So, he knew that this status belonged only to God, and so he also knew that as a man, he could not be able to experience this glory he had with the Father before, as he did when he was God as spirit. Therefore, when he asked that he may be glorified again, as he was with the Father, he was speaking to the future from the past, at present, into eternity, which was the reality of his existence presently, in a different state of being.

Now that he was in a man, he understood his limitations. Knowing this, he, therefore, spoke of the future, beyond time, back into eternity, as exemplified in his life. We need to know and believe this truth, so our faith becomes alive in the Most, High God. (Phil. 2:8, 1 Peter 1:21, 4:1-2.)

Consequently, having all knowledge, power, and being Omnipresent, which he did not have while on this earth, still would not cover all the essential attributes of the one true eternal God. However, to have all these attributes with Glorification, then one is indeed God almighty. He wasn't while he lived on earth as a man. Remember, this was what he prayed for, to have again. Besides, God will never pray to any other to get his glory. Therefore, we see again that Christ was not God while he lived on the earth. Matt. 28:19. This position of being God only applies to him before his birth, when he was one with the Father, and not after his second coming, when he came back to earth after his death, burial and ascension, when he was recognized. He will only display this glory again at his third coming. Not a second coming that occurred already, as most Christian falsely believe. His first coming was as a baby, his second was as the triumphant redeemer, and his third will be as King of Kings. (Luke 2:11-13, Luke 24:33, 36-49, John 20:11-21, Mark 16:12, Rev. 1:7.) {Those who are looking for the second coming, without the true knowledge of Christ appearing the second time before, as stated in John 20: 16-30, will be deceived of the appearance of the antichrist coming the second time. (2 Cor. 11:14, Matt. 24:25-27)}

However, this was the one attribute Lucifer wanted to have: glory. This way, he could be like the most, high God. Therefore, he went to war with the Most, High God for it. (Isaiah 14: 12-14, Rev. 12: 7-9.)

Now, let's look on the other side of the coin. Glory was also the attribute that the messiah prayed for, so he could be one with the Father again. Interestingly he did not pray for knowledge, or power, or omnipresence, but **Glory**. (John 17:5.) He, on the other hand, was obedient to the Father, even unto the death on the cross so that he could be glorified with the Father again. He was willing to give up his glory for the saving of our souls, and in so doing obtained glory again from the Father through his obedience to the Father's will. This prayer also reveals to us that the messiah recognized that he was one with the Father before, during eternity in the spirit. (Hebrews 2:9-10, Phil. 2:6-11.)

 Remember, the messiah had told the woman that the Most, High God is spirit. He would have known because he was the word that was with the Most, High God, and was one with the Father as the true and living God, who was also spirit. This knowledge was revealed to him by the spirit of God in him. So, we have proof and can accept his words. (Luke 2:52.) Therefore, the living word that was the spirit, who was the truth, and one with the living God, became flesh or most appropriately came into the flesh. (Luke 2:27,49, John 1:1-3, 14, 4-5. Hebrews 10:5)

This revelation also exposes the truth that those who believed that the messiah was just a true prophet will have to accept his words. Now, if you think he was a true prophet and accept his words, his own words tell us that he was the word that was one with the Most, High God, and was the true and living God before coming into the flesh. Therefore, we have no excuse than to accept him as the true and living God before coming into the flesh. If you accept him as a true prophet, you have to accept him as the messiah, who was the son of the living God in the flesh. (John 1:14.)

After becoming flesh, the messiah is considered by many scholars and others as the 'second Adam' for many years after his death and ascension. Adam here referring to the first physical man. This position indicated, and we know, that he succeeded the first Adam, as the co-operate man where he the first Adam had sinned, having the fallen nature of Adam. (Romans 8:3.) Therefore, the Messiah could and was ready to reveal who the true worshiper was at this time. He, coming into man, then picked up, so to speak, where the first Adam left off. Not only did he take on the flesh of Adam, but he also took on Adam's fallen nature. (Romans 8:3. Hebrews 2:14-18.) Emphasis on verse 16. His coming into flesh was the only way he could have redeemed our spirits and paid the price demanded by the law of God for us by becoming one with and like us.

He specifically told the woman that the true worshiper of the Most, High God was not indicated by a particular external location or showing: not on the mountain, in Jerusalem, or the flesh as a 'Jew.' As much as it stated that he had mentioned that salvation was of the 'Jews,' he made the point that the true worshiper is not indicated by being a 'Jew' or a Gentile for that matter; not the "race" or tribe you were born in; you can't play the 'race card.'(Gal.3:26-28. Romans 2, 10:12-13,) But one who worships in spirit and truth, for the Father seeks such a one. Races are categorized flesh, not spirit, and flesh can't please God. (Romans 8:8-17. 1 Cor. 15:50.) This knowledge is one of the reasons many who claim to be 'Jews' both blacks and whites hate the messiah. Simply because he has destroyed the false notion that the Most, High God prefers one nation over others because of lineage. Not in the new covenant. God is not interested anymore in a bloodline worshiper, but a spiritual worshiper, because God is spirit.

Similarly, God is not interested in the offerings of the blood of animals or sacrifices of man, but a broken spirit and a contrite heart. (Psalms 51:17. John 4:23.) That might have been in the past as a temporary symbolic expression, not anymore, since the messiah's death, today, or in the future.

We have to worship the true and living God only in spirit and in truth. (John 4:23-24.) Not with blood and flesh, or sacrifices, gifts, or tithes and offerings. (Psalms 51:16.) (Isaiah 1:11. Romans 6:10. 1 Cor. 15.) Therefore, whatever stock you are off

*is not relevant, or irrelevant to your salvation, and God, but a
broken and contrite heart is required. (Psalms 51:17.) Neither is
he interested in a particular location outside of the heart/mind
of man. Not in Jerusalem, Mecca, Rome, or your church. But
wherever you are, if you accept the spirit's bidding, he will
come in and sup with you.*

The messiah was a "Jew," yes, however, being of this lineage was not a qualification for him to be a true worshiper either. He had mentioned that some call themselves 'Jews,' but are of their father, the devil. Meaning they did not worship the true and living God, though they claimed to have lineage, but praised the devil by their deeds. Therefore, calling yourself a "Jew" or "remnant" does not qualify you to be of God. However, how you live will tell if you are of the devil or of the Most, High God, not what you call yourselves. Remember though, not all real 'Jews' were and are of the devil, but fake 'Jews' were and still are, because of their continuous lying. Neither are all whites racist, nor all blacks, slaves or Leaders stupid, nor all Asians smart, nor all those who say Allah or God terrorists, nor all Jamaicans smoke 'weed.'

 Now the Messiah was the son of the Most, High God, so he should know. (John 8:33-44, Rev. 3:9.) Therefore, it is never about a race, lineage, a tradition, a status, or a place; but always of a spiritual connection. These physical legacies are a total misconception of the truth of the gospel by those who seek to see themselves as better than others because of their traditions, be it stolen or not, and, or bloodline, in all these forms.

The fact that the messiah was born with the same nature of fallen Adam; therefore, he was inclined to sin. Luke 22:42. The fact that he had tainted blood running through his body, therefore he hungered and thirst, as like unto a common man. Consequently, it was not the blood that qualified him to be the pure Lamb of God, but the life he lived, being spiritually connected to his Father. (John 14:30.)

If it were the blood that made him acceptable to the Father, then we could play the race card and get away with it, but we would still be lost, and he couldn't help us. However, his blood was tainted, just like any other human being. (Romans 8:3.) The fact that he could be tempted and could have fallen, but did NOT fall to these temptations, indicated that he was a true seed of Adam, Abraham and David, and our blood brother; while at the same time, the spirit of the Most, High God was in him. (Heb.2:11-18, Romans 8:3-29.) The messiah was also made a high priest of the Most, High God by God's order. Yes, even a priestly seed from the lineage of man; flesh, but of the order of Melchizedek: spirit. However, a true

115

worshiper of God while at the same time condemned by the religious leaders of the day. Now, having all these gifts and contradictions did not give him an excuse for living a sinful life, while in a sinful body. And he did not but became perfect through obedience, and we certainly should not either. But also become perfect through obedience, through the power of the spirit vested in us, by the son. (Hebrews 5:1-10, Romans 8:1-4.)

I know that in the old testament, it said that "life is in the blood." (Gen. 9:4, Deut. 12:23, Levit. 17:13-14) However, this, too, needs to be distinguished from the symbolism usage of the expression in the old as it relates to Christ in the new. This usage refers to the eating of the flesh of the animal. The blood in the animal contains life or is the life source of the animal. If you eat the blood with the flesh or the blood, you are not eating just the meat, but the animal. Partaking of the flesh this way was and still is an unhealthy practice both on a spiritual and physical level, which was forbidden. In the sacrificial system, however, the blood was the main component that was used in this ritual, after the animal was sacrificed, for the completion of the process of the symbolic transference of sin. Many, it seemed, have confused the two with the text. (1 John 1:7). Many have said and have been taught and is teaching that the blood of Christ is the main component that cleanses us from sin, not realizing that verse 6 in 1 John 1 is where the meaning of the text rest. The word "walk" within the proper context is referring to how we live. This teaching comes out of substituting the real with the symbolic, which means that the spilled blood of animals was just a symbolism of the real-life of Christ. Now that Christ was here, in reality, living, there was no more need for the symbolic. Meaning we no more look at the blood but look on the life of Christ. Also, the death of Christ was the answer to the demand of the infallible law of God. "Without the shedding of blood, there is no remission of sin." (Heb. 9:22.) Meaning Christ had to pay the penalty of the law, for us, by giving his shed blood as corroborated by 1 John 1:7. However, more appropriately, it was him giving his life by living first the life; hence, the expression: life is in the blood, and that's it. (Remember Adam had blood in him before he had life: Ge. 2:7.)

Hebrews 9:12, speaks of Christ entering once into the holy place, by his own blood. This entering by his blood does not mean like the high priest he would sprinkle his blood in the holy place; no, this entering is speaking of his sinless life. The expression: life is in the blood, has now manifested as one; this is where reality takes precedence over symbolism. We see Christ the whole of salvation; our all in all in the holy of holies, not as a symbolic blood sprinkler like the high priest, but as the perfect living lamb of God. (Rev. 5: 6-10.) Therefore the 'walk' and 'light' mentioned in verses 5 and 6 of 1 John 1, is not referring to the symbolic or literal blood of Christ but the life of Christ in the believer. This life is what makes the blood of Christ effective for the purpose for which he came. Both in his life first and then his believers live as well.

I know many songs tell us about the precious blood of Christ that will never lose its power; however, the power contrary to popular belief, is never in the blood, but in the life of Christ. You see, the blood is the carrier or sustainer of the physical presence of the body; that's all it does period, nothing else. The life that is lived by us through the spirit is where the power lies. So, the proper or correct wording of these songs and poems should be, "the life will never lose its power." That is the truth that is consistent not only with the word but also with our own lives. With this proper understanding, we will see the power of the gospel is also in our own lives, and leave the 'bloody' rituals, that are now superstitions behind.

Chapter 21

The true worshiper does not sin because he is of a sinful nature.

Christ became sin, who knew no sin

(Romans 8:1-11.) However, we have an advocate with the Father if we fall. Hold on a minute; I understand that might sound strangely contradictory. Notwithstanding, it is crucial to note the truth here because this is the only way we can know that we worship in spirit and in truth, too, as the messiah did, and live without sinning as he also did; yes, while in a sinful body. (Heb. 10: 5. Romans 8:3. Heb. 2:14, 16-18.) First, we have to acknowledge the truthfulness of our condition; yes, we are sinful by nature from the fall; however, we are sinless by the spiritual life of redemption through the son of the Most, High, and him sending his spirit to maintain this privileged status in us. (Romans 8:1-17, John 16: 7-14.) That means that though you live in a sinful body with a sinful nature, you are not considered as a sinner in God's eyes after you are redeemed and is living by the spirit, but rather sons of God, as the messiah when he walked this earth. (Romans 8:14, 1 John 3:1-10.) How is this possible? Well, we have just read that he, Christ took on our sinful nature or body of sin and conquered sin and death in his flesh. So, the righteousness of the law is now fulfilled in us, who accept the gift of redemption through the spirit. (Romans 8:3.) He walked in our fallen flesh so that he could give us his righteous mind.

By accepting the redemption of the Most, High God through his son, you now become one with the Father and the son through the spirit. (John 17: 20-26. Psalm 103:1-5.) Yes!! Let that sink in, meditate on that truthfulness, bask in that glorious truth, yes! Let it marinate your minds.

Only by allowing our sinful nature to take control of us, are we then drawn away by our fallen desire to sin, after we are redeemed. (James 1: 13-16.) However, we do not have to allow this to happen, because the Most, High God has given us the power through his indwelling spirit residing in us, to stay away from sin; while in a sinful body. We also have the most excellent example of this life in Christ. (Gal. 5:16-26. Romans 6.)

Now, if the messiah were able to do so, live above sinning because he was of a sinless nature, then it would be unjust, by God's law, for God to seek such a one from among us to do so. The messiah could not then be considered as one of us, or be an example to follow if he were of a sinless nature. He could not have represented us at all. Therefore, he had to have been one like us in every way; "as a man of sin acquainted with grief." (Isaiah 53. Romans 8:3, Heb. 2:14-18. 2 Cor. 5:21.) Also, he could not have been touched with the very feelings of our infirmities, if he were not one like us, having the same fallen nature as us, yet without sin, as in sinning. (Hebrews 4:15. Isaiah 53:1-12.)

Now the obvious question should be if the messiah took on the sinful nature of Adam, Abraham, and David, just like us. (Luke 3. Romans 8:3. Genesis 1:26.) Then, how was it possible for the spirit of the Most, High God to dwell in him, for him to be a true worshiper, knowing that the spirit of the Most, High God left Adam because Adam had sinned? That is a great question, wouldn't you say?

To answer this question, we have to go back to this beginning again, John 1:14, which tells us that the Word became flesh. Therefore, to answer the above question, we need to start by looking at these questions first: what type of flesh did he become? And what does that mean concerning the question?

Now, there are only two types of flesh: sinless and sinful.

The creation account tells us that Adam was perfect after God created him. Meaning he was off sinless flesh or nature, but he committed a sinful act and became of sinful flesh and, or nature. Therefore, everyone who is born into a human family is born with a sinful nature. If Adam was the Father of all nations, who had sinned before the birth of his first child, then every baby that was, and is born of a woman after Adam sinned, was and is born with this fallen, sinful nature, including the messiah. (Gal. 4:4, Romans 8:3, 1 John 4:2-3. Heb. 2: 14, 16-18.)

There is no way around it. Some will argue that the spirit came upon the woman, and she conceived; therefore, no man had anything to do with her being pregnant, so the baby was pure of sin. However, those who propose this argument forget one vital piece of the biological chemical equation. The host of the seed is the one that supplied the original blood flow to the placenta, for the nourishment and life support for the baby and the body which was formed within that environment or womb. Consequently, the seed would not survive in this physical state that was needed, to be the sacrifice, without the host. Now, if the woman were pure: without sin, then her blood would not be tainted. Then that argument would make sense. However, that was not the case, but she was fallen just like all of us. (Romans 3:23.) She was a seed of sinful man, herself. Now being a virgin does not mean pure of sin but simply not being sexually engaged, as every virgin will confess, and calling he the mother of God does not change the truth.

We, however, now need to be careful in making the righteous distinction between what is a 'sinning' and what is the 'sinful' nature or flesh.

'Sinning' is the present continuous verbal participle, while 'sinful' is the adjectival conditional present tense, as in tainted. One shows the current continuous action of the individual. The other describes the present situation of the person. One denotes action, while the other is describing a condition. Therefore, in God's sight, he, Christ, was innocent of sin, (sinning) while being made sinful for us, (sinful) he suppressed his sinful will or nature and lived for the will of God. (2 Cor. 5:21. Luke 22:42.) Which meant he had the nature of sin, but he did not do the act of sin. I hope we got that.

Now, who lived without sin, but was made sinful by coming into the falling nature of man? (Luke 22:42. Isaiah 53:7-12.) Christ did. How do we know this? Well, the answers are in these questions: Did he express a desire opposite to the will of God, and why? (Luke 22:41-42. Romans 8:3.) Could he have disobeyed the will of the Father, and if so, would he have sinned?

If you answer yes to any of those questions, the answer will confirm to us that Christ, the messiah was indeed in 'sinful' flesh.

Note the scripture in 1 John 3:5, last phrase: "in him is no sin." What does that mean, if he was in sinful flesh? Well, just looking at this text and others similar to it, at face value, you would think that Christ did not take on the sinful or fallen nature of man. However, the text is explicitly speaking to what was in or possessed the mind of Christ, not the body of Christ, which was the spirit of Christ and the spirit of God, not what the body contained or constituted off, as in flesh and blood. Therefore, when the text stated that "in Him is no sin" we now know that it is referring to the spiritual nature or spirit of Christ, and not the flesh, but what was in the mind of Christ. That is the reason we are encouraged to be transformed by the renewing of our minds, having the mind of Christ. (Romans 12:2. Phil. 2:5-8.)

On the other hand, when the scripture state as in (Romans 8:3.) "God sending his Son in the likeness of sinful flesh, and for sin, condemned sin in the flesh," and similar text messages, the subject here is referring to the content or nature of the flesh, and not the spirit. (1 Peter 4:1-6.) Therefore, "in him is no sin" is referring to the mind of Christ, where the spirit dwells, while "God sending his Son in the likeness of sinful flesh" is referring to the body or flesh, where the brain is, but the mind dwells in that brain. This teaching is also reflected in 2 Cor. 5:21.

Now, when a baby is born, he/she is born into this sinful world with a sinful nature; however, remember now that the baby is innocent of sin because the baby is not knowledgeable of sin in his mind and does not act consciously in sinning, though the baby is born into sinful or fallen flesh or nature, therefore, the baby is sinless in mind, as in thinking sinful thoughts. We call that being innocent, which is also a legal term. Meaning the moral laws protect his/her innocence. The nature of the baby is sinful; fallen, however, the baby is innocent of sin in his/her mind. That state or condition of being in a sinful body, but innocent of sinning, renders one innocence of the act of sin. (Psalm 51:5.) In 1 John 4:2-3, we are told that the messiah came in that same flesh. Romans 8:3, tells us that the messiah was not just birth into flesh, but into fallen humanity, resulted in him coming into sinful flesh or nature. (Hebrews 2:9, 14, 16-18. Romans 8:3.) In Gal. 3:16, and Romans 1:3-4, we see factual corroborations also that the Messiah came from the seed of Adam, Abraham, and David, who were sinners not just by birth but by act also. Meaning the bloodline of his family tree was infected by sin, all the way back to Adam. However, like the baby who is in sinful nature, but does not sin; the messiah maintained this innocence of the baby throughout his life, as a man, while in this sinful body of flesh. That right, there is a mind bomb!! The fallen fleshy nature is an inheritance of his sinful parent, but he maintained his innocence. (Phil.2:8. 2 Cor. 5:21.) WOW! That is so amazing, but truthfully a mystery being revealed. To the Most, High God is all the glory, honor, and praises. This teaching here makes it abundantly clear that we have no excuse to sin because we are in a sinful body. Christ was, but he did not sin, we can too, and he has given us more power not to. (Heb. 5:7-9.)

I know some might be astounded by this. How is it possible for the messiah to be sinless if he took on the sinful nature of man? "Impossible!" they say.

Well, let's dig deeper, so we can look a bit closer at what did happen. Shall we?

So, while the body of the messiah was flesh and tainted with the nature of sin, the mind was never tainted with such. He was innocent of disobedience and sinning, by him not breaking the law of his Father, as stated before. However, remember the statement the Most; High God made after man sinned. He said, "the man has become like us, knowing good and evil." (Gen. 3:22.) Just as the devil had said to

Eve. (Gen.3:5.) However, knowing good and evil is not being sinful, as God knows both, but to know good and evil as a man, man being without sin, innocent, was the result of man sinning. Therefore, the man had to have sinned to know both. Indicating that the messiah obtained a sinful nature as a man, though he never sinned, being the seed of man, but only through inheritance, knowing both good and evil. (Acts 13:22-23, John 5:30.) In other words, to know both good and evil as a man, the man had to have broken the code of innocence by sinning or inheriting this sinful nature. Consequently, the Messiah coming in the form of a man, not as God, knowing both good and evil, shows he had inherited the true nature of fallen man, though he never sinned. (some will say: well he was God, that's why he knew both good and evil. Well, we will correct that false theology of Christ being God when He walked this earth shortly.)

In whatever way, we now know that Eve had to have performed an act of disobedience to arrive at that place of knowing sin, as Adam also did. Now the child that is born does not readily know good from evil or is consciously aware of the differences. But has the mixed nature inherently, as a result of his first parent's acts, resulting in this fallen nature. After a child who is born of a woman learns the difference between good and evil, that child is then able to make conscious intellectually independent decisions to do good or evil after becoming accountable to God. Likewise, the messiah did not act disobediently to know both good and evil as a member of the human family but inherited this trait just like all of us do through our first parents, was taught the difference, yet he remained innocent and never sinned, but we all have.

Now, this is the reason, I believe, the Messiah told us to be like little children. (Matt. 18: 2-3.) You see, the child though sinful by nature or inheritance, still has an innocent mind, as described above. So, this is the similarity to having the mind of Christ. (1 Cor. 2:16. Romans 12:2.) *(However, we should note the difference between being childlike and childish. Childlike speak to innocence and humility, Matt. 18:1-5, while childish speaks to the immaturity of mind, in a mature adult body. 1 Cor.13:11. Heb.5:12-14.)* This is why a child has to be taught to be evil as in being racist. Though he is born with these sinful inclinations, he still has to be taught.

Therefore, this also tells us that having a mind that can make the distinction between good and evil in us, in itself, is not sinning. However, it shows that we have been exposed to the sin germ, our fallen nature, and is subject to the first death, being sinful. Our action toward the gift of God will now expose us to condemnation or justification. This justification is not saying your action or none action has any merit by itself. However, if the messiah had the fallen nature, and we have proven without a doubt, with biblical text messages, that he did. If he had sinned, he too would have also needed a savior. Therefore, his action would have condemned him, but because he acted according to the spirit of the Most; High in him, though he was in sinful flesh, he did not sin but was obedient even to the giving of his life, his actions justified him. His mind was as innocent as that of a little child throughout. So, this is why he was able to conquer death and sin, in his sinful flesh, and worshiped in spirit and truth at the same time. By his willingness to be humble and maintaining his innocence like a little child, he could say "now is," speaking of himself. He realized that those in the temple and on the mountain were neither worshiping in spirit and truth nor could they. Because they were both sinful, not only by nature but by their very own immoral acts, not knowing themselves, but "he had made him be sin for us, who knew no sin; that we might be made the righteousness of God." (2 Cor.5:21.) Again, this 'made sin' is here referring to him coming in sinful flesh, while the 'he knew no sin' speaks to the state of mind he had possession of, the spirit of God. He was innocent because of the lack of experience in sinning. The word "know" is speaking to an act regarding sinning.

Now because they, the leaders, did not accept the Messiah, they ultimately rejected the Most, High God.

He nevertheless, who found himself in fallen flesh, did not use it as an excuse to sin, but suppressed his own will in the flesh for the will of God to be manifested. Likewise, we can do the same because he has proven to us that we can, knowing he has also redeemed us back to God and has given us that redemptive power through his victory and spirit. This is the good news of salvation, this is the true gospel of salvation; that we can live without sinning while in sinful flesh, because of him, taking on our sinful flesh, and living a sinless life, hence conquering sin in the flesh, and he has given us the same power to do so. (1 Cor. 15. John 15, 17.)

We also must remember that those who have been taught to say he did not come into sinful flesh, have been deceived, and have become deceivers and antichrists themselves. Receive them not, neither listen to their false teachings. Some innocently by default, and others willingly for money, position, or association. The word in the text message, which is translated as "Flesh," in the last clause of Romans 8:3, is vague and should be translated as "in his sinful flesh." As the context within the text reveals and bears witness. (Romans 8:3.) Without a correct understanding of the accurate translation, most have missed the real significance of the messiah's coming to earth in sinful flesh. (2 John 1:7-11.) In other words,

Roman 8:3 bears witness to 2 John 1:7, which also should read "sinful flesh" (Heb. 2: 14, 16-18, Romans 6:23.) Remember that no one can taste death unless they taste sin first, by either committing it or becoming it. The law of God permits death only on these two counts. (Romans 6: 23, Heb. 9:22. 2 Cor.5:21, Ezekiel 18:20, John 3:16, 1 John 2:2.) For the messiah to have died, he had to have taken the sinful nature of man upon himself, for the law of God to be justified of his death. Consequently, he became sin, who knew no sin, to redeem us from sin. (2 Cor. 5:21.)

(Just a side note: correct or incorrect translation of scripture, can always be verified or corrected by the proper context of the account)

Chapter 22

The power to or not to sin, where is it?

This text message states, "Every man is tempted, when he is drawn away of his own lust, and enticed...." (James 1: 14-15.) Meaning that the redeemed individual has the power to sin or not. You do not have to act upon the fallen, sinful nature you are exposed to, but you can subdue the inclinations by allowing the spirit of God to take control of your heart and mind; which are your emotions, and conscience or consciousness, by accepting the gift of the Most, High, and allowing the spirit of God to lead you. (John 16:13.) Your fallen "will" will then be overruled by the "will" of the Most, High God, and you will not be subjected to the result of sin, the judgments of men, demons, or the second/ eternal death, just as the messiah was not. (Romans 6. 1 Cor. 2:15.)

The essential point is, we all have come under the condemnation of the first death, even the Messiah was subjected to this because he came into the sinful nature or fallen flesh. However, the second death has no power over us. (Romans 6:9-11. Rev.20:6.) This freedom is not only through the death of Christ, but more so, the example of the life of Christ. If he did it, he certainly is telling us we can also live the perfect life while having the nature of sin. This truth is the ultimate contradiction. However, we need to have accurate knowledge as possible of this truth. When we are aware of our real condition, we will be able to live above sinning. The condition is this: we have been redeemed back to God through the life of Christ, by him conquering sin and death, in his own body of sin. (Romans 8:3.) How did the messiah do it?

Well, firstly, he kept his mind focus on the Father's will. Likewise, our minds have the potency of the power of God to conquer sin and bind sin in our bodies, right here and right now. By focusing on the will of God through the power vested in us, we the redeemed activate the spirit and power of God in us. (1Peter 3:21-22. 1 Cor. 2:16.) However, we have to remember that, though we have been redeemed in our minds; spiritually, we still have the fallen nature of our flesh to deal with physically, that we live in. And so, there is a constant fight between the two forces in our consciousness and our emotions, or spirit and body. (Romans 7:14-23.) However, we must also remember that we are the ones who have the right and the power to make our choices. The devil has no power over our ability to make a choice, and God does not infringe on our individuality or rights to do so. (Joshua 24:15.) Without this true knowledge, we are doomed to indulge in the acts of our sinful nature, thinking we have no choice or control in the matter of choosing.

Ignorance is a tool of the devil, which keeps us under subjugation to the power of the fallen nature of sin. Those who do not understand this truth can't live the truth and will not be able to present the truth; therefore, they perish. "My people perish through lack of knowledge." (Hosea 4:6.) "You will know, if they preach or teach not according to this word, it is because there is no light in them." (Isaiah 8:20.) This word is the truth of the Most, High God. This truth has been revealed to us by him coming into sinful flesh. (1 John 4:3. Romans 8:3.) *"And this message of the kingdom shall be preached into all the world as a witness, and then the end will come."* (Matt.24:14.) The message of the kingdom is in a nutshell: **we will live without sinning because we have been redeemed by the Most; High, through the living gift of his son, and his spirit in us. We now have the power over sin and death, while in a sinful body, just as he lived without sinning while in sinful flesh on this earth. (John 3: 15-17. Romans 6: 14-16.)**

This gospel is the living gospel that has been preached and continues to be through our lives as witnesses. Therefore, this was the gospel that was a witness by the messiah, through his life. Living in sinful flesh, yet without him sinning, this is the good news of salvation. When we live this perfect life, while in this sinful flesh, the world will see clearly and hear loudly, the good news of salvation through our lives as witnesses. *"Christ in me the hope of glory."* (Col. 1:25-28.) We shall then light up the world with his glory reflecting from our lives. Praise be to the Most, High God of all gods. Then the end will come. (Matt. 24:14.)

Just for clarity on the word 'witness.' A faithful witness, within context, is one who speaks what he lives. Not only speaking qualifies one to be a faithful witness. ('Mouth cut cross-way; it can chat anything')

That is the reason, in a court of law, a witness is cross-examined to establish the truth from such a person. This procedure is simply because the lawyers, the judges, and the jury might not have seen for themselves the account in real-time, that is, now argued, and they need corroborating information to establish a proper case for the right verdict.

Now a true witness is one who the lawyers, judges, and jury see doing or experiencing through their senses what he/she stated happened through their testimony. Once the judge and jury can see the truth, they will accept or reject the witness's testimony and present a verdict.

Those who need the gospel will only truly see and judge the gospel in our lives as we live out the gospel as testimonies, which is the power over sin through Christ.

Chapter 23

Do not be deceived by emotions

Many of us still ask, "why do I feel like this even after accepting salvation and is striving to live for God?" This question about feelings is ubiquitous but reasonable. Pay keen attention to the following explanation.

Romans 7 and 8 explain that there are two sets of enemies warring within the soul of a man. One of the spirits of God and the harmonious spirit of man, against the flesh, the sinful nature of man, and the rebellious spirit of man. (Romans 7:21-25.) The messiah's mind was of the spirit, not of the flesh or emotional, while in a body of fallen flesh and emotions. Our mind is not flesh while in an environment of flesh. The head is flesh, muscles and bone, the brain: grey matter. The brain hosts the seat of consciousness, which is in the mind of man. However, this brain is a part of the body, therefore, while the sinful nature has a lasting effect on the body of flesh, in this present life: the physical. However, not so in mind, though, the mind can become corrupted. Now, this same mind can be transformed right here, right now. (1 Cor.15: 34-50.) Unlike the body that will only change at the third coming, (some say second coming, but Christ came the second time already when he came into the upper room) or if there is translation before. (1Cor. 15:51-52, 2Kings 2:1-11) Because the body is of the elements of this earth, physical and is subject to the earth. (1 Peter 3:21.) Remember, though; the body is neither sinful or holy; it is neutral but bears the effects. The nature and spirit of man within are what is sinful or holy, which is in our minds. Therefore, when we say sinful flesh, we are talking about the fallen nature of man.

Remember, the elements of the mind are from above: spiritual. (1 Cor. 15:45-49. Romans 12:2.) Also, the man was made from this earth that is now in a fallen state; he became consciously aware only after the breath of life, and the spirits of God, which came from the creator, were put in him. (Gen. 2:7.) This breath of life and spirit came from God above, who is pure, that made man conscious. This breath through the redemption of Christ has resuscitated man back to his conscious spiritual state, those who have accepted his gift. (Col. 1:14, Eph.1:7-11.) Though this breath of life that gives consciousness to man is in man, man still is given a choice to reject or accept the righteousness of God. He is also able to allow his mind to be influenced by either the spirit of God or the devil.

Haven't you read that the breath goes back to God who gave it, and the body goes back to the earth from which it came upon death of both the righteous and the wicked? (Eccles. 12:1-7.) But Choose you this day who you shall serve. (Joshua 24: 15.)

Now for those of us who feel a certain way, I am here to remind you that you have the power over whatever circumstance you find challenging. Please understand that those unpleasant and challenging feelings are not the facts of your actual condition, but a reflection of a struggle or war that is occurring in your being; to distract you from your true reality. They would rather draw you towards the circumstances around you, than towards the power of God through his spirit within you. (Matt.14:28-31.) Knowing that you already have the victory will propel you to change your attitude toward your circumstances, and you will find that you are now energized with the power and might that come only from the Omnipotent God, whose presence is within you. (Phil. 3:14-16, 2 Cor. 4:16-18.) When you have realized that you are in partnership with God for your salvation, and his spirit dwells within you, you will express an effervescent radiance and power within and around you, and your circumstances will have to bow down to the power that is within you. (Matt. 16:19, 2Kings 6:16.)

A quick reminder. Remember when the Omniscient God created Adam, he made him first a body, then he breathes into his nostrils, and man became a living soul. Job testifies to this; Job 33:4. Within the body, we have all the physical functional attributes.

Within the "breath" of the Most, High Gods contain the elements of his spirit, "he spoke, and it was done he commanded, and it stood fast." This creative force indicates the power of the spirit by the breath of God's eternal might. (Gen.1:3, Job 32:8, Heb.11:3, Psalm 147:18, 148:5, 33:6, Lam.3:37, Ezek.24:14.) By putting life into the man, he was now able to put his spirit into that life that was in man, with the spirit of man that he also placed in man. This act resulted in man becoming a "live-in-soul,"; living soul. He was now consciously aware of himself as a whole. Not just a body, but of mind and spirits. The spirit of the Omnipresent God, and the spirit of man dwelling in harmony together, in man. Job. 32:8, 1 Cor. 2:11 Romans 8:8-16, emphasis on verse 16. The body of man contains life, which equals the soul of man: body and breath. However, they are two different entities. One is physical and the other spiritual. Therefore, the true identity of the man is both spiritual and physical. Those who see themselves as just a body with a brain

129

do not have the spirit of God in them. If they did, they would have known the truth. So, once you know this, you have just activated the power in you, by accepting this truth of self. Remember the body is just a container, it is not what a man puts in his body that condemns him, not the food you eat, but what comes out; the state of mind that does. Therefore, the statement that states, you are what you eat, is incorrect or limited to the physical. However, the correct thought is, you are what you think; therefore, you will act accordingly. The text messages: Prov. 23:6-7. Romans 1:18-32 corroborate this truth.

 Back to Romans 7 and 8, these text messages teach also that the messiah, while being in sinful flesh, walked not according to the flesh, but according to the spirit, and by so doing conquered sin in the flesh. This statement could not be possible if the messiah lived in sinless flesh. Now, if he were not in sinless flesh, it would not have been necessary for him to need to walk to the spirit, and not to walk to the flesh. Therefore, it had to have been a sinful flesh that the messiah was in, to make that statement true. (Romans 8:3.) However, he chose to walk or lived not according to the fallen flesh, the body he was in, but the spirit that dwelt in his mind, while he was in this sinful body. Remember, he has given us the power to do the same.

He also emphasized the importance of suppressing the physical will, of the fallen nature that he was in, by doing the spiritual will of his heavenly Father. (Luke 22:42.) These prove that he was focused in his mind to conquer the nature of the sinful flesh he was in and willed to walk in the will of the Father through the power of the spirit in his mind. This understanding also tells us that the spirit of the Most; High dwelt in the pure mind of Christ while he was in sinful flesh. Yes! The mystery has been revealed to us his chosen. If you are reading this with a true understanding, then you have been chosen. What will you do with this knowledge of the eternal truth? Will you leave your water pot for this gift of truth? This revelation is the correct explanation of the concept of divinity in humanity. Humanity was the flesh as we all are, which he took on. The divinity is the spiritual mind of Christ, that he gave us access to, to be like him, being one with him, as he was one with the Father while on earth. (John 17:20-21, Romans 12:2, Phil. 2:5, 12-15.) Will you now do the exchange?

Chapter 24

Whose flesh, and whose will?

Whose flesh did he conquer that was in sin and shaping in iniquity, and why did he do this? (Romans 8:3-4.) His flesh, his container, in which he was born. (John 3:5-6. Heb.2:14, 16-17.) To walk according to the flesh was to do the things of the flesh; live according to the fallen nature of sinful flesh that he was physical. And to do so, he had to have been in that sinful flesh. These things are contrary to the will of the Most, High God. But the messiah had more of an internal struggle than an external one. He struggled with the carnality of the fallen flesh in his mind, which is his consciousness. Now, this is where the real fight against sin and the devil happens; in the consciousness of man. That is why he said, "not my will (fallen nature), but thy will (spiritual nature) be done." The will is a conscious spiritual effort that is totally within the mental capacity of man, however, is manifested in the flesh, because we are physical. To struggle with sensuality is to be tempted to do the things that please the flesh; the 'my will,' against the things that please the Most, High God; the 'thy will.' He struggled with this, but never gave in to this sinful nature or inclination to sin. (John 4:34.) It is the 'not walking after the flesh' he demonstrated, which shows how he conquered sin in his flesh. We also struggle with this, but, as sinful men. (1 John. 4:1-6. Matt. 4:1-10.) However, we also have been given this same power through the redemption of the messiah, to walk in like manner as he did. (John 17: 3,8,14, 19-26.)

As stated, "he was touched with the very feelings of our infirmities." (Heb. 4:15.) To be touched with such feelings is to have the same germ of sin; he spoke about his will of the flesh, conflicting with the will of the Father before he was on the cross. How could he have a will that conflicted with the Father's, if they were the same? If his fleshly will was the Father's will, or if he was God when he walked this earth? There would be no conflict of wills between them, if he were God, and without a sinful nature. However, there had to have been opposing wills for him to say, "not my will, but thy will be done." The 'thy' is of the Father's perfect will, and the 'my' is of the son's fallen nature or will of the flesh. One is of the spirit, and the other the fallen flesh. However, he was able to put his fallen will under the subjection of the will of the Father by the spirit of the Most, High God in him, his mind. And could not only say, but live the life of "nevertheless not my will (the fallen will), but thine, be done (the will of God)." (Luke 22:39-42.) It clearly shows that the will of which he called 'my,' was not the will of the Father's spirit in him, but that of the fallen nature of the flesh, while he was in sinful flesh.

Notwithstanding, he consciously chose to allow the spirit of the Most; High to lead him while suppressing or rejecting the will of his flesh. To God, be all glory and praise for the acts of his son. We call that in legal terms 'overrule.' He allowed the spirit of the Father's will to 'overrule' or rule over his own will. This example that was given by the Most, High God to us, through his son, shows that we now have that same power through our redeemed minds to live the same way he, the messiah, did. Though he was tempted yet, he never yielded to temptation and sin. We can allow the spirit of the Father to overrule our sinful nature, and live that same sinless lives now, while we are in this body of sin. The difference, though, between him and us is, we live in a sinful body and also have sinned; however, he lived in a sinful body but never sinned. All glory and honor be to the Most, High God, for the sinless life of his son. (Romans 8:3-4, 1st Peter 1.) Therefore, it was not just the flesh of the son, but more so the will of the Father that mattered in the redemption process of humanity. We will forever thank the son for taking our fallen condition, to redeem us, and the Father for his perfect will through his son.

Chapter 25

Error at the cross

The erroneous teaching by some is that Christ suffered the sins of the world once in his body when he was on the cross for man, this is a fundamentally flawed theology, so much so that the devil is having a field day with this erroneous teaching. This teaching also presents no hope for change in us, the fallen, in our present state. The text message 1 Peter 2: 24, is misunderstood and taken totally out of context, if verse 21 and 22, are not considered along with Phil. 2:8, Luke 22:41-42, Heb. 2:14, 16-17, Romans 6:23, and Romans 8:3, because these verses speak to an example that Christ left us to follow. What is this example? Simply, that we can and should live without sinning while in our sinful bodies, as he did.

Some will say and teach that it is impossible to live a sinless life while in sinful flesh, which is an indication of the little god they serve; powerless! Well, nothing is impossible with the true and living God that we serve, and Christ could not leave us such an example if he did not live with the same conditions as us. He could not expect us to live without sin in our sinful condition if he did not live without sinning while he was in our sinful condition. How did he do it? Again, Christ's mind was in constant communion with the Father, though he lived in this sinful body of flesh. (Romans 8.) However, he allowed the spirit of the Father to overrule. This body he had from conception was just like ours. Phil.2:8. Verse 24 of 1 Peter 2, along with those others mentioned, are telling us that he bore this sin nature from birth even unto the death of the cross. (Phil. 2:5-8.) The without spot and blemish is referring to the sinless life he lived, while in a sinful body, not his blood. The blood of Christ was only accepted because he lived a holy obedient life to his father, not because it did not have the infirmities of sin, which it did. (Heb. 10:29, 4:15.) Notice that Romans 6:23 reflects in Romans 8:1-34, both are telling us that Christ, who came in the fallen nature of man, who was condemned by the pure law of God, was also the gift of God to man by his pure life through the spirit, as we should too. The text message in Leviticus 17: 11 is not referring to the physical blood in the new testimonies; this is not the testimony of the Messiah. The testimony of Christ was the life he lived, therefore, the real spiritual

133

understanding of Leviticus 17: 11 is that real life is not the blood, which was a symbol in the old testimony but was the actual life of the redeemer in the body, in the new. The 'life in' the blood, can only be seen by the action of the individual, which shows the true testimony or presence of the spirit of Christ in the person, as Christ did. The reality of our lives is not the blood in our bodies while we sleep, but the actual actions we are engaged in while we are awake.

So, what is the correct teaching here? Did he find himself bearing the sin of humanity only when he was on the cross, as some would argue? However, as the scriptures tell us, he knew of his condition when he found himself as a man, long before the cross. These scriptures also tell us that as soon as he realized he was a man, Phil. 2:8, he knew he was born in this body of sin and understood what he was sent to do. (Luke 2:40, 52, 4:18. John 10:10.)

It is absurd to think that the messiah only knew that he was in sinful flesh when he was on the cross. If we were to follow the illogical logic of this erroneous teaching, it would conclude that his blood became tainted just before he offered up himself as a sacrifice on the cross. Just think about that madness. That he was in a pure body all his life until it was time to be offered as a sacrifice for sin. His sacrifice would have resulted in a polluted sacrifice, which the Father would have rejected, which would also have left us without even a hope of redemption. This erroneous teaching has no substance in truth and is a lie from the enemy. His condition was the only reason he asked his Father to glorify him again as he was with the Father before the world was. (John 17:5.) He knew he was in sinful flesh. *"Why call me good, there is only one..."* (Matt. 19: 17.) There are more pieces of evidence proving he knew his condition as he walked this earth, and Christ wasn't on the cross then, but knew this throughout his ministry, that he was in sinful flesh. Therefore, being in this condition, he was able to fight the good fight and won for us all. Setting an example for us to follow on the way to victory, while in sinful flesh as we are. (John 17: 1-4.) He is the purest example given for us to follow. That he would take on our corrupt state and lived a sinless life in it, to prove to us, we can do the same, while conquering sin and death. Praise be to the Most, High God for his son!!!! (***We now have been given this privilege to demonstrate the power of the redeemer Christ in our lives, not only as witnesses but also as victors over sin and the devil***.)

Let's get even more profound. Heb.2 explains this truth further. Let's look at a few relevant verses in this chapter. In verse 7, we see the man, not Christ, but Adam, being made a little lower than the angels and given glory, the same as in Psalm 8:4-5. This glory that man had was taken away from him when he sinned.

(Gen.3.) However, we see the messiah being made in the same state as the man was but lower because of the sin factor, him taking sin upon himself. Heb.2 verse 9, Romans 8:3, but given the same glory and honor, that man had before Adam sinned because he was without sin though in sinful flesh. In verse 10, of Heb. 2, we see the Messiah coming in that condition also to bring many sons back to the glory; the glory they had with the Father before man had sinned; their first estate. This act of the messiah, Heb.2, was established in John 17:22. Verse 11-13, continuing this confirming of John 17:22. Verse 14 of Heb.2, specify the physical condition of the Messiah; that he partook of the same flesh and blood as those he came to save, Romans 8:3 confirming the type of flesh he took on; sinful flesh. In verse 16 of Heb. 2, we see the imperative emphasis being placed here to make it abundantly clear that the messiah, Christ took not on the nature of angels, but the life of fallen, sinful man; Abraham. Verse 17 and 18 continuing the confirmation. (Remember angels were made higher than man. Heb. 2:7,80, and Christ was made lower than the angels, verse 8.)

It is therefore apparent then that the messiah took on the sinful nature of man, being in sinful flesh long before the cross. Doing so was the only way he could have conquered sin in the flesh, through his living, not his death. (Romans 8:3.) The dying on the cross was for the fulfillment of the demand of the pure law of God, and he could not die if he were not in a tainted body; the law would not allow his body to die if he were pure of the fallen nature. (Romans 6:23, Heb.9:22. Romans 8:3.) He was only able to die because of the sinful body he was in and be raised because of the sinless life he lived, while in this body of sin, as an example for us, through his living, not by his physical blood.

What we need to understand is once the mind of a man is right with God, as was the case of the messiah, meaning that our spirit is being in harmony with the spirit of the Most, High God, as was his. This state of being will make our sinful bodies to come under subjection of the spirit of God, through the renewing of our minds daily, (Romans 12:2), the same way Christ did. This condition will keep us secured by the spirit of God being in us because of the gift of the life of Christ. Our true self will never taste death because we, through the precious sinless life of Christ and his sacrifice, have been redeemed.

Remember, however, that though our bodies are now under the subjection of the will of God, there is still a struggle as we have seen and experienced. A fight that continues, because of the sin nature, until we are transformed not just in mind only, but also in the body. (1 Cor. 15:51-57.) Therefore, the internal fight was in the mind of the messiah, spirit over carnality. These were and are the true realities of his and our conditions, and did not, and will not change totally until after death or translation, as was for him and will be for us. (1 Cor. 15:52-53, 1 John 3:2.)

That is the reason he insisted that they should not touch him before he went to his Father after his resurrection. (John 20:17.) Remember, they were the ones who handle his body upon death, John 19:25, Luke 23:50-43, but now were refrained from touching him simply because this sinful body was now renewed by the spirit, because of his obedience to the Father. However, it had to be confirmed by the Father. (1Cor.15:50-58.) Remember, immortal and incorruptible can't die. Therefore, what died on the cross was mortality and corruption, but because of his obedience to his Father, he was given the victory over both: death and the grave. Praise be to the Most, High God, for his resurrection power as a result of his son's sinless living.

 Neither the religious leaders, politicians, the common people, nor the devil and his angels, could sway the messiah. It did not matter what they said about him, did to him, or plotted against him. He chose to fix his mind on the will of the Father by the indwelling spirit of the Most, High God in him. That is what kept him. This same power is ready within us by the same spirit of the eternal God, if we choose. We can start using this power by looking at the resources of our talents and gifts that the Most; High God has entrusted to us and use these gifts and talents for his glory in every capacity of our lives. By using these gifts and talents for the Most High's glory, we will start to exercise the resident eternal spiritual power that God has entrusted to us. The prophets did, the messiah did, the disciples did, and many others. I have also been experiencing this power of the Omnipotent God over the years in my life. The Most; High Gods have been great! I hope you do too.

Chapter 26

No Excuse for sin Adams

You can now realize and see that the relationship that Adam had with the father, before sin, was one of a spiritual nature in his mind. It was not about the emotions of the body, but a steadfastness of the mind. However, it was the emotions of his body that led him to make that fatal decision, even while being perfect. That is the reason why our emotions have to be under the subjection of our spiritually conscious minds.

The messiah, on the other hand, though he inherited the fallen nature of Adam, maintained his spiritual connection, in his mind, with the Father. Therefore, though he was in a body of sin and in all points tempted as we are, he did not sin. (Hebrews 4:15.) It simply meant that he had to have been in the same fallen state as we are. How could he be tempted as we are if he did not have our fallen nature? Consequently, he had to have inherited a body of sinful inclination unlike Adam before sin, but everyone and Adam, after sin, yet he yielded not to temptation, by putting his fallen emotions and will under the subjection of the spirit of God, within him. (Gal.4:4-7, 5:16-18.)

How did he do it?

Be transformed by the renewing of the mind, having the mind of Christ. Romans 12:2, which can't be overemphasized, that the thought of Christ was and is the mind that is stayed on the Father, as Adam did before he decided to sin, though Christ was in a sinful body of flesh and was aware of his physical condition. Nevertheless, he purposed in his mind to subdue his carnal physical will and live for his Father's spiritual will. (Luke 22:42.)

Let's not believe this was a walk in the park for the messiah. No, this was a challenge every day, every hour, every minute, and every second. The devil made sure of it. And you and I are no exceptions. Think about it: how long have you lived without sinning? How about a day. How did you accomplish this? Do you remember? Did you have to lock yourself up alone in a room with no distractions?

Even then, did your mind strayed? How were you able to accomplish this with all the temptations and distractions, both physically and mentally? For this to happen, your selfish nature had to have died. And for that to have happened, your mind had to have been right; having the mind of Christ. Even then, there is still a struggle, as we see in the life of the messiah. We have to acknowledge the willingness of the messiah to suffer deprivation of the flesh, to the point of dying daily throughout his life, to the dying on the cross and do the same. (Heb. 5:8, 9.) We have to acknowledge and understand his love for us. So, this expression of "having the mind of Christ" is having a disciplined mind toward the will of The Most, High God. That includes living truthfully, regardless of what the devil and his agents say or do to you, which is true love in action. (1 Peter 3:8-18. Romans 8:35-37.)

This rightness of the mind is in the eighth verse of Philippians four.

Finally, brethren, whatsoever things are true, whatsoever things are honest, whatsoever things are just, whatsoever things are pure, whatsoever things are lovely, whatsoever things are of good report; if there be any virtue, and if there be any praise, think on these things.

We have to determine that we will fix our minds on the things that bring praise to the living God. We have to realize that the messiah had real struggles, and had to make every effort to maintain his mental integrity. He was not a superhuman with supernatural powers, but he was one like us who had more than supernatural powers available to him while he was here, the same as we do. (John 5:30, 17:22.) Only by having a transformation of the mind, a disciplined mind like that of Christ, can we live like him, to present our bodies and emotions as living sacrifices, and live in that same power as he did. (Romans 12: 1-2.)

Chapter 27

Before and After Kingdom Citizens

We have to remember also that before the existence of the word as flesh, the devil as Lucifer had always wanted to fight and destroy the word after he became proud. (Ezekiel 28: 1-18. Isaiah 14: 12-14, Rev.12:7.) Also, after the word became flesh, he tried to kill him. He had been plotting for his death before he was born. (Matt. 2:1-14, 16, 19-20.) The messiah and his parents had to take evasive actions, both spiritually and physically, many times to avoid an untimely death while on earth. (Luke 4:28-30, John 10:31-39, John 8:57-59, Matt. 2:13.) Though his time had not yet come, his parents were cautioned by the angels to take evasive actions. Though his time had not yet come to die, he was still cautious of the devil, the devils' angels, and the devil's followers. He did not trust any of them, and neither should we. (John 11:53-54.) Therefore, we should be wise as a serpent and harmless as a dove, in the ways we deal with those types around us. (Matt. 10:16.) A word is sufficient for the wise. (Proverbs 12:15.)

To maintain his connection with the Father, however, as he grew, he fed, meditated, pondered, investigated and studied the ways of God, and sought out diligently the things of the spirit. These things are known as the mysteries of the Most, High God. These truths, however, are revealed to us, his servants only, by the same spirit of the Highest being in us, who have the minds of Christ. (1 Cor. 2: 6-16. Eph. 1:9. Col. 1:26-27.)

The formula is simple: "**Seek ye first the kingdom of God and his righteousness, and all these things shall be added to you**." (Matt. 6:33.) We only get the things of the Most, High God through the spirit of the Most, High God being in us. If you have not his mind, you are none of his: Romans 8:9 and can receive nothing of his. Before you can seek the kingdom, you have to know what the kingdom of God is. This way, you will see when you have found it. When the spirit of truth has come, he will guide you into all truth.

Now, the kingdom of God has to be understood correctly, through the spirit of God.

Firstly, the kingdom of God is not of this world, while in this world. (John 18:36.) It is not a physical kingdom but a spiritual one. (Just like the mind of Christ in the body) Luke 17:20-21. By looking at these two text messages, we see that there is not an institution in this world, be it religious or political (which are the same) that reflects the kingdom of God. Neither is it an external presence because it is within the children of the Most, High God. Therefore, the expressions of the kingdom of God are in our witnessing; the way we live. The way we live in this wicked and perverse world will tell of which kingdom we are. (Matt. 5:13-16.) Consequently, only those who are living the kingdom life will know what this kingdom is that they seek. Interesting! Wouldn't you say?

The messiah made it very clear by describing the real citizens of the kingdom of God in this sin-cursed world. The actual citizens are poor in spirit, humble. We will mourn, to go against or grieve for the wickedness we see, but we shall be comforted. To morn for the immorality, is to show our deep disagreement toward such vices. We are meek, and the wicked ones think this is a weakness and have robbed us of many thinks, but we will inherit the earth. We hunger and thirst after righteousness: for we shall be filled because this is the only thing that can fill us. We are merciful, pure in heart, and are peacemakers: we are the children of the Most, High God. Because we are not of this world, we reject the doctrines and teachings of this worldly "morals" of calling evil good and good evil, in and outside the churches. (Isaiah 5:20-23. Matt. 21:13.) Therefore, we shall be persecuted for righteousness sake, and we shall be slandered and falsely accused of many things for righteousness by the world and the organized religious churches. We do rejoice and are exceedingly glad because great is our reward in the kingdom of God. (Matt. 5:2-12.) We have been experiencing great rewards now and will receive even greater rewards then because we have been experiencing this kingdom living currently and will continue later. Praise be to the Most, High God.

Christ experienced an example of such great rewards after he spoke to the woman at the well. He told the disciples that he got refreshed without eating the natural food they had gone to buy. Our refreshing is beyond this world's offerings because it is spiritual. (John 4: 31-34.) We also need to understand that the organized church and the body of Christ are different in functions and structure. The organized churches are constructs of man and are structured and governed by human laws. Those who manage these institutions are educated and qualified by man, as we see in the leadership of these organized churches. To be a leader in these organized churches, one has to have credentials from these organizations that are temporary gifts to him or her, after being trained and educated in these secular institutions, that have been approved by this secular government of fallen men. Therefore, the curriculum of these organized churches educational institutions will have to meet the approval of this secular government first because they are the same in principles, laws, and structures.

However, the children of God are alien pilgrims in this world but are citizens of the kingdom of God. The body of Christ, on the other hand, is structured and functions on the moral laws of the eternal kingdom of the Most, High God. The servants of God are given their abilities and assignment before birth by the spirit of God and not of man. (Jeremiah 1:5. James 1:17.) Their qualifications come from God himself. (1 Peter 4:11, 1 Cor. 12:8-10, Romans 12:6-8.) Therefore, human qualifications can't qualify anyone to be a servant of God, but only of the world. Man can't qualify or ordain man for the work of God, only the Most, High God can do such a thing. And those who are set apart by God, do not thirst after this world's earthly goods. However, those who are qualified by man, with their human degrees, will do and say just about anything for this world's earthly goods, because they do thirst after such. Neither do they understand, nor can they the mysteries of the Most, High God.

However, those who seek shall find, and those of you who knock, it shall be opened unto you. (Matt.7:7.) The mysteries of the Most, High God is only revealed to us; his people who are of his kingdom. (1 Cor. 2: 7-10.)

These principles used by the messiah and are still sure and true, relevant, and available to us today.

The opposite is also true. To be overwhelmed by the things of this world: looks, feelings, material possessions, associations, money, fame, the lust of the flesh, the pride of life, and religions, renders one carnally minded, and far away from The Most, High God. (1 John 2: 15-17.) There is nothing wrong with pursuing one's temporary goals and be blessed in doing so. (3 John 1:2.) However, we should do so with the intent of helping others who are less fortunate, know the limitations of these gifts, and spread the gospel of the truth of the Most, High God, in serving him daily. In other words, these gifts should be used to enhance our spiritual relationship with God, the brethren, the world, and to fulfill our purposes, which then will show we are kingdom citizens of the Most, High God.

Part 5

Understanding your purpose

One's purpose is his/ her reason for being. Each person has a reason for being right here, right now. Your life is not without an intended purpose. It is for you to find out your reason for being here. That should be one of your main priorities. Without knowing and fulfilling your purpose or purposes, you will be like a song without a tune. (Proverbs 8.)

Chapter 28

His will is mine; How to know the real purpose of your life

 To be carnally minded is to feed on these things of the flesh, but to be spiritually minded is to feed on the elements of the spirit. Those who are carnal-minded can't know the mysteries of the Most, High God and will teach others the same, because they do not know God. (Romans 8:8.) However, to 'feed' here means to spend a significant amount of our time, talents, and gifts to live the kingdom life; the truths that God gave us a passion for; Investigating, learning, and the sharing of these truths.

The messiah was passionate about the will of the Father to be in his life. Therefore, he lived and fed on the Father's will. (John 6:38, John 4:34.) This spiritual food was what the messiah fed on, through the gifts granted him. The messiah demonstrated all the attributes shown in Romans 12: 6-8, 1 Cor. 12:8-10, and 1 Peter 4:11. This principle indicates spiritually how powerful the mind of the messiah was, and this mind is still available to us today. Subsequently, the spirit of the eternal God could dwell in him (Romans 8:9) because he gave himself up totally for the Father's will. The question is, what is the Father's will for you?

The messiah meditated many times throughout the day outside of the temple made by hands but within the temple built by God, in mind by the spirit, on the things of the essence of the spirit. He was also in prayer and communion always with the Father. That is how we are encouraged to having the same mind as Christ. If you have this mind of Christ, which was the intent he had, you will know what the Father's will is for you. You will know that your qualifications are in the form of the talents and gifts you have. Then you will live the purpose of your life, by using those gifts and talents. Your gifts and talents are the chart and compass on your roadmap of life, to your successful purposes for being here. Find and use your map and compass, and you will live your purpose.

Chapter 29

Ready and prep, here I come

The mind is the seat of consciousness where the spirits of the Most, High God and man sit and have Harmonious fellowship together, which is the true worship in the right temple.

We need to separate ourselves from spending too much time on those worldly affairs. As often as we can, we should begin to meditate on the things of God as the Messiah did and to transformed by the renewing of our minds. Ponder his ways and follow. He introduces us to the spirit by which we are sealed and have become one with the Father. (Eph.1:13-14, 2Cor.1:22, Eph.4:30.) Let's, therefore, fellowship with the Father through his spirit, rather than having this fellowship with the world, which will result in us being in the world, but not of the world. Just like being in the church, but not of the church. Why? Because the church has become like the world, there is now no difference between the church and the world in these times. The messiah was glad to be in the temple to teach, but not of that temple's functions, as he taught. (Mark 11: 15-19.) So much so that he left that temple. (Luke 13: 35.) He then told them that they would not see him again until he came back with power. The same should be true of us today. Then we like the messiah can say "now is" and take our gifts and talents to the streets as he did.

Chapter 30

Loving and showing your true self

There was and is something within the self we need to know. The Self is the correct spiritual composition of man that would serve us well to identify, as it served the messiah. And that is to know about our spirit and the spirit of the Most, High God in us; this is for those who have had a rebirth by the spirit; this is critical knowledge. The self of which we speak here is referring to the same self the Messiah told us to love. He said, "love your neighbor as you love yourself." (Mark 12: 30-31.) Now, the question is which self was he speaking off?

Many say and teach that self should die. (Romans 6-8.) There, however, is no contradiction here, but a misunderstanding. All these text messages speak to two different natures of self; the nature of sin, and the nature of holiness. The true nature of sin controls this body of death. This body, which we are in, is subject to death because this body has fallen into sin and is subject to going back to the nothingness from which it came: dust or translation. However, the image of God that's in this body is the self; the essence of the true man; the spirit, the true self, which is holy unto God. 1 Peter 1:15-16, is been redeemed back to God. This redeemed spirit is the self that we are told by Christ to love, and we can't love this self unless we know this self. Now, to know this self, we have to become consciously aware of who we are and what is our composition.

This consciousness will then remind us that we are redeemed back to the self that was without sin. (2 Cor. 5:17.) However, we will also know that we are in this sinful body of condemned flesh. It now becomes clear as to the reason Paul speaks of the war between the carnal nature and the transformed mind, which is spiritual. You see, this mind of the redeemed has the spirit of God within, while that brain which contains the mind, remains in this sinful body of flesh. So, this is why the true condition of man needs to be understood thoroughly through truthful knowledge. So, we can know who we are. That is the only way we shall know the truth, and the truth shall set us free.

(**side note**: SOME THOUGHT THEY COULD HELP GOD BY KILLING THE BODY TO FREE THE SPIRIT. HOWEVER, THAT WAS A DISTORTION OF THE TRUTH, AND 1 COR. 5:5, WAS TAKEN WAY OUT OF

Yes, "self"; the carnal nature of man is at enmity with God. (Rom.8:7-8.) Therefore, there has to be a distinction between the two different types of selves. The true and the false selves; self, which is the image of God, and self, which is the fallen nature of man. Self before sin; the redeemed self, and self after sin; the fallen self. Because Christ has redeemed us back to the father, and we walk not according to the fallen nature of sinful flesh, though we are in sinful flesh, selfish. But walk according to the spirit of the most, high in us: the redeemed self, within the mind. (Romans 8:1-15.) With this true knowledge, we are now able to understand and recognize our true selves again.

In Romans 7, Paul describes this conflict. Simply that there are two natures and two laws that are working within man, the law of sin unto death and the law of the spirit unto life. Now, having an understanding of the functions of these natures and laws are essential to not just knowing self, but more so living the victorious life presently. The law of sin unto death will not change because we are redeemed, the body must first die or change for the law to be satisfied, even though Christ died for us. We need to know that Christ did not die to save the flesh of man, but the spirit of man, this is what was redeemed back to God; the spiritual man. Yes, from a rebellious spirit back to a harmonious spirit. Therefore, while we live for the Most, High God in our minds, spiritually, the law of sin unto death still exists in our bodies. So, there is an ongoing war for territories within man: one of the spirits, in mind, the other of the flesh, in the body. (Romans 7, 8:1.) This war will continue until death, translation, or the return of the messiah. So, there is no sinning until Christ return for the redeemed, no! That is a lie and a trick by the evil one and his side-kicks. Though there is a war going on within, because of the condition of man, we are still able to live without sinning, right here, right now, which happens only by the renewing of our minds by the spirits vested in us by Christ, bringing our spirit back in harmony with the Father's: making us one again.

With this understanding of self and the steadfastness of the mind, the messiah was able to maintain his spiritual connection with the Father through his spirit, being in constant harmony with the spirit of the Most, High God-self in him. Yes, he had the spirit of a man like any other man. However, within his mind, he was able to maintain that vital connection with the Father through the spirit of the Most, High God being in harmony with his own spirit, which gave him the power over sin, resulting in him living the victorious life in this body of this fallen flesh. This life, we are also able to experience if we yield our spirit to the spirit of God's leading. (Romans 8:16-17.) He depended totally on the guidance of the spirit of the Father in him. (John 5:30, 14:10, 16-20, 26.) That is the only way to live like the messiah and be able to proclaim the good news by us living a sinless life in a sinful body, the same way the messiah did. Yes, he lived a sinless life in a sinful body. Then we will be able to witness to this world our true self, the same way the Messiah did, to the saving of many souls and the proclaiming of his glory. (Romans 8:19-21.) Praise be to the Most; High. (Romans 8:1-5.)

Part 6

Christ knew his purpose

Christ understood the source of his giftedness. Him having been made aware of his talents, gifts, and the source, which was of and from his Father. He purposed to find out the will of his Father and to apply his giftedness to the Father's will. By doing this, he was able to fulfill his purpose for being here. (Luke 2:52, 22:42, John 13:3.) We can all do the same.

Chapter 31

The Word VS the Flesh

In ancient times a name given to a baby was not as casual as is today. The name is given then had much significance to it and carried within it the purpose of the life that bore it. This act indicated that the parents then were more aware of their responsibility to their children and God, to at least introduce to their children their purpose.

The words "Christ" and "Messiah" refer to the 'word' after coming into the flesh, not before, he was now the anointed one after coming into the body. This 'word' was God, before becoming flesh, but not after becoming flesh, which is very important to understand. This misunderstanding within the religious world has caused much confusion for a very long time.

There is a timeline that is misunderstood by those religious practitioners who claim to know who the messiah was, but don't. Without understanding this timeline, these religious practitioners are like a pilot flying in the dark without the modern state of the art navigational tools and skill, just relying on the sound of the engine.

Let's remind ourselves that time is the distance between two points, and eternity transcends time. Meaning that time is like a speck of dust on the ocean face of eternity, that disappears when the big picture is understood. There are differences between eternity and time, which we also notice within the timeline. There is the existence of the living word in eternity, before coming into time. (John 17:5.) There is the time when the word became or came into man, John 1:1, and the time after his crucifixion as a man, Luke 23:46. Both these last time frames are dust particles on the road of eternity as significant as they are.

We know the word was God first; in eternity, before the word came into flesh: in time, as a man. Then, before his death, the man asked the Father to give him back the glory he had with the Most, High God before the world was: eternity. Remember also the Most; High God is spirit. (John 4:24.) Meaning that the word that was with the Father, who was also God, before becoming a man, was also spirit.

Now, the correct usage of the term "God" is not a noun, but an adjective that refers to a position of supremacy, not a person or being, but a government. This understanding is a must for those who are seeking to know God.

Once more: word=spirit=God. But Christ=Messiah=flesh. John 1:1-3, 14, 4-5. John 3:6. Romans 8:3. Therefore flesh is not the word, nor is flesh the spirit, or is flesh God.

Christ or the Messiah was never the word. Christ or the Messiah was never the spirit. Christ or the Messiah was never God. Christ or the Messiah was the flesh. Christ or the Messiah was the man.

The anointed was the spirit that was in the one flesh.

The expression 'living word' does not refer to the flesh, but the spirit of God living in the flesh. Also, the word God does not apply to the person or being, but the position of these supreme beings.

That is why it stated clearly, "and the Word became flesh, and dwell among us." To 'become' simple means changing from one state or position to another; however, within the proper context, though, this means "come into" not become; this is the truth that happened as stated. The meaning is clear, and the evidence bears witness. The word came into flesh and dwelt in the flesh, then flesh died. Therefore, the proper rendering of this text message should be: "the word came into sinful flesh, and dwell within and among us."

The messiah testified to this truth when he said these truths. "I of myself, do nothing...." Speaking of the flesh. John 5:30-31, "my God, my God, why has thou forsaken me?" Speaking of the spirit of God. The "God" here speaks not of the flesh but the spirit, which is God, and also the spirit of God. (John 4:24, 1 Cor. 2:10-14.) The "me" here speaks of the flesh, the man. (Matt. 27:46.) Therefore, the questions are; who did what, in what, and who left what?

(The reason why this is so, we have to remember after God created Adam, he had the spirit of God in him, but he rebelled and the spirit left. The spirit has never taken residence in man permanently since. However, upon the birth of Christ, spirit coming into sinful flesh. The mystery was both contained in him and revealed through him. (Heb. 10: 5) In this text, who is the "me" that is speaking, the spirit or the flesh? The spirit. That is so because the body now contained the spirit of God while being in a sinful state. A contradiction of nature and law, however, the law allowed him, because of his purpose and his sinless life. (Heb. 10:7) We give all the praise, adoration, and glory to the Most, High God and his son, for sending his son, who has redeemed us back to himself.)

When the messiah said, "If you see me, you see the Father," to his disciples. He was not talking about the body of flesh that was called Christ or messiah, but the spirit of God that was within the flesh: the word. (John 14:8-11.) Now, the logical question to ask is, how could they see the Father through the flesh, if the Father was the spirit within the flesh? Think about that for a minute.

Well, to "see" here is more than just looking, but having an understanding of what is happening. Christ had to understand who he was and what he was about, that is the "see" we are talking about here.

Well, he answered when he further explained to his disciples, in the same text messages, by telling them to look at the works he did. He then said, "I am not the one doing the works, but the Father that is in me, does the works." If you noticed he just switched from the physical, his body: flesh "I," to the spiritual; the one in me, the spirit. How does the Father dwell in him? Through his spirit, of course! The spirit of the Most anointed him to do the works he did in the flesh. (John 14:12-21, Luke 3:22 Acts 2:17.) The expression: 'anoint by the spirit' in context means "to be filled" or "poured into." Only a container with volume or a body with capacity can be filled or poured into, which showed that the man Christ was filled or poured into of the spirit, from the Most, High God. Therefore, it was the spirit of the Father in him; the flesh, that did the work. The manifestation of the work done tells who was in him doing the work. It was the same Spirit of God that hovered or moved upon the face of the waters in Gen. 1:2. It was the same spirit of the Father in him that left him also while he was on the cross, when he said: "my God, my God, why has thou forsaken me." (Matt. 27:46.) The word 'forsaken' here means to leave or get out of something or someone. It's clear, isn't it!? On the day that he had baptized, the spirit anointed or filled him, the opposite is also true, on the day he was on the cross; the same spirit left him.

Now for those who would try to argue that the spirit of God can't "be poured" into a sinful body of flesh. By sighting the parable of the messiah in Matt. 9:14-17, Mark: 2:21-22 and Luke 5:33-39. I would absolutely have to agree except for them overlooking one fundamental truth. The spirit of God did not go into the body of Christ. I will repeat for emphasis; the spirit of God was not poured into the body of Christ, but into the mind of Christ, which is not physical. Neither will, or has the spirit been poured out into our bodies, but our minds also, which is the most sacred place in the body. The old testament sanctuary exposes this truth. In brief, in the temple, the presence of God was only in the 'holiest' place (the mind); however, the sanctuary had many compartments, such as the 'holiest' place, the holy place (the body), the outer court (the world). The man is a body, then the breath of God breathes us (the spirit) into that body, in the mind of the first man. Therefore, our bodies are the containers temple, and we now dwell inside. Now for us to be redeemed, the spirit had to have been poured into a body like ours in all respects, giving us the redeemer, Messiah, the Christ. (John 1:1, 14.) Now, our bodies also can be quickened by the spirit, only because of the presence of the spirit in our minds. (John 6:63.) This truth also reveals to us that those who say they "are filled" with the spirit of God, if their minds have not changed; having the mind of Christ, they are lying and are possessed by another spirit, if any.

In verses 44-50 of 1 Cor. 15, and 2 Cor. 5:1-8. The two different bodies spoken of: one is natural of the earth; being flesh and blood, the other is spiritual of heaven. The first man was of the natural; earth, the second man, became as a result of the spirit coming from heaven, and came into the fallen flesh, like unto the first man. (John 1:14.) Therefore 1 Cor. 15. Has to be understood within the context of Romans 8:3, John 1:14, and related text messages. It now shows clarity as to how the spirit functioned in Christ, while he was in sinful flesh. That is the reason we are called to be transformed by the renewing of our minds, having the same mind of Christ. (Romans 12:1-2.) Also, to present our bodies as living sacrifices means to be dead to the desires of the fallen nature through the transformation of our minds by the spirit, and live just as Christ lived. If you are your body, and you sacrifice this body, you exist no more. But the text says to present 'your' body as a living sacrifice. Now, who is 'your' or 'our' here? Meaning you are not your body, but you are in your mind; your body only contains you, which shows we are now like Christ, showing now that we have now become like him, the opposite, as he became like us to redeem us back to himself. (*I know, I know this is very difficult to understand by some, but if you are truly seeking the truth. Just pause at this moment and pray sincerely that the spirit of God will open 'your' mind to understand his truth.*)

The renewing of the mind is a pure, transformed mind. If we noticed that the mind is the only entity that is changed, but the body stays the same, however, it is presented as a sacrifice. It means that the body of sin is now overruled by the renewed mind, which is in harmony and "is filled" with the spirit of God. It is the dying of the flesh, that is referred to in 1 Cor. 5:5, within the proper context.

Therefore, when the Messiah said, "I am the way the truth and the life, no one comes to the Father except through me." He wasn't talking about the body of flesh he was in, but the harmonious union of his spirit, and the spirit of the living God in his mind, as reflected in his living. (Romans 8:16, John 14:6, 10.) Granted, but how do we go to the Father through him in practical terms? That can only happen through the spirit that was in him, being in us. This same spirit he said would come and guide you and me into all truth: the spirit of truth. (John 16:13.) It clearly shows us that we indeed are like the messiah when the spirit of the Most; High dwells in us, in our mind, and we have, in fact, the same spirit of Christ. (John 14: 17,18.) Therefore, we are no more under the subjection of this body of flesh and death, though we live in it. (Romans 6:23.)

Remember, the Messiah was a man at this time, not the Most, High God, as the confused ones would want you to believe. Neither was he a hybrid as in; part God and Part man. Besides, this duel nature possession does not render one as the living God, because that condition does not exist and never did outside of us. (Romans 7.) We know he had the spirit of the Most, High God in him. However, some believe because he had the divine Spirit of the Most, High God in him, he was the Most, High God, while he was on earth. Well, that was not true. Romans 8:3. The Messiah came in the likeness of sinful flesh; therefore, he couldn't be God. God is sinless in both essence and existent. God is also a spirit and exists as a spirit. Christ, on the other hand, had the spirit of God in him but lived not just like flesh, but in sinful flesh. (Heb. 2:14-18, Romans 8:3, Phil.2:8.) Therefore, he could not have been God while he walked this earth physically, as one of us.

Consider this: The angels in heaven are also divine beings having the divine spirit in them, but they are not Gods. They do not have the fallen nature of man as the messiah did, only the nature of perfect beings, but they are still not Gods. They did not sin or took the sinful nature of man, but again, they are not Gods. They were not gods before the creation of man, not gods during the forming of man, not gods after creation, and they still are not gods today; however, they are divine beings. They were made higher than the man Christ, that the word came into or became. (Heb. 2:6-7. 9.) OK, now answer this, how then can the Most, High God, ever be lower than the angels, when there is no variableness with or in God?

155

(James 1: 17.) The argument that God walked the earth as a man does not make any sense in heaven or on earth. The correct statement should be: God walked the earth in man. And he is still doing the same today in us the redeemed.

Even having the divine spirit of the Most, High God, through his spirit being in Christ, while he was here, did not qualify him as the Most, High God. It takes more than that. As we now have this divine spirit in us also, and we are still not Gods. If we can get this understanding, then we will know that we can live just like he lived on this earth, in total obedience to our Father, as he did while in this body of sin. (Romans 8:3. 1 Peter 1:15.)

There are two main reasons the messiah showed for him not being God while living on this earth.

The fact that the messiah only gave worship to the Father, who is in heaven and never took praises for himself. Neither did he do anything of himself. Should tell us that he never saw himself like the Most, High God. **God worships no one**. Remember, he became flesh, and out of his mouth, he said: "the Most, High God is Spirit." He was flesh at the time he spoke this. He also said to the rich young ruler, not to call him (the Messiah) good, because there is only one who is good and he is in heaven. (Matt.19:17, Mark.10:18.) He also gave praise and worship to the Father: "Holy be thy name" (Matt. 6: 9-13.)

The Messiah was on earth when he said those words. We know that the Most, High God is good all the time, and all the time the true and living God is good, but we conveniently, for demonic religious purposes, continue to lie about what the messiah said about himself, as not being the Most, High God when he walked this earth. The Messiah was here in the flesh when he said that he should not be called good. And, if he did not see himself as good, then how did he see himself? Yes, as one like us, lower than the angels. (Heb. 2: 14, 16-17.) I know the text message of John 10:11, 14 comes to mind in that regard, however, understanding the context here tells us that Christ became the good shepherd only after giving up his life for his sheep: verse 15, 17,18 bearing witness. ('action, action, not a bag a mouth')

He was also condemned to die the eternal death because of sin. (Heb. 2:9.) That was the only way for him to be able to die for us; he had to have become as one like us, of the fallen nature, verse 11. And to conquer death through this life, living to die the eternal death to redeem us, verse 14, as demanded by the law. (Heb. 9:22-28.) So, if he said we should not call him good, what or who gave us the authority to call him God when he said not to do so? He told the ruler then and now, not to call him good while he lived in this earth, in the fallen flesh as a man of sin and acquainted with grief: Isaiah 53:3, 1Peter 2:24, Romans 8:3, as also indicated in verse 28 of Heb. 9. He came bearing the sins of many the first time; however, he will come again, this time without sin, but with righteousness to judge. Now, the rulers had ignored his words and are now calling him God when he walked the earth. That gives way to considerable confusion within Christianity, making that teaching a doctrine of demons.

It is essential to know the truth about the messiah. That he was a man like us in every way, and the same power that was available to him is ours, too, and more today. The spirit of the Most, High God, the power of the Most, High God, and the mind of Christ. 2Tim. 1:7-10. Also, because of his victorious living over sin, death, and the grave, we have been redeemed. Therefore, we can live the same victorious life, because he did. We only have to depend on the power sources he has availed to us.

This truth has been turned upside down by the devil and his religious workers to confuse the people and to trick us into believing it is impossible to live as the messiah did because he was different from us. Total Nonsense!!!

Chapter 32

What of taking praises and forgiving sins?

Some would insist, well, the messiah not only took the praises of man, but he also forgave sins, only the Most, High God can do those things. Well, let's look at these two assumptions, which by-the-way, I agree, are solely the prerogatives of the Most, High God: to take the praises of man and to forgive sins.

Let's address these assumptions by first drawing a contrast between Lucifer and the messiah; it will give a broader perspective on the matter, that will make it even more transparent still.

While in heaven, Lucifer, because of his position, splendor, and the magnificent constitution of his being, was looked upon with awe and wonder by all other angels under him. However, all these admirations were not a bad thing, if Lucifer would take all the praises and give it to the one and only, who deserve all glory, honor, and praises, who is the Most, High God. Remember it was the Most, High God who made Lucifer with all these features and attributes, then placed him in that position of leadership. He was a created being, created with certain qualities for the Most High's glory. (Ezekiel 28: 13-18.) That was also his test.

There was nothing wrong to send praises through him, for the glory of the Most, High God, as The Most, High was working through him, Lucifer, for the Highest's glory. We must remember that there is a difference between accepting praises and allowing praises to flow through us to the Most; High. That was the real issue here.

 Therefore, he was to acknowledge to the angels the sovereignty of the Most, High God, and direct their attention and praises to the Most, High God. In other words, he was to be a vessel through which praises flow to the Most, High God, from the angels and himself. However, he did not do so, but became rebellious and selfish in his heart/mind and took the praises for himself. But as an angel with these abilities given to him by the Most, High God, to direct the others to the

Most, High God, he forfeited his responsibilities and position by attempting to bring glory to himself. (Isaiah 14:12-13.)

He was not just a director of the choir of heaven for singing praises, but also for directing all these praises to the Most, High God. (Job 38:7, Isaiah 14:12.)

We have to remember that all created beings in heaven, on earth, under the earth, and in the sea; every living thing created, were created for the selfsame purposes of praise, adoration, and glorification of the Most, High God. (Rev.5:13.) Praise be to the Most, High God.

The messiah, on the other hand, though in a different situation, was still governed by the same principles. Being born a humble man with the given gifts from the Most, High to do the works he did, was no exception. However, he did not take any action to bring praise to himself. (John 12:49.) That is very important to understand. This understanding will open our eyes to who the messiah indeed was when he walked this earth.

The messiah, however, while on earth recognized that he was an instrument of the Father and, as such, gave all the praises and adorations to the one and only true God, the eternal Father. He did not refrain from receiving the praises; *however, he did not take those praises for himself*, but gave all to the Father, and acknowledge the Father as the only one we all should praise, and taught us the same. "Our Father, who art in heaven holy is **thy** name **thy** kingdom come; **thy** will be done…" (Matt.6: 9-13.) And the messiah answered, "Why call me good? There is only one, and he is the Most, High God." (Luke 18:19.) "I can do nothing of myself; I do what I am told, I do not do my own will, but the will of the Father who has sent me." (John 5:30.) "If you see me, you see the Father." (John 14:9-11.) "The Son can do nothing of himself…." (John 5:19.) There is nowhere in the life of Christ; we see him taking any praise for himself, nowhere!

The messiah knew he was an instrument the Father was using to bring his people and his glory back to himself. All the praise and worship he was given, he did not take for himself but gave everything to the Father. (Heb. 5:7-10.) In Matt. 8:2, 14:33, John 9:38 and other similar text messages, you would notice that the acknowledgment of Christ being the son of God and not God was consistently presented not only by the people and the demons but also by the messiah himself. Everything that Christ did was by the power that was commanded by the Father. (John 10: 18.) He stated that he did nothing of himself. (John 5:10.) All the works were done in the Father's name or authority. (John 10:25) Meaning that all the praises went to the Father and not the son. All the works came from the

Father, through the son. (John 10:32.) In these text messages in John 10: 32-38, Christ explained that the 'Jews' were hypocrites because their laws call them gods, therefore what was the big deal if they call him god also.

However, notwithstanding, he clarifies again, stating presently, for the record that he referred to himself as the son of God and never God, verse 36. They were the ones with the identity crises and accused him of calling himself God as many are today, which he did not do. The messiah knew who he was, and he knew he wasn't God. Again, in verses 37 and 38, he redirected their attentions to the one who was in charge: The Father, the one true God. Therefore, he was the perfect director, directing all the attention, praises, and glory to the Most; High. An assignment Lucifer failed. (*we must be careful not to join with the confused, even though they are many, but stand firm against such, as our "God is not the author of confusion." 1 Cor. 14:33.*)

Now, sometime after the resurrection of Christ, he was able to accept worship, praise, and honor again because he now was given the power and glory he had before, now being made one with the Father again, not just in spirit, but also glory. Remember that he had prayed to the Father for this glory. (John 17:5.) This glory was given back to him sometime after his resurrection and not before. (Matt. 28:9, 17-18.) This glory is the same as that mentioned in John 17:5. However, it is different from the glory spoken of in Hebrews 2:9 and John 17:22, while these are the same. Therefore, without having this glory, he was unable to accept any praise or adoration as a man. Let's not get it twisted, he was a man, not God, while on earth.

Let's illustrate for more clarity. Think of yourself being an ambassador for your country, being in another country, in your capacity; you represent your country's government in another country. In your performances, you excelled in all areas of your work, because of your exceptionally high quality of leadership representation over the years. This country in which you are working seeks to give you the highest recognition that only belongs to the president of your country. Question: do you accept this recognition for yourself, after all, you are the one doing the work? Or, do you refer these enthusiasts, to your superior or president? Because you know that your authority and power to perform come from your government, your president, and not from yourself. Therefore, you refrain from the temptation to accept such an honor. What's the protocol here? Well, you also could accept this recognition on behalf of your country's president, but not yourself, if your president allows you. However, if you somehow became president later, only then you are now able to accept this same honor by this country, without any conflict of interest or breaking of the laws, if they were to offer it then.

We know that Lucifer tried to accept such on behalf of himself and failed, but we also understand that the messiah did the total opposite and passed the test. (Phil. 2:8.) Praise be to the Most, High God.

Similarly, there is nothing wrong with other men showing praises for the working of the Most, High God in our lives. But we always must remember to give these praises to the Most, High God and to direct those people to the one and only true God; so, they too can become channels through which the Most, High God can work, and receive his glory and praises, which was what the Messiah did. Praise be to the Most, High, forever.

Several examples: you have a genius mind, and everything you touch turns to gold; remember to give all the praises to the Most, High God, take none for yourself. You become the president of the free world or not so free world; you give all the praises to the Most, High God, take none for yourself. You studied hard and got accepted in all the Ivy League colleges; you give all the praises to the Most, High God, and take none for yourself. You are hungry and can't pay your bills; however, you received all that you need; You give all the praises to the Most, High God, and take none for yourself. You are homeless, but not sick; give praises to the Most, High God, and take none for yourself. You are in a hospital bed sick, but not dead; give adoration to the Most, High God and take none for yourself. And if your loved ones die, and you are still alive, give praises to the Most, High God, and take none for yourself. Whatever condition you find yourself in presently, if you are redeemed, you will give praise to the Most, High God, and take none for yourself. Let everything that has breath, praise the Most, High God Almighty, Praise ye the Most, High. (Psalm 150:6.)

That is what you will do when the spirit of the Most; High God is in you. Giving praises to the Most, High God for what others think you have done and is doing in your life as a witness, yes giving praises to the Most, High God regardless of your present condition. And remember these are spiritual exercises.

Only spiritual people do spiritual exercises.

I must hasten to remind us again that the Father had reestablished the son back to his position as the true and living God, being one with the Father, as he was before the beginning when he was with the Father as God. (John 1:1-5, 10—15, John 17:1-5. Acts 1:6-11. Psalms. 24.) Therefore, the Father and the Son deserve our praise and adoration today, as the true and living God: the Elohim. (Rev.5:11-13.) No more is he the Christ, but now God Almighty!

Chapter 33

The Real Good News, is it more than his death?

On the question of the forgiveness of sins. We have to remember that the messiah was sent here to redeem man from his sinful state and to reestablish the relationship man had with the Most, High God before sin. That could only happen if the messiah lived a perfect life in a sinful body of flesh. **Because the messiah was used by the Most, High God to do so, he was also qualified as an instrument to be used to forgive sins; as one who was one with the Most, High God in spirit, who had no sin in himself. Meaning he did not commit any sin while being in this body of sin, but he took on the sinful nature of man, in his flesh to redeem man. (Roman 8:3)**

This type of life no one else could have done or can do, outside of Christ. Because all others, who were and are born of a woman, have not only been born in sin and shaping in iniquity, but have also sinned, and we all are guilty. Except for babies and mentally ill people who are born in a sinful body, and have died without consciously sinning. Yes, while they are born into this condition, they are innocent of committing.

HOWEVER, WITH THE MESSIAH, WHILE HE WAS BORN INTO SINFUL FLESH LIKE US, AND BEING AWARE, HE DID NOT FALL TO SIN, MEANING HE DID NOT SIN. THAT WAS A DEMONSTRATION OF HIS VICTORY OVER SIN IN HIS BODY BEFORE THE CROSS AND THE RESURRECTION. (PHIL. 2:6-8.) HE WAS SINLESS WHILE IN A SINFUL BODY, WHICH WAS USED BY THE MOST, HIGH GOD AS A CONDUIT THROUGH WHICH FORGIVENESS WAS ASSURED. REMEMBER HIS WORDS: "I DO NOTHING OF MYSELF," HE SAID, TESTIFYING OF THE POWER OF THE FATHER IN HIM, NOT HIS OWN POWER. (JOHN 5:30.) THAT INCLUDES THE FORGIVENESS OF SINS, WHICH WAS A TESTIMONY OF THE POWER OF THE MOST, HIGH GOD IN THE LIFE OF OUR REDEEMER: HIS SON. THE LIFE OF OUR REDEEMER WAS WHAT'S MOST IMPORTANT, NOT HIS DEATH, AS IMPORTANT AS HIS DEATH WAS IN PLEASING THE LAW. (HEBREWS 9: 22, 26-28.) DYING, HE HAD TO DIE, EITHER WAY. HOWEVER, TO BE ABLE TO BE RAISED FROM THE DEAD, HIS

LIFE HAD TO HAVE BEEN IN PERFECT HARMONY WITH THE FATHER'S WILL WHILE IN SINFUL FLESH. HIS LIVING ENSURED THAT HIS SACRIFICE WOULD BE ACCEPTABLE, AND HIS DEATH WOULD NOT BE IN VAIN. HIS LIVING QUALIFIED HIM SO THAT HE WOULD BE RAISED FROM THE DEAD. THEREFORE, THE POWER IN THE CROSS, IS, IN REALITY, THE POWER IN HIS SINLESS LIFE, WHILE IN A SINFUL BODY OF FLESH. THE CROSS AND GRAVE ARE JUST SYMBOLS OF BOTH HIS DEATH AND VICTORY. THIS POWER HE DEMONSTRATED THROUGH HIS LIVING, BY THE SPIRIT IN HIM, SHOWS THAT WE NOW CAN ALSO LIVE WITHOUT SINNING, WHILE IN THIS BODY OF SIN, HAVING THE POWER OF THE SPIRIT OF GOD IN US, BEING REDEEMED.

YES, WE ARE SINFUL AND ARE CONDEMNED TO DIE THE SECOND, ETERNAL DEATH. (ROMANS 5:12, 14.) HOWEVER, THE MESSIAH HAS DIED THIS DEATH FOR US, AND IN DOING SO, CONQUERED DEATH IN HIS SINFUL FLESH BECAUSE OF HIS SINLESS LIFE. (ROMANS 5:15-21, ROMANS 8:3.) NOT ONLY GIVING US AN EXAMPLE BUT HAS MADE US CONQUERORS TOO, RIGHT NOW, THIS MOMENT, OVER THE SECOND DEATH AND SIN, WHILE IN THIS SINFUL BODY OF FLESH. THAT IS THE ULTIMATE CONDITIONING OF THE BELIEVER IN THIS LIFE, WHO IS IN CHRIST, TO LIVE IN A SINFUL BODY AND WORLD, WITHOUT SINNING OURSELVES. (ROMANS 8:31-39.) THAT IS THE GOOD NEWS OF SALVATION; THE REAL AND TRUE GOSPEL!!

Most of us, especially Christians, are not taught right, so we do not know this, but we have to acknowledge this for it to be a reality right now in our lives, while it has always been a reality around us. However, how can we recognize it if we were not taught? And how can we be shown if we do not have a teacher of truth? And how can we have a teacher of these facts, if they do not know? And how can they know if they are not sent? And how can they be sent, if the Most, High God did not inspire them? (Romans 10:15.) So, we have to ask for the spirit of the Most, High God to come into our heart/mind as David did, to inspire and lead us into this truth. (Psalms 51.) That is the gospel, the good news of salvation, present in us, and to us to present to the world, through our lives, in the way we live.

So, the messiah was demonstrating this to us and the world, that he came into sinful flesh. However, he had the power over sin because he did not sin while in this sinful body of flesh. This power over sin is a demonstration of the power over death because death is only a result of sin. (Rom. 6:23.) Now he has given us that same power/ glory to live over sin and death while in our sinful body of flesh.

(John 17:22-23.) (*This is similar to having the power over the law in your country. Though you are under the law. However, if you did not break the law, you would not be subjected to the penalties of the law. This living above the law, while being subject to the law, gives you power over the law.*)

Because he lived in the nature and body of sin, his flesh was subject to the law. However, he did not sin; therefore, he was above sin and the law. Consequently, he was and is the conquering of sin; thus, he exercised power in him to forgive sin, but he did not own that power. The power in him, meaning that the spirit that was in him, was the spirit and power of God, the Father, working in harmony with the spirit of Christ. This is the reason he acknowledged that he was not the one doing the forgiving, but the Father, through his spirit in him, who was the one that doth the work. (John 5:30, 6:38, 8:28, 12:49-50, 14:10, Matt. 26:39.) (Giving all the praise to the Father again!)

We, too, now have been given victory over sin, to live without sinning while in this sinful body. And must remember to give the Most, High God the praise and glory, each time we demonstrate this victory. Notwithstanding, because we had sinned through Adam and continued to sin, we cannot forgive sin as a man. Only through the messiah could this have been accomplished, because though he took on a body of sin as a man, yet he did not sin. (John 1: 1, 14. Phil. 2:6-8. Romans 8:3, 2 Cor. 5:21.) If he had sinned, he too would have needed a savior.

No man has ever walked this earth before, or live in this earth presently, outside of the messiah, that have demonstrated the forgiveness of, and power over sin through living a sinless life while in a sinful body. We all have sinned and have come short of the glory of the Most, High God. (Romans 3:23.) Did you get that? **Only through living a sinless life, while in a sinful body did the messiah demonstrated, maintained, magnified, and obtained salvation for us and the glory of the Most, High God for himself. (2 Cor.5:21, Romans 8:3 John 4:34, 5:30, 17:4.)** Therefore, we lift humble hearts and praise the one and only true God for sending his son, and we praise the son who came and gave his perfect life as a ransom for our sins and has retained his glory with the Father in doing so. We will forever praise both the Father and the son. Because we have been redeemed by the life and death of the son, as a gift, and sealed by the spirit of the Most, High God. (Rev. 4:11, 5:11-14.)

Now we must also remember that he, the Messiah, said he did nothing of himself; it was the spirit of the Father in him. Therefore, even the forgiveness of sins he acknowledged as the work of the Father in him. (2 Cor.5:19.)

165

THE QUESTION IN THE LAST DAYS WILL NOT BE WHETHER THE MESSIAH EXISTED OR NOT, BUT RATHER, DID HE LIVED WITHOUT SINNING AS A MAN OF SIN? THE ONLY PROOF WE HAVE TO SHOW IS US LIVING AS HE DID. LIVING TESTIMONIES TO THE WORLD, SHOWING THE GOSPEL OF TRUTH, LIVING WITHOUT SINNING WHILE IN SINFUL BODIES. NOT JUST TALKING ABOUT IT, BUT LIVING IT!!!!

Chapter 34

Sinless, Sinful, and Sinning: what's the difference?

The messiah took on the sinful nature of man but did not sin. That made him sinless. The body of sin housed the mind of the messiah that was stayed on the Father by the indwelling spirit of the Most, High God. The messiah decided or chose always to focus on the things of the Most, High God.

Again, the messiah forgiving of sins could not be on the merit of human nature, which he got from the fallen nature of man. But the nature of the Spirit of the Most, High God; the Father in this man. It was never about the fallen nature of Christ. The fallen nature, however, was also used to show that he contained sin in his flesh. (Romans 8:3.) However, more than that was to reveal the presence of the power of the spirit of the Most, High God in the mind of the messiah, while being in that fallen nature of sin. (2 Cor. 5:21.) It is clear right here in the text message. It states, 'he was made to be in sin,' meaning he took on the body of sin. But the scripture goes on to say, 'who knew no sin,' meaning he was innocent in his mind, by not sinning. Therefore, he was able to Bind and subdue this fallen nature of man, to the point of conquering sin and death in his flesh, and redeeming man back to the Most, High God, in the process. Romans 8. It was a cooperate victory over sin, similar to the cooperate sin of Adam. (Romans 5. 1Cor. 15:21-22.) Because of his total obedience to the Most, High God while in fallen sinful flesh. The Most, High God could use him by his power working through him to forgive us of sin, while he was in the flesh, but not of the flesh. Remember, again, and he said I (the man) could do nothing of myself, speaking of the fallen nature of the flesh. Therefore, the text message Matt. 9:6, speaks to the power of forgiveness been demonstrated through the son of man: the messiah, by the indwelling spirit of the Most, High God in him. Because he is now the true son of man and not just of Adam, but having the fallen nature of Adam without sinning himself. (Heb. 2:14-18.) He was also the true temple of the Most, High God, where sin has been forgiven. Not just as a symbolic gesture, but a reality in time for eternity. Him knowing the difference between the presence of the spirit in his mind and the presence of the nature of sin in his body chose to allow the spirit of

God to demonstrate the Father's will in him. (Luke 22:42.) And by so doing subdue death and sin in his flesh. (Heb. 2:14.)

Now, the only difference between the cooperate sin of Adam and the cooperate redemption of the Messiah is; the children of Adam had no choice in having a sinful nature; however, for those who will be redeemed, they have to choose to accept or reject this gift of redemption. (John 3:16.)

All the inspired scriptures and accounts have to be inconsistent agreement. There, the messiah: the man of sin did not forgive sins, as is erroneously taught by many, but proclaimed forgiveness of sin and, as such, was not shown to be God while in sinful flesh. Instead, the spirit of the Most, High God was in him because he lived a perfect life without sinning and was totally in obedience to the will of the Father, doing the work of the Father. Because of this, the Most; High God was able to demonstrate the power of forgiveness of sin through him, him being sinless while having a sinful nature, as the true and living sacrifice. He, the Most, High God brought glory to himself and not to the messiah, however, through the messiah. (John 3:16, 17.)

Therefore, there is a difference between forgiving sin and proclaiming forgiveness of sin. God, the Father, is the only one that forgives sin, and the servants of God are the only ones that give the proclaiming of the forgiveness of sin. (Exodus 32:32, Isaiah 43:25, Psalm 9:5, Nehemiah 13:14.) Now, Luke 5:20-25, and Luke 7:48 are centered in and confirmed by John 5:30, 8: 28, 12:49-50. Christ was here doing the will of the Father; therefore, he was a servant of God proclaiming the forgiveness of sin, not only in words but more so in his sinless life.

The messiah also had to ask for glory from the Father. (John 17: 4, 5.) That meant the messiah knew that he was not God, and didn't have the glory of God while on earth, but was God's instrument, being used by the Most, High God for God's glory, while here on earth. Yes, though he was in sinful flesh, he was able to satisfy the law and the will of the Most, High God at the same time. Praise be to the Most, High God, for his marvelous works in man, for us, man! Therefore, sinless is one who has never sinned; Christ never sinned. Sinful is one who has the nature of sin; however, he took on this nature. While sinning is committing the act of sin, Christ never committed an act of sin, which made him the perfect sacrifice, redeemer, an example for humanity. Therefore, while he was sinful by taking on the nature of fallen man, as the law looked at him in that way, he was never a sinner, sinning, or sinful by the act. There is no mystery here; this is as plain as day. To God be the Glory great truth he has given.

Chapter 35

The Truth revealed on the mount

The account on the mount of transfiguration experience has had many thinking and teaching that the messiah revealed his glory to the disciples. This event, they say, shows that he was God, while he was on earth. This misrepresentation of the account has left many confused.

 If we should take that text message at this time and look at it carefully, we would note. Verse one of Matt. 17, states that after six days, the messiah took Peter, James, and John the brother of James on a high mountain. Verse 2 says that he transfigured before them. And his face shines like the sun, and his raiment was white as the light. Now, this is the text message that has most thinking that the messiah was showing "his glory."

 Well, let's look at this carefully. The word "transfigure" within context means Christ's outward appearance changed into a spectacular sight. In this change, the face and clothing of the messiah shone like light, even as the sun. These expressions speak to how bright the light was on and around him, to those who are describing it. Now the next verse, verse 3. Gives us an indication as to why there was such a light. It states that: "And, behold, there appeared unto them Moses and Elias talking with him." That is very interesting because Moses was dead. In Duet. 34:5-6, it states that "Moses died in the land of Moab and buried in the valley of the land of Moab over against Beth-Peor, but no man knows of his sepulcher to this day." However, in Jude 1:9, we see an interesting development occurring. An argument and fight between the angel Michael and the devil over the body of Moses. Well, Matthew 17 testify to the victory of Michael over the devil regarding Moses, because of his appearance here on the mount with Elias. Therefore, we can safely say Moses came down from a glorious place we call heaven, with the glory of the Most, High God around him, not with his own glory. That is the first thing we should notice.

Now, the name Elias is mention as the second man seen talking to the messiah; however, some text messages referred to him as Elijah. Regardless, the messiah after speaking to the disciples, it states in verse 13, that they knew he was talking about John the Baptist. If we should accept what the scripture state in this text message, many theologies will be in question. Because John the Baptist had not died a long time ago like Moses did and was not shown to have been translated or taken up. Therefore, there is a question on the resurrection theology of many. However, we will stay on the present path. Regardless, we know both men came down from the presence of the Most; High in heaven.

Also, we must remember that Moses had a similar experience, being in the presence of God before he died, on the Mount Sinai. (Exodus 24: 18.) In chapter 34, Moses again, as he went up to commune with God, and in verse 5, it states that the LORD descended in the cloud and stood with him there, and proclaimed the name of the Lord. In verse 29-35 of the same chapter, we see the skin on Moses Face shone because he was in the presence of the Most; High. So much so that the people were not able to look upon him, and he had to cover his face when he came from the mountain. That shows that Neither Moses, Elias, Elijah, nor the messiah reflected any glory of their own, but only shone because the presence of the Most, High God, was around them. In verse 5, of Matt.17 it states that "while he spoke, behold a bright cloud overshadowed them: and behold a voice out of the cloud, which said, 'this is my beloved Son, in whom I am well pleased; hear ye him.'" The brightness was only there when the bright cloud appeared, and a voice spoke from this bright cloud.

That should make it even clearer still to us, that the only one with the glory was the one everyone could hear talking out of the bright cloud, and that was not the messiah, but the Most, High Eternal God. The God of Moses, Elias, Elijah, John the Baptist, and the messiah. The messiah had not this type of glory to show, as he was a man and not God, but the glory of his Father overshadowed him. (Phil. 2:6-8. John 1:1, 14. Romans 8:3.) Remember, he had not received the glory he had with the Father before the world was, at this time. Therefore, he had no glory to show, except the glory he would restore to man, that man had before man fell, which was not comparative to the glory of the Father, but was favored by the Father to be returned by the son. (Heb. 2:7-15, John 17:22.) However, the Father demonstrated his favor by surrounding them with his own glory at this present time.

That also is a privilege for us to be used by the Most; High God to bring glory to himself, in many different ways, and for his glory to overshadow us also. The messiah said we should do greater work than he did. This work means we shall light up the world, by being used by the spirit of the Most, High God to show his love to a grossly sin diseased world. And in so doing, bring glory and praise to the one and only true God, the father and the word in these last days.

The messiah, however, did show an example of the glory and dominion he had as a man. (Gen. 1:26.) This glory he gave back to us, man. (John 17: 22.) One example is found in the story of Christ calming the sea. (Matt. 8: 23-27.) All the miracles that we see Christ performed, that glory has been given with the dominion stated in Gen. 1:26, back to the redeemed. Praise be to the highest God.

Chapter 36

Being divine doesn't necessarily mean being God, what!!?

Another erroneous argument is that the Messiah was divine, and therefore he was God. If that were the case, then all of us who have been redeemed, and have the spirit of the Most, High God in us, are Gods; because we have the same divinity as Christ. Yes, you read that right; we now have the same spirit he had when he walked this earth. Romans 8:1-17, emphasis on verses 11, 14, 16, and 17.

The word 'divinity' and 'divine' have stupefied and mystified many because of the erroneous teaching on the subject deliberately or not. Most are taught or tricked into believing that the word divine only means God when it also means godliness or of God. This godliness or being of God speaks to the relationship of the person referred to, towards God. Those who are in harmonious relationships with God are, in fact, divine. Why? Because, to be in a harmonious relationship with God, the spirit of God has to be residing within that person or being; being in harmony with the spirit of that person or being. Those who are in such a relationship know who they are and are just as Christ was, as a man is with the Father by the same spirit. (John 17:20-23.) If the divine spirit of God that dwelled in Christ made him divine, also dwells harmoniously in you, then you are now a divine being, meaning you are now of God and belongs to God. Not like God, but of God, there is a difference. (Romans 8:16-17.) Most are afraid to claim this truth, because of their so-called religious leaders not teaching such truth, because these teachers do not know such truth.

 This absence of true knowledge is one of the problems with ignorant Christians today. Most are taught and therefore think that this divinity was only available to the messiah and, therefore, that made him the true and living God when He walked this earth. That is utter foolishness and ignorance. This plot of the devil has caused many to stumble and have used this argument as a crutch for sinning. Remember Romans 8, tells us that we have that same divine spirit: emphasis on verse 11. There is only one divinity. We have to keep reminding ourselves that he, the word, was with the Most, High God, who was also the true and living God. He who was with God then became flesh. He the word came into sinful flesh, verse 3. He was subject to death because of sin, not only being in this sinful world but also within sinful flesh. The Most, High God cannot exist as sinful flesh, or ever, ever, ever die! The Most, High God can't die. If the Most, High God ever die once, he ceased to be the Most, High God forever. More than that, he would have shown he was not the Most, High God in the first place, but an imposter. He would have been a total fake. Also, sin can't dwell, not even, in the presence of the Most, High God, let alone in his body of flesh. That is an impossibility throughout time and eternity because God is not flesh, but spirit. The messiah that you call the Christ; the flesh was never God because he was in sinful flesh, Romans 8:3, but the Most, High God, dwelt in him by his divine spirit. (John 14:8-11. John 15:26. John 16:13-15.) The same way the Most, High God lives in us by his same divine spirit today. (1 Cor. 3:16. Romans 8:9-11.) Therefore, he was holy because of his relationship with God, by the divine spirit of God that was in him; this is the only way he was divine. Now he has made it possible again for us to be holy like he was; by accepting his gift of divine grace because of his life, death, resurrection, and acceptance by God. Praise be to the Most, High God, and his divine son, our savior.

Now, because he was one like us, in sinful flesh, except without sin, he was a man, not God, subject to death. And we know, the Most, High God cannot be subject to such. Remember the flesh he became was sinful flesh, Rom. 8:3. This text message uses the word "likeness" this word is the same in meaning as "likeness" used in Gen.1:26. The context is clear. The same way God was pure and perfect during creation, the man was made pure and perfect, but at a lower level, even lower than the angels before he sinned. (Heb. 2:6, 7.) So here the messiah who was in the "likeness" of sinful flesh. And only sinful flesh can be subjected to death. Adam was not made subject to death as a man, no he was made in the likeness of the Most, High God, sinless and of God: divine. It was after he had committed a sin that he became subject to death, and started to die.

However, the messiah took that fallen nature of Adam after the fall, the likeness of sinful flesh as a man. Yes, he also came in a lower state than Adam when Adam was created. That was the only way Christ was made a curse, and subdued sin in his flesh, while subjected to death. (Gal.3:13.) There is no mystery here for those of us who have the divine spirit of the Most, High God in us. Sin cannot enter into a perfect, sinless body by osmosis. It had to have been an act of the Most, High God or Adam that cause him, the messiah to be born in sinful flesh, who knew no sin. Also, if the messiah who you call the Christ was the living God, the effects of sin could not be in his body, and he would not be in sinful flesh, being subject to death, and then dying, but we know he was divine or of God, being the son of God.

Remember!! The Most Holy God is Spirit and will always be Spirit. Being spirit and manifesting himself into other kinds. Example: the cloud by day, the fire by night, the burning bush, the still small voice, flesh, nature, etc. (Exodus 13:21, Exodus 3: 2, 4. 1st Kings 19:11-15, Psalms 19:1.) So, the messiah being in sinful flesh was not the living God, but the living God was in him, through the spirit of God, the same way he is in us today, those of us who are redeemed. We have to remember that all that we see physically, can touch physically and hear, are manifestations from the true and living God, not the essence of the true and living God, who is divine spirit.

Consider after the resurrection of the messiah: the Christ, doubtful Thomas was able to touch the risen savior after he returned from heaven, being accepted by the Father. However, the only true essence of the living God as revealed to us, who are spiritual, is Spirit so, for Thomas to be able to touch the risen savior after he had gone to his Father and came back to earth. (Remember he had told Mary that she should not touch him because he had not yet ascended to heaven. But Thomas was allowed to touch him, indicating he had gone to the Father and was back.) This condition he was in shows that he was not glorified at the time and as such, was not God even at that point, however, was divine. (John 20:16-17, 26-29.) The remarks that are written that Thomas made after, verse 28, has to be taken within the context of the entire inspired word. A sinful man can't be in the presence of a Holy God, let alone touch him. Also, Pentecost had not yet happened, and they were not refreshed by the spirit as yet, to be one in the spirit. He was indicating that he had not retained his power as God even at this time.

Therefore, going back! For the Messiah, the one you call the Christ, to be the living God and to be in all point tempted as we are, and to have the temperament to sin, and then to die. He would have had to have sinned at least once for the law to allow that to happen; if you think he was God on earth. That would also prove he was not the living God, but a living man who had sinned, and that argument falls flat in its grave, as he would be today. Isaiah 53, bears witness, emphasis on verse 11-12. To bear/ take other's sin or iniquities, and to be numbered with the transgressors, is clearly to be one like them: (Romans 8:3, Heb. 2:11-18.) Yet, without sin, while in sinful flesh.

Therefore, Christ was indeed divine, but was not God while he walked this earth as a man, and so are we as he has redeemed us.

Chapter 37

Who raised who?

Many believe that he was able to raise himself from the dead because he was God. That is not true and is a deception of the evil one. The Father rose him. (1 Peter 1: 21, 2 Cor.4:14. John 5: 21.) While he was alive, he stated that he could do nothing of himself, but only through the spirit of the Father in him. (John 5:30, 2 Cor. 5:19.) It is therefore conclusive that while he was dead, he definitely could not do anything, let alone raise himself from the dead. Only the Father could do such a thing, which would be consistent with the entire inspired Scriptures. John 10: 17-18, 32-33, 35-42, 19:7, have to be in corroboration with John 3: 16-17, Eccl. 12:7 and Romans 8:11.

Verse 18, of John 10, has puzzled many scholars to this day. Especially the clause that states that "I have the power to lay down my life and take it up again." Most think this meant that the messiah was God because only God could say such a thing. However, if we were to carefully observe the full text within the entire context of these text messages, we will note that both verses 17 and verse 18 stand or fall on the last clause of verse 18. This clause states: "This commandment have I received of my Father" Which simply means that this act was not something that he was able to do on his own, but the Father was able to do this wonderful work through him because the son was willing to first, live for the will of the Father, and allow the Father to work through him by his spirit, which is not subject to death. John 6:63. Remember, he said he does nothing of himself, nor does he speak his own words. Therefore, to say, "I have the power to lay down my life and take it up again." was not his own words but the proclaiming of the Father through him by his spirit. That is the true example that is left for us by the messiah if we are willing to allow the will of God to be in our lives. Through his spirit in us, we will then be in harmony with God, as the messiah was, in proclaiming and doing God's words and works. Now, by him plainly saying, "no man can take it from me, but I lay it down of myself." That means just as is stated, no one could kill him, and no one killed him. He volunteered to give his life up for us sinners. As dramatic as the crucifixion was, they still could not take his life without him volunteering it. The obvious question would then be this: How was his life taken if he were God?

The scripture explained what happens, but we can see this only if we read the scripture with the spiritual eye of the spirit. The explanation is as follows: the spirit of God had to have departed from him, for him to have died in the first place. He confirmed this when he said: "My God, my God, why has thou forsaken me? " While he was on the cross. (Matt. 27:46.) Indicating that the spirit of God left him. He also said shortly after, "Father, into thy hand, I commit my spirit." (Luke 23:46.) He was speaking this time of the spirit of the man that was in him also. This spirit of his, he commended to the Father; "into thy hands, I commend my spirit" (Luke 23:46.) That also proves that no one killed him by putting him on the cross, or piercing him in the side. He voluntarily gave his life. This spiritual principle is also applicable to us. No man can kill us physically unless the spirit of God and our spirit leaves our bodies. (Acts 14:19-20. Rev.11:7-11.) Whatever men do to our bodies, if the spirits remain in the body, we will not die. We only die when the spirits leave.

These truths also tell us that he had no power in the grave. It was the spirit of the Most; High that had, and retained that power. Upon reading and understanding these scriptures, it is clear that the Father is the one with the power, who was working through the son. (2 Cor. 5:19.) He is the one giving the love and the sacrifice through his son, who was willing to do the will of the Father. (John 3:16, 2 Cor. 5:18, John 4:34.) Again, have you not noticed that the last clause in verse 18 of John 10, tells us that the commandment to lay down and take up his life came directly from the Father?

Now, because he had the divine spirit of the Most, High God in him, he was able to obey, even unto the death of the cross. Therefore, this commandment to lay down and take up again came only from the Father to the son, through the divine spirit. Not from the son to himself. I hope we noticed that too. The son was always subjected to the Father, doing the father's will and allowing the Father's will to be done through him. (1Cor.15:28. Luke 22:42.)

That also calls for a little reminder. We have to remember that man is made of a body but is constituted of breath, the spirit of man and spirit of God. When the messiah said he gave his life, he is talking about the body as a sacrifice and the breath; that is the cessation of this physical functional life. The spirit of God and man can't die. We know that the spirit of God goes wherever it wills, while the spirit of man goes back to God who gave it, upon death. (John 3:8, Eccl. 12:7.) The spirit of man and the breath of man are two different essences. The spirit of man is consciousness, while the breath is not a conscious entity, but is essential for the physical life of man to function in this realm. (1 Cor. 2:11. Gen. 2:7.) That is why, upon death, man (body) ceases being conscious and functional because his spirit goes back to God. His breath expires into the atmosphere, and his body returns to dust. Therefore the "I" in verse 15 of John 10 is referring to the spirit of the man Christ: the conscious. The word "life" in the same verse refers to the body as a sacrifice and breath. This same "I" is referred to in verses 16, 17, and 18. In verse 17, the word "life" again refers to the body. The last "I" usage in verse 18, expresses the harmonious existence of the spirit of the Father and the spirit of the man Christ, in the life or body of Christ.

Some might argue, however, that Christ went to Hades and preached to the spirits in prison. (1 Peter 3: 18-19.) Therefore, they say he wasn't really dead. Well, now, if we read these same text messages carefully again, we will notice some undeniable truths. (1) We see that Christ was put to death (he gave up the spirit.), meaning he died, and we know the body without the spirit is dead. 1 Peter 3: 18, James 2:26. (2) We see that Hades is where the spirits are: a spiritual environment. Therefore, it was the spirit of God that left Christ that went there, not the body of flesh that was dead; but the spirit of God that was in the body. And for the spirit to go there, it had to have left the body of flesh first. (3) It clearly states that the body was put to death, but was quicken by the spirit. Which means it was sustained in an incorruptible state, while not functioning or functional because the spirits and breath were not in the body for it to function or live. Without the spirit, there is no life. Similar to how Adam was before he was made alive by the breath and spirits of God. (John 6: 63. Psalms 16:10. Gen.2:7. 2 Cor. 2:11. Rom. 8:16.) (4) Also, we must remember that the spirit of a man, like that of Christ, goes back to the Father from whom it came upon death. (Eccles. 12:5-7.) And Christ knew this truth, as we see him commended his spirit to the Father, then he died.

Therefore, the correct understanding is that the spirit of God that was in Christ was the one spirit that went to hades, not Christ, or the spirit of the man Christ, but the spirit of God. (2 Cor. 5:19.) Remember, Christ was flesh, though he was the anointed son of God, he was still the flesh that died. (Acts 10: 38, John 1:29, Romans 8:3, Phil. 2:8.) But the spirit of which we speak in is the spirit of the Father and the son: the one spirit. This same spirit is the spirit that was in Christ and now is in us, with our spirit that makes us one with the Father and son. (John 14: 16-18;

17: 20-26.) It was the spirit that went to Hades, the spirit of God that was in Christ also. The spirit of the man Christ that every man receives in this earthly life is the spirit that went straight away, back to the Father. (Eccles. 12:7.) We also see corroboration of this truth in David's prayer.

In David's prayer, Psalm 51:10, 11. David asked the Father not to take away his spirit from him. It was after David had committed that terrible sin, being a sinful man. Moreover, the spirit he was referring to was the same divine spirit that was in Adam before he sinned, and the messiah. He first asked for his rebellious spirit to be renewed, the spirit of David, which was defiant against the spirit of God. Even David acknowledged that two spirits dwell within a son of God, as shown in Romans 8:16, 1 Cor. 2:11. Then he asked that the Father does not leave him by taking away his holy spirit from him: the spirit of God.

Similarly, the messiah asked that this will, which was his will not to be done, the will of the sinful cooperate, man. The will he referred to was the flesh and not the spirit, which made him a living sacrifice, but that the will of the Most, High God gets done; the spirit, the divine will. (Luke 22: 42.) Brethren, we have to know that the same divine spirit that was in Christ is also to be in us, being in harmony with our own spirit. (Romans 8:8-11.) If we accept this truth of the spirit of the Most, High God, his 'will,' will allow our rebellious spirits to come into conformity with the divine spirit of God if we let him. Then we will live and teach sinners the truth of God's ways, and they will convert to the Most, High God, and we will sin no more while on this sinned cursed earth: living in a body of sin, but living as the messiah did, victoriously now, because Christ lived a sinless life, while in a sinful body on earth, and God was able to raise him from the dead by his divine will because of His sinless life. Amen.

Part 7

The spirit, self, and God

The thesis also of this book is God is a spirit, and they that worship him must worship him in that same Spirit and that same truth. Also, to worship in this truth, man has to acknowledge and accept who he is, being in the image and likeness of God, and God being his creator, sustainer, redeemer, and King. (John 4:24.)

Chapter 38

Self or selfish, what's the difference?

Self:

Definition:

1   A: the entire person of an individual
    B: the realization or embodiment of an abstraction

2   A (1): an individual's typical character or behavior. Her true self was revealed (2): an individual's temporary behavior or character. His better self

    B: a person in prime condition. I feel like my old self today

3   : the union of elements (such as body, emotions, thoughts, and sensations) that constitute the individuality and identity of a person
4   : personal interest or advantage
5   : Material that is part of an individual organism. The ability of the immune system to distinguish self from non-self. *(Merriam Webster Dictionary)*

Selfish:

Definition:

1. Selfish (Ethics) Believing or teaching that the chief motives of human action are derived from a love of self.
2. Selfish Caring supremely or unduly for one's self, regarding one's own comfort, advantage, etc., in disregard, or at the expense, of those of others. *(Webster's Revised Unabridged Dictionary)*

In today's world, just as in every other, the understanding of self is a very important concept that defines life for good or ill.

Many people think that self has to do with their physical appearances, their achievements. Their looks they call it, or image that they can see. But what does the word "self" really mean? More appropriately, what is the concept of self really, in its truest sense? Some today, look at self as their net profit, their financial value.

However, most of the world's understanding of self couldn't be further from the truth, and as such most of us continue to live in a fantasy world of not knowing self. Therefore, it is very imperative to know the difference between 'self,' 'image,' and 'looks.'

By knowing these things, we will have the right understanding of who we are, and this will reveal to us the path to knowing God. It is impossible to know God without knowing your true self first. Let me repeat that for emphasis: it is impossible to know the Most, High God without first knowing self! Also, this is a similar principle for you not being able to love God, without first loving your brother, who you see. (1 John 4: 20.) With the understanding that your brother is more than what you see, as you are too.

Therefore, we have to expose what self is. What most do not know is that self is not what you see in the mirror; the way you look. Neither is self what you put your clothes on in the morning; frame. I know this knowledge will be shocking to many people. It took some time for me to have an understanding of self, and I am still learning from the spirit of the Most, High God, so much about my "self." I want to share the basics of knowing "self" with you. In the hope of you coming into a clearer understanding of who you are, so you can know who the Most; High God really is. And by knowing self, we will remember that whatever we do should be done to the honor and glory of the Most, High God. (1 Cor. 10:31.)

First, let us take note that the meaning of "self" is quite different than the word "selfish." Many have mistaken the two as having the same root. In the English language, the argument would be that both words have the same root or origin of 'self' in them. Therefore, they are from the same family tree. That would be acceptable if the dimensions of man were all the same, which means that there are many dimensions in the classification of man when it comes on to the existence of man. However, there are two main classifications. One is the physical that we see; in our presence and action, and the other is the spirit that we discern; in our thoughts, motives, and speech.

Consequently, this understanding of self has to be from these different perspectives. The physical self-explanation which has been exhausted we will not expound on any further here, except to say; we know that what we can physically see, touch, and feel; the body of a person is referring to as self. Therefore, we will look at the spiritual self, the real self, or the person or personality within the body.

When God created man, he made the physical, form, or frame of man from the earth. It is interesting to note that there was no life in man as a form. Then he, God, placed within man the spiritual or the "self" the person of man from himself; the Most, High God, the image of himself, after he blew the breath of life in man. Now we know that God is a spirit; thus, the image of God has to be spirit also, which is a reflection of himself in man. Therefore, the image of God that was like himself must be the spirit of man that God placed in man. (1 Cor. 2:11-15.) As we have mentioned before, that the body, a form of the man, is like unto a container, and the spirit, which is the "self" of man operates from within that container. Therefore, when you get up in the morning and look into the mirror, what you see is not "self," but a reflection of a form that self operates through. But you are taught by conventional beliefs that you are looking at yourself. This teaching is not of the deep things of God, but the shallow deception of the devil.

In the Holy text messages, we read that the Most, High God 'form' man from the dust of the earth. Then the Most, High God blew his breath of life, which is of himself, into this form and 'than' man became a living soul. (Gen.2:7.) The word 'living' in its most accurate context is Godly, which means Godly soul, or of God. Because living is from life, and life is from the Most, High God. Therefore, there is no life outside of the Most; High, because the Most; High God is life.

Consequently, God gave a part of himself, life, into this form, and man became a live-in-soul. Meaning God now lives in man through his spirit. That is how the Most; High God made the man into his image. To have a part of God in you is also to have the image or spirit of God in you, a part of the Most, High God 'him-self'.

Therefore, this image is not of the earth or flesh; else, it would be physical. If that were so, then the form that the Most; High God made would be his image, his physical looks. And would not need breath to live, but would be living as a form. That, however, is not so, as we know, the structure has no life of its own.

Remember, also, we were all made in God's image, but we all look different. If our physical looks were a reflection of God, then there would be as many different Gods as there are many different looks of people. Again, the form is not the image, but the presence of the Most, High God that is in that form man, that is called self; that is the image, which is the spirits of man and spirit of God. This image is the likeness of the Most, High God. Not of the physical, but the spiritual, because the Most, High God is spirit. And this image is consistent; there are no changes in its essence. Therefore, when the Most; High God put his breath into man. The Most; High God also gave of himself to the man the spirit of man, which is also referred to as a part of the self of man. The other part of the person of man is the spirit of God. Both of these essences make the complete, authentic self of man. This self is the actual image of God in man. Therefore, to distort the image of God is to have a rebellious spirit towards God.

Having a proper understanding of this truth will now reveal to us who we are and give us an introduction to who the Most; High God is. That is the reason the messiah could say to his disciples, "if you see me, (see here means, understand) you see the Father." Not referring to the physical, but by showing them the works that were done through him by the spirit of the Father's self in him, the spirit. (John 14:8-11)

An example would be looking at the appearance of a father and his son. If the son looks physically like his father, we would say: "he looks just like his dad." However, if this same son who looks physically like his father does something terrible, that is opposite to his father's character, we would then say: "he is nothing like his dad." Why the change in our expression? Well, because the character or nature is reflected in the spirit of the person, his consciousness, not the physique or appearance of the person, and we all know that's most important. Hence the image is in the container, earthen vessel, or house but is not the container, vessel, or house itself. The opposite is also true. If the son does not look physically like his father, but his disposition and manners are like that of his dad. We would say he is just like his father, proving again that the actual image is not the looks, physique or body (container) of a person, but the mannerism, dispositions, personality, and character, which is a reflection, an image, or spirit within the person. That is the consistency of the truth of the true essence of man.

Many illustrations within the scriptures speak to the value of what's in the container or body, as opposed to the container or body. In John 14:9, the messiah tells his disciples that if they see him, they see the Father. However, he tells the rich young ruler that there is only one who is good, and he is in heaven that is the Most, High God. (Mark 10:18.) Sound contradictory to the carnal ears, but not so to the spiritual. (1 Cor.2:14.) So, when the messiah tells his disciples that they should look at the works that he does and these works were not done by him, but the Father that is in him, through the indwelling Spirit of the Most, High God. In John 14: 10, he was telling them how to look to see the Father's image, not speaking of the physical that they saw, but of the spiritual self of God's spirit in him, the image of the Most, High God, through the actions or manifestation of the spirit in him. He knew that the body he was in was just a form, a container, an earthly house or vessel. (Heb. 10:5, 2 Cor. 5:1-2.) The works that were through this container, however, were demonstrations of the power and presence higher than what they could see as a body, which reflected the image of the Most, High God in the son. Yes, the manifestation of the work, speaks to the spirit that dwells inside, this is the image or self of which we also speak.

Let's look at an everyday example of this. There are many brilliant people in the world today, doing tremendous and excellent things in many different areas. The question is, what makes them so intelligent and not someone else? Is it their looks? Well, we all are made up of similar parts. Is it our bodies, the container, or is it what's inside of us? Be it talents or gifts. I believe it is what is inside of us, the spirit that gives these gifts. There is a power that transcends the physical container, which is operating through this physical space, which is a spiritual power, be it of good or bad influence.

Consequently, the work that's done is not by the container; the body, but through the vessel; the body, by the spirit that is within that body. Many brilliant works will continually be done through us in this world by the spirit of the Father and Son, for their glory again. And many brilliant works have and will also be done by a demonic spirit in many others. So, the question is, which spirit or image are you reflecting?

Some might also ask, how is it possible for the Father to be in heaven and on earth at the same time?

To answer that, we have to remember that the spirit of the Most, High God is the presence of the Most, High God, in man. Remember also that God has a spirit of himself, as man also has a spirit of himself that was given to him by the Most, High God. (1 Cor.2:11.) *"For what man knows the things of man, except the spirit of man that is in a man? Even so, the things of God know no man, but the spirit of God.*" This text shows the reflective properties or image of God in man. It is evident that the spirit of man is not another man, but the essence or reality of the true consciousness of man, the same as the spirit of the Most, High God is not another God, but the true essence, presence or reality of the Most, High God. Therefore, God is a spirit, and indeed God has a spirit. The carnal mind will never understand these truths. (1 Cor. 2:14.) What this means, in a nutshell, is that the Most, High God is a spirit, as in existence, and also spirit as in function. However, there are not two fathers, but one. Consequently, the Most; High can be in heaven while his spirit is on the earth and anywhere he desires, while there is still only one Father. So, the presence of the Most, High God can be felt in many different places, through his spirit, at the same time.

However, in the case of man, his effect can only be felt in one place at a time. This one effect can be accumulated over some time for man's impact to be in many places at one time, but not his presence. That shows a restriction or limitation of movements and influence within a given time for man, while he contains the image of God. However, the Most; High God is unaffected by time and space.

Remember, an image is a reflection of the same characteristics that are within the original. The spirit of man within man only appreciates all the qualities that the Most; High God gave man off himself. And can only be recognized and appreciated by the spirit of man adequately. (1 Cor. 2:15-16.) The form, container, or body is just there for the spirit to operate through. When the Most; High God made the man, he gave him dominion over everything on earth, as he; God has authority over everything in heaven. Note carefully, though; it was after he placed his image, the spirit in man, that man could receive dominion and power. (Gen. 2:7, 1:26-30.) This spirit is also another image quality of God in man.

Yes, this is of the true image of the Most; High. As the Most; High God also has a spirit in himself, he also puts a spirit inside of man; the spirit of man, which is the true reflection of his image and how the Most, High God operates. The Most; High God tells the man to be fruitful and increase. The Most, High God is always fruitful and have been multiplying since before forever; another part of the true image of the Most, High God. Then to solidify his image in man, he puts his spirit also into the man in a harmonious union with the spirit of man, which shows in the intelligence of man, another reflection of the image of God in man. This intelligence was also what we saw in the Messiah, the true image of God demonstrated.

185

Chapter 39

If you see me, you see the Father, WOW!! REALLY!!!?

Yes! When the bible says that God is a spirit, this statement is referring to the self or essence of the Most, High God. As we have discovered that the term "God" is not a noun, when used in the proper context, but instead refers to a position of supremacy, an adjective that describes a position. Remember, there can be, and there are many gods; however, only one has the right to and occupies the supreme position of supreme creator and sustainer of time and eternity, and everything within and without the source.

 The true identity of the Most; High God is spirit. The self of the Most, High God is spirit. While the true identity of the man is flesh (Gen. 2:7 first clause), but the true self of the living soul is the spirit within man (Gen. 2:7 second clause), as in, the self of man. Therefore, the first step in knowing the Most, High God is to know self, as was stated, which is the image of the Most, High God in man. If you do not know self, the image of the Most, High God in you, you can't begin to know the true God. Because the Most, High God has put a part of himself in you to learn of him. This arrangement is the closest we have been with the Most, High God, yet most do not know this. Yes, the devil has distorted our minds so much so that many are not aware of this truth. Whenever our minds are confused about the truth, the image of the Most; High will appear distorted to us. This distortion is a deceptive strategy of the devil to hide the truth from us by intoxicating us with the Babylonian pagan wine, or false teachings.

 The messiah understood this truth. And as a man, could say: "I am about my Father's business," "my time has not yet come," I do nothing of myself," "Lord, not my will, but thy will be done," "into thy hand I commit my spirit" and so on.

 To say "I am about my Father's business," like the messiah, one has to subdue the fallen natural desires of the flesh, the container, and acknowledge the spirit self that is within, and this is a spiritual exercise. To acknowledge that we do nothing of the fallen nature that we are in, but of the spirit of the Most, High in us, just like the messiah, is a spiritual awareness that comes from the spirit of the Most, High

God in a conscious mind. One of the most effective tricks the devil uses is for us to look on our container as sinners with a fallen nature, and think that's all we are and will ever be. (Romans 7:25.) We have to destroy that lie that is coming straight from hell. And we can only do this by becoming aware of who we really are. We must remember we are redeemed and have been made more than conquerors in Christ. (Romans 8:37, 1 Cor.15:57.) In other words, our truest identity is the spirits that are in us and not the body we function through.

To say "lord not my will, but thy will be done," is also a humbling of the soul that only a mind that has chosen to give everything to the Most, High God, can express. This also tells that the messiah was aware that his fleshly will was not the same as the will of the Most, High God in him, which reveals to us that there were, and are two wills: The will of the flesh and the will of the spirit. The intention of the flesh is always in opposition to the will of the spirit. The will of the flesh is stronger than the will of the spirit in the carnal man, because of the dominance of his fallen nature that he was born with. This nature was the nature the messiah took upon himself as a man. Therefore, the scripture is true in saying he was in touch with the very feelings of our infirmities. (Heb. 4:15.) Infirmity here is the germ of sin in the flesh. Though he was not a sinner by committing any such act, he became sin by acceptance of this sinful condition of fallen man upon himself. (2 Cor. 5:21. 1 Peter 2:24. Romans 8:3.) Regardless, he conquered sin and death by the power of his mind, in full obedience to the will of the Father, through the spirits in him. Likewise, you can conquer this fallen will by the renewing of your minds as the messiah acknowledged that his true self was within the veil of this flesh. We should likewise be aware and also live by the Father's will, having our minds renewed. (Hebrews 10: 12- 20.)

The expression of the messiah "into thy hand I commit my spirit," tells four central truths: (1) Christ who was flesh knew that he had a spirit, apart from the spirit of the Most, High God. This is called the spirit of man, which is a part of the true self of man. This spirit was given to him, as is given to every man, sometime between conception and birth. (2) He had the right to commit his spirit/self to the Most, High God or not, just like we all do. Just like we saw with David when he asked the Most, High God to renew a right spirit self within him. (3) That also tells that man has intelligence, control, or influence over his own spirit from his fallen nature, hence the rebellious spirit. (4) The messiah also had the freedom to decide not to be in harmony with the Father as Adam did; however, he chose to remain faithful.

We can only make these statements of facts if the spirit of the Most, High God is in us, and we are made aware of this. No religion or doctrines of religions can teach these truths or introduce the Most, High God to you. Only the spirit of the Most, High God within, can do such work. What the various religions have done over the many centuries, is to distort the truth that has been revealed, and continue to teach lies as truth to manipulate the masses. They can talk about what they think the Most, High God is, and present these theories as God; however, they are wrong. Only the spirit of the Most, High God in you, can teach you about himself. (John 16:13, Heb. 8:11.) No one in this world can teach you the true knowledge of the Most, High God as the spirit of the Most, High God does. As the messiah said, "When he the spirit of truth comes, he will guide you into all truth: for he shall speak not of himself; but whatsoever he shall hear, that shall he speak: and he will shew you things to come." (John 16:13.)

Therefore, the teachings that are in most churches, which states that self must die, without distinguishing the true self from the false self, is erroneous. What we need to do is learn about the truth of "self," and what it is, then we can understand by having a true knowledge of self. Hosea 4:6.

Self-being the spirit of the true man that is within. The correct teaching, the spiritual teaching, is; the fallen nature must die to self, not that self must die. In other words, the sinful nature of the flesh is the "you" in the statement which must come under subjection of the spiritual nature of man, self, and of the spirit of God-self. This dying of self is the death that is spoken off here in 1 Cor. 15:31, which was demonstrated in the life of Christ while he was living on earth. (Roman 8:1-16.) And it should be shown in our lives today, for anyone to know, love, and live for the Most, High God. He first must understand that 'self' is off the Most, High, and God's presence is in him. Remember, man is dust, and if a man does not exist by his own self, then by which self does he exist? Has to be the self of the Most, High God's presence in him. Therefore, there is no such thing as a man's self-outside of God. But his existence is from the self, existing God. Then that self that is in man is a part of the Most, High God that came from the Most, High God. Remember, the man was made of the dust of the earth and only became alive by the breath of God that contains the spirit of God and man. That there is the true self of man, the spirit of man, that comes from the Most, High.

We will now look at several verses that illustrate the right understanding of this self.

Gal.2: 20. "I have been crucified with Christ, and it is no longer I who live, but Christ lives in me; and the life which I now live in the flesh I live by faith in the Son of God, who loved me and gave himself up for me."

There are four "I's" in this text message. The first two are referring to the fallen carnal nature of sinful flesh, the rebellious spirit David spoke off, the fallen self of man. The second two "I's" are referring to the renewed spirit of man, David also referred to in Psalms 51: 10, the redeemed self of man. These are first the rebellious self or spirit of man, then the renewed self or right spirit in man. Remember man is flesh; dust; dirt. Having a rebellious spirit is equal to being just functional dirt. However, having the spirit of God, being in harmony with the spirit of man, is not only being alive but living the right life, verse 11. Also, this body becomes quickened by the spirit of the Most, High God within. Romans 8:11.

Eph. 4:22-24. "That, in reference to your former manner of life, you lay aside the old self, which is being corrupted in accordance with the lust of deceit, and that you be renewed in the spirit of your mind, and put on the new self, which in the likeness of God has been created in righteousness and holiness of the truth."

The former manner of life and the old self is referring to the rebellious spirit of man. The fallen, rebellious spirit of man is at enmity with God. The renewing of the spirit of the mind is changing from the rebellious spirit to the "self" that God had created in righteousness, during the creation of man and now has redeemed man back to his righteous "self" by the truth; the living word. I hope we noticed that it was stated that we are renewed in the spirit of our minds. That is where the spirits of both man and the Most, High God dwell. That is where the renewing takes place. This newness of spirit that is in righteousness and holiness of the truth is the true image of God in our minds.

Matt. 22: 27- 39. "And the second is like, unto it, thou shalt love thy neighbor as thyself."

This exposition is one of the heavy-hitting teachings from the messiah. This teaching, if applied righteously, will reveal the Most, High to the world. However, it must be appropriately understood first.

The question then is, how can we be counseled by the messiah to love self, if self must die? What's going on here? Which "self" is Christ talking about when our religious teachers tell us that self must die, but the Messiah says that we should love ourselves? Who is right? Also, in 2 Tim. 3:2, there is a negative connotation to men being "lovers of themselves." In Mark 12:30-31, we are also told that the first command is to love the Lord with all our heart, soul, mind, and strength. And the second is to love our neighbor as we love our self. The imperative question is;

189

which should we love first: our neighbor, God or self; if in 1 John 4:20 we are admonished not to be liars, if we claim to love God who we can't see but hate our brother who we see, and we are told to love our neighbors as we love ourselves? (Mark 12:31.)

Now, this teaching has not been taught correctly by our religious practitioners for one of two reasons or possibly both, and that is for mind control and manipulation, or they are just clueless.

First, let us not misunderstand what or which "self" we are talking about here. You see, there are two "selves," as was presented earlier, the true self and the false self. The true self is the self that was placed in man after man was created. This arrangement was the harmonious union of the spirit of God and the spirit of man within the man. (Gen. 2: 7, 1Cor. 2: 11-12.) The false self is the fallen, rebellious spirit of man. (1 Cor. 2:14, Psalm 2:2, Daniel 9:5-9, 1 John 2:18, 2 Tim.3:2.) This same self was redeemed back to God by his son. (1 Cor. 2: 15-16. Gal. 3:13.) That is the self the messiah is telling us to love.

Remember, he also said, how can you love God who you cannot see and hate your brother that you see? (1 John 4:20.) Here we are admonished to love our brothers as we love our self. (Matt. 22: 27-39.) But, how can you love your brother, if you do not love yourself first if you are to love your brothers as you love yourself? And how can you love God if you do not love your brother, who you have seen? (1 John 2: 6, 9-11.) The next imperative question, which is the root question is, how can you love yourself if you do not know the self? As we all should know, it is impossible to love someone or something you do not know. Therefore, it is essential to know and love 'self' first to know and love your neighbor and God. That knowledge right there is the missing key in this love equation. This self, being the spirits of God and man. (1 Cor. 2: 11-12.) By our understanding and loving this "self" that is in us, we will love our neighbors, and we will love God. (1 Peter 1: 22-23.) Because the true self in us, is the reflection or image of the true God, and God is love. Therefore, having that true knowledge will guide us to loving ourselves; which will result in us loving our brothers, because we see ourselves in our neighbors, resulting in us loving the Most, High God, as he is the reflection, the image in us and our neighbors that are loving and being loved by God. (The carnal minds can't understand this love.) Now, that is the love that passes all carnal understanding.

Now we can conclude that the first to be loved should be self; after having a true understanding of self, then we will love our neighbors just as we love ourselves. By doing these acts, we would love God naturally a true reflection that we are loving

God because God's spirit is being in harmony with our spirit, and our neighbor's. This love in us is also the image of God, which is the beauty of following the true words of the spirit of the Most, High God in us, and not the erroneous teachings of man. Praise be to the Most, High God.

Now on the other side, there is also the teaching of the messiah; to deny self, taking up your cross, and following him. The text continues in verse 24 of Luke 9, to reveal that those who will try and save their lives will lose it, but those who lose their lives for his sake will keep it. We need to remember firstly that the words 'himself', 'self,' and 'life' first must be understood properly to have clarity on what the messiah is saying. The words 'himself' and 'self' are referring to the selfish fallen nature of man, here. While the word 'life' here is referring to the breath that leaves the body upon death, therefore, those who are willing to die for the gospel will live, while those who will try and preserve their life by denying the gospel will lose their lives.

Therefore, the loving of 'self,' this self is the redeemed nature of man, through Christ, is to live the gospel. While the denying of 'self,' this self is the fallen or rebellious nature of man, through the devil, is to oppose the gospel.

Now, the deceptions that have taken a super subtle form is the misunderstanding of "self." This deception is manifested when you believe who you are by the introduction of many false gods. Such gods are intellectual gods, emotional gods, financial gods, wood and stone gods, and pie in the sky gods. By accepting these gods, you automatically, without knowing, distort the truth of the true and living God that is resident in you. Because these gods take you away from the most accurate knowledge of self, you now think that acquiring these gods will satisfy you and show who you are because of your sinful nature. However, not coming into the true knowledge of self will leave you empty always, and you will never know the true God. Because, without the knowledge of the true God's spirit in you, and the knowledge of your spirit in you, which is the total constitution of the true spiritual self, you will not be able to know self or worship in spirit and truth, because you can't worship what you do not know.

Consequently, most worship a god that does not exist in reality, because of the absence of true knowledge of self. (Deut.28:14, 5:32, 17:19-20.)

We have to remember that the true and living Gods put in us a spiritual image of themselves at creation. If we do not know the image of the true Gods in us, we will never know the true God. (Gen. 1:26.) Hence, we can't worship what we do not know because we are disconnected. That is one of the greatest mysteries ever told, not that Christ only came and died, but he has redeemed us back to the true God's perfect image of 'himself,' or back to his 'self' in us. He has reconnected us back to our truest self presently. Now that we have been redeemed to our truest "self," we must now look again at the image of the true God's self that he had put in us at creation that we now have access to once more and learn of him.

Therefore, the messiah could have boldly testified to this; "if you see me, you see the father." What was the reason for him saying that? Well, he recognized that the self in him was of the Most, High God, and he acknowledged his nothingness. He stated, "why do you call me good; the only one good is the father in heaven." (Luke 18: 19.) This text also shows that what he referred to in himself as doing the work, was the spirit of the Father. As the Father was in heaven, but the spirit of the Father was in the man: Christ, while he was on earth. (Luke 4:18. John 5:30-32. Matt. 3:17, 17:5.) The absence of this knowledge is a self-destructive plague that has retarded our living to just a mere existence, in a doomed world on this earth, caused by religion. However, you shall know the truth, and the truth shall set you free, from religion too.

These false teaching of self are the main reasons why the churches and the religious world are so confused about the true and living God. This confusion is known as Babylon. They have created these external false gods of wood, stones, emotions, and intellect. While the image of the true God is within us and hidden in plain sight, which is Christ in me the hope of glory. (Coloss.1: 11-17, 19-21, 26-27.)

Therefore, until we have become aware and understand "self," then and only then will we start to have the right knowledge of the true God. This understanding is totally contradictory to the conventional ways we, as a society, have been taught to think. The true God is not a physical structure or an emotional high-velocity Roll-a-Coaster ride that we would know the true God through these means but is revealed to us by his indwelling spirit in us.

Consequently, for us to know the true and living God, we have to go inside the mind of the redeemed soul of man, where the true and living God resides by his spirit. When this acknowledgment of the true self is done, we will meet the spirit of the true and living God there, and the spirit will explain and guide us into all truth that he has for us, of ourselves, and of the Most, High God. (1 Cor.2: 9-12. Romans 8:14.)

The bible tells us that we are the temple of the Most, High God. The symbolic temple that Moses built in ancient times, the true and living God dwelt in it, by his spirit. Exodus 25:8-9. This act shows how gracious the true and living God was in the dwelling with his people in a temple of wood and stone then, even after sin, his glory was in that temple. (2 Chron. 5:14.) However, after the Most, High God had redeemed and reinstated us back to himself through the life of his son. He now dwells no more in a temple made by human hands, but he is more gracious now to dwell in us. We are now the true temple of the Most, High God once again, where his presence dwells, yes in us. (1 Cor. 3:16, Romans 8:9.) Therefore, we are reflectors of the true self of the Most, High God. All servants of the Most, High God can now say: "If you see or know me, you see and know the Father." (John 14:7.) Can you say that, as a fact?

Chapter 40

Polonius: "This above all; **to thine own self be true**, and it must follow, as the night the day, thou canst not then be false to any man."

THE TRUE SELF OR MONEY

This knowledge can't be explained to you by your fake pastors. Because they are an institutionally brainwashed group of workers, and as such, have to represent their institution's theologies, interest, and by-laws to be paid. Therefore, they are compelled not to think on their own, so they know not their true "selves." Consequently, the spirit of the Most; High is rejected by them for human credentials. Those ministers who are made professionals by their institutions, have to comply with the dictates of their respective organizations, as these organizations are the ones that qualified them and gave them their credentials and employment. They are not sent by the Most, High God, but by those institutions that are greedy for your money, which is one of their first gods. Therefore, they do not have the spirit of the true and live-in God in them to lead them and yourselves, as they do not know "themselves."

That indeed is a sticky situation to find oneself in as ministers, when they are to represent the truth to the lost people. In such a case, they as pastors, instead, present what they are told to by their institutions so that they can keep their jobs, rather than the truth. However, in doing so, they have sold their souls to the devil and have put the souls of many others in a precarious position.

These are the ones who consider their Pastoral duties as career activities within their respective institutions, as more important than the souls of men. Money, position, possession, and association are the gods that have clouded their minds. These are the ministers who are paid to lie to the people, so they can keep a position and keep that worldly currency flowing. They have denied the truth and the power of the true and living God for their false gods of money, status, possessions, and association. They instead serve mammon than the Most, High God. This condition is also applicable to the independent preachers who lie to the people for their monies. (2 Kings 5:22-27. Exodus 23:8. Deut. 16:19.) However, there are still genuine spiritual men of the true and living God in our world today. All have not bowed their knees to Baal or his images these days, but they are few and far between, comparatively speaking.

These are some of the ways to identify real ministers of the gospel. Genuine preachers do not trade the word of the true and living God for money, or any of the above commodities mentioned. They will not receive all gifts, nor will they accept payments for preaching the truth. (2 Kings 5:15-16. Gen. 14:22-23.)

All televangelist or preachers who tell the people to send them money for their preaching are fake, and they do not know the true and living God themselves. They are all professional liars and thieves. No one should present the word of the true and living God for money. The messiah did not, nor did any of his disciples. Neither should we. However, a gift is ok to be accepted without any attachments, obligations, or favors. Not for the truth you present, but because of the willingness and affordability of the people to whom you minister, without pressure from anyone. Yes, only from those that can afford this, or has a conviction to give a sacrificial gift. (Acts 4: 32-37, Mark 12:44.) Also, if there are plans to help others that are in need, those who are ministers of the gospel can partner with others to bring relief to the needy. However, proper accountability should be, as God loves a cheerful giver, but he will hold us accountable, and we should hold each other accountable also for proper accounting.

Now let us not get carried away by evoking the widow with the mite as a faithful tithe payer, as lying preachers have been teaching. Firstly, this was not a tithe, as she was unable to give a tithe, which is a percent of one's increase. (Deut. 14:22.) But she had no gain from which to give. The book says she gave all she had: a sacrificial given. Her story only caught the messiah's attention because it reflected his own life and what he came to do. (John 10:10. Mark 10:45. 1 John 2:2.) That was to give his all, also.

You see, like the widow, he gave all he had, without reservation. He, like her, was not looking for anything in return. He, like her, knew that the Most; High would prepare his way out as he usually does, out of no way. He, like her, cared not for his own life over his mission. Therefore, it was not about the money that she gave, that got him excited, no, it was about the giving of her heart, her mind, her entire being. This act for her demonstrated her conviction, regardless of her situation. She didn't do this, so God could bless her, save her neither for her to go to heaven; these are a few of the lies that are told in these deceiving churches today by these lying ministers. Nor did she do it to be seen, as she did it from a heart of love. That's what made the difference. Are we serving from a spirit of love, or are we working and giving for kickbacks, a financial return, or some other earthly favors? What is the real reason you call yourselves Christians and give? Is it because of the temporal benefits you think you might receive, for yourself or your children?

We must also remember that he had contrasted her with those who had lots to give, but never gave their hearts, but only gave to be seen and to get the usual kickbacks, thinking of themselves as being in favor with God. By making that comparison, he, in effect, is comparing himself as the example through the widow to follow, and not the others. Therefore, those preachers of the true gospel will be taken care of, only if they have enough "action faith," to believe in what they are teaching. That the real, living, and loving God always takes care of his own 'self.' In other words, they will live the gospel. Therefore, if they have the spirit of the Most, High God in them, they will not worry about their livelihood, because the True Eternal Father always takes care of his own "self" in you. So, you will not lie to obtain a living or to take care of your family. If you do, you have demonstrated that you have a lying spirit, and you are not of God but the devil.

Now understand, if there is a method of presenting the good news that requires financing, then there is no reason not to obtain funds or make an arrangement, not by lying though, to get the message to the desired recipients. That in itself is not selling the gospel. However, to charge money for your preaching is selling the word, which is not of God, whether you are independent or a part of an organization claiming to represent God.

Therefore, those who sell the gospel for money or favor, and think of preaching as a career do not experience the indwelling spirit of the true eternal God. There is nowhere in the scriptures that show any of the true prophets of God or disciples of Christ, trading the truth for money, favor, or position (credentials). Acts 22:5 shows that those who act on the credentials of the church in opposition to the truth of God represent the works of the devil. Not unlike what we see happening in the churches today.

Also, the text message that speaks to those being supported by the gospel, if you preach the gospel. (1Cor.9: 13-14.) Means to exercise "live-in faith" in the gospel that you preach, not to be compensated by a system because you teach what they tell you to, even when it is a lie, and you know it.

If we should look at the following verses 14 and 15 of 1 Cor. 9, Paul, however, understood that those who took this-worldly pasture became corrupted, and are used to hinder the gospel. He was one such person before conversion. Knowing this, Paul resolved in his heart after conversion to preach the gospel without the glory of man, meaning status and financial gain, verse 15-16. He now speaks to preaching the gospel willingly in love, by him coming into a knowledge of "self," he then knew God would reward him. But not against his will, meaning if, by a bribe, he will "be cut" off, verse 17. He now makes it very clear in verse 18, by stating that he will not charge for preaching the gospel of Christ, what would his reward then be? If he did, he would be abusing his power. (*Remember Paul knew exactly how the system worked. He was not only a scholar but the right hand of the general council: the Sanhedrin. (Gal.1:13-14.) Therefore, he knew what he was talking about; circumcised the eight-day, of the stock of Israel, of the tribe of Benjamin, An, Hebrew of the Hebrews; as touching the law, a Pharisee; concerning zeal, persecuting the church; touching the righteousness which is in the law, blameless. Phil. 3: 5-6.)*

In other words, you should not be taking from the poor, but you should be giving to the poor. Then look to the master for your blessing. If the poor have enough and are willing to share with you, that is fine. However, the principle is that the poor's gift should, if taken by a minister of God, be multiplied so all can be blessed. (2 Kings 4, John 6:1-14.) However, to lie to the poor and ignorant by telling them they have to pay a tithe and or offering, to receive a blessing or make it to heaven, is just pure demonic. Many liars are and have infested the churches as preachers, because there is easy money to be made, as these lazy pastors (LAPS) hate real work. They know that the people, in general, are ignorant, eager, and desperate to have the truth, and will give just about anything for peace of mind, to believe that they are saved. So, they use this weakened state of mind of the poor and ignorant to manipulate and steal from them, while selling them what they call the gospel. Pathetic! (Proverbs 30: 7-9.)

 Someone might ask, so what about the pastors who went to college and spent all that money to obtain a career in becoming a minister? How do they make back that money and survive?   Well, the same answer as given above applies. It is not about you; you are a means to an end. Many do not like to hear that. However, it is the truth; you are just a vessel that God is using for his glory. That should be sufficient for your efforts. With all the money and efforts you put into obtaining a career in the ministry, you would have considered it a joy to be used by the Most, High God. If you knew God and had the right intent, you would not have a problem with your present condition, if that is your calling. Therefore, if the spirit of the true eternal God is in you, you will not have any needs that are not met, be patient, and believe. Remember the true and living God takes care of his own self, which you are a part of. Most Christian pastors do not know or understand this, hence the problem of scheming and lying to survive. They think they are separate from God and have to make individual efforts to come to him and to take care of themselves. As many have promised their wives or themselves a 'good' life, however, because of their position, they can't afford it but are determined to accomplish this by any means necessary. That is a wrong way of thinking, which has so distorted our relationship with the Father. Why tell the poor to have "faith" in God when you don't? Why preach to the people that God will take care of them when you really do not believe that for a second? So, you align yourself with an organized religious institution to cover your un-beliefs. You know that what you are telling the people are lies and deceptions, or things you do not believe yourself. However, because the organized religious system employs you, you think this gives you cover from the scrutiny of the ignorant people. You think you are just doing your work, and you do not make the rules, so you do what you are told. However, you forgot one thing, you can't hide from the Most, High God, who you claim to serve. (Jeremiah 17:10.) You have to decide. Remember, God looks at each heart individually. Is it God or Mammon? When you choose the ways of the highest God, the spirit of truth will come in and strengthen you to get out of these Babylonian ways of thinking and living.

The truth is the Most, High God, has put his image in us, for us to acknowledge that we are his craft that contains his spirit, his breath, and his life. We are all his; our true self is his. We are nothing on our own. All we need to do is acknowledge these facts like David, and yield ourselves to him. And he will always take care of his own in us. Then we will be able not just to teach righteousness, but live righteous lives to the glory of the Most, High God.

Unfortunately, these ministers are taught otherwise, to depend on their career growth by obtaining as many degrees as possible, to be qualified for bigger paychecks, to cover their unnecessary expenses. The result is no dependence on God or true knowledge of God, but on their money, associations, and positions, given to them by their institutions. Therefore, for them to obtain and keep these fleeting gifts or gods, it now becomes necessary for them to lie to themselves and the ignorant.

Many of these pastors knew of the true and living God before, because the spirit of the Highest convicted them. However, it was easier for them to accept the partial glitter and benefits the world and its churches offered them. (Matt. 4: 8-9. 2Kings 5:20-27.) If you are not living under a rock, you will know that most of our religious leaders today are just in their religious operation for the money, positions, and associations. The messiah had addressed this condition in Matt. 4:

10-11. Most religious institutions also have financial issues because of greed, resulting from stealing within these same religious organizations. They often boast about the money they have made from the ignorant people, then turn around and steal the same. (Rev. 3:17.) They have made the house of prayer to become a den of thieves. (Luke 19: 46.) This is the self that must die, this self that is portrayed in the attitude of these religious leaders today, as we saw in the manner of those in bible times. That is the false carnal self that must die; the pride of life, the lust of the eyes, etc. (1 John 2:15-17.) This is the self that false teachers love. However, this was not the self the messiah was referring to, for us to love like unto our neighbor. The person he spoke of was the self that was from the Father, the true self of man. The spiritual self that esteem others above, the carnal self, who is his brother's keeper. The self that the true and living God shines through. That is the self we are counseled to love, but only the spiritual can do so. In Phil. 4:8-9, we are urged to meditate on the truth, honesty, justice, purity, loveliness, goodness, virtuousness, and praiseworthiness. Yes, we should think of these things and love this "self." That the speaker said is seen 'in' him. I pray that this same 'self' of the Most, High be seen in us all, Amen.

Chapter 41

A story of "self" in time

The story of Nebuchadnezzar, in Daniel 4, gives another perspective of the difference between the selfish nature of man and the "self" of the true God in man.

Nebuchadnezzar was probably one of the greatest kings ever lived, who God favored. He was claimed to be the one who builds great Babylon with its beautiful hanging gardens, so beautiful that they are still considered in memory to be one of the many wonders of the ancient world. He was described as the king of all people, nations, and languages in all the earth. That is huge!

In the third chapter of Daniel, we see Nebuchadnezzar acknowledging the true God of Shadrach, Meshach, and Abednego, because their God was also able to save them from the fiery furnace of the king. As much as he had seen the work of their true God, he still did not accept him as his own.

However, not too long before, the King needed help. Daniel 2, which is a setup for chapter 3. Having had a significant dream and was now troubled by not remembering the dream. But he needed to remember the dream to know the meaning of it. You see, he knew that dreams were a way for the gods to reveal mysteries and the future. He had solicited his wise men to reveal the dream and the interpretation to him before; however, they couldn't. This made him very angry, so he decided to kill them all. If they could not give him the true dream and its interpretation, why have them around, he must have reasoned.

 Now Danial was also considered as one of the wise men of Babylon, who would undoubtedly be among the wise men to be killed along with his fellows. Daniel heard the king's decree from Arioch, the captain and responded with counsel and wisdom, so he could come to the king, and be used by God. Daniel was able to receive from the Most; High God and was then able to reveal both the dream and its interpretation to the king. Therefore, Daniel was now respected by the king. Interestingly, the King acknowledged the God of Daniel as the God of gods, verse 47. Again though, he did not take him as his own God while accepting the words of revelation coming from Daniel's God.

Once again, the Most, High God showed favor to the King in a dream, chapter 4. This time, however, he remembered the dream and related it to Daniel. In the vision of his dream, he spoke of a great tree. That was so great, "its heights reached the heavens and could be seen from the ends of the earth. The leaves were beautiful, and its fruits plenty. It shaded all the beast of the field and was a resting place for the fowls of the air, and all flesh was fed by it. But a holy one came from heaven and cried aloud saying, hew down the tree, and cut off his branches, shake off his leaves, and scatter his fruit: let the beast go away from under it and the fowls from his branches. Nevertheless leave the stump of his roots in the earth, even with a band of iron and brass of the field; and let it be wet with the dew of heaven, and let his portion be with the beast in the grass of the earth: let his heart be changed from a man's, and let a beast's heart be given unto him, and let seven times pass over him. This matter is by the decree of the watchers, and the demand by the word of the holy ones: to the intent that the living may know that the Most, high rules in the kingdom of men, and giveth it to whomsoever he will and set up over it the basest of men."

Then Daniel was astonished for an hour, after which he gave the interpretation.

The interpretation also tells that the king would be taken from his position and kingdom and be placed with the beast of the wild, living as such. Until he knows that the Most, High rules in the kingdom of man, and giveth it to whomsoever he will. You see, he, Nebuchadnezzar, had acknowledged the true God of the Hebrews and his might, his wonders, his kingdom, and dominion, but did not accept their God as the ruler of his world. He thought that he was a god and all other gods should conform to his wishes, or show him many favors. Yet, again, he was told by Daniel that his kingdom would not pass from him if he 'knows' that the true God of heaven rules. The word "know" here indicates not just acknowledgment, but also acceptance and having a close relationship with the true and living God, accepting him as the one and only true God of the universe.

Daniel also asked the king to accept his council and brake off his sins, of unrighteousness and iniquities, by showing mercy to the poor. Now for the king to do such things, as was suggested by Daniel. He would be acknowledging that he was also a sinner and need to ask for forgiveness. This subjugation would show that the king would be a subject of the KING OF KINGS, the true God of heaven and earth. This Nebuchadnezzar could not bring "himself" to do as his false pride of self; selfishness, could not allow. This was a manifestation of his rebellious spirit, along with a measure of arrogance. The same kind that David spoke off in Psalms 51.

Now twelve months after the interpretation was given, he the king of Babylon walked into his palace and proclaimed "Is not this great Babylon that 'I' have built for the house of the kingdom by the might of 'my' power, and for the honor of 'my' majesty!"

This "I" or "my" attitude also tells of the false identity of the king.

He was defying the knowledge of the true and living God with his "I" and "my" attitude, which is a false identity of the true self of man. The true self of man will never identify the form or the rebellious mind of man as self. At that instance, the fulfillment of the dream came to pass. He lost his mind, totally mentally incapacitated. He became, in quick succession, as like unto a wild beast living in the wilds, eating grass, hair growing like eagle's feathers, and having nails like birds' claws.

This desperate condition of man can only occur when the spirit of God leaves, and the spirit of man becomes rebellious in the person, but the breath is still in that person. The spirit of the evil one now can take over the function of the body and the mind. This demon possession is the reason Nebuchadnezzar was described as a mad man. We must remember that the spirit of man is essentially the essence of his cognitive self, meaning his consciousness and all that it contains in it, which comes from God. (1 Cor. 2:11.) While in this condition of madness, only the Most, High God can overrule such a state of possession, because he is the only one that can allow it in the first place to happen; even though the king made all the wrong choices that led to this. The power that is displayed here by God is Similar in the Job situation but different in the reason why he allowed the devil to afflict Job. (1. 2:1-7.) The difference between Job and Nebuchadnezzar is the devil was not permitted to possess Job, only to torment him physically of all he possessed, including his body, even his wife, because Job's spirit was in harmony with the spirit of God; nothing or no one can come between that. However, he was permitted to claim Nebuchadnezzar for seven years because he had allied with him before, and the devil had the right to claim him because of his prior choices.

At the end of his time in solitary mental confinement, the time allotted for the devil to do his work. The text message says that he lifted his eyes unto heaven, and his understanding came back to him. Meaning the rebellious spirit was changed, and the right spirit or consciousness of the man came back to him. The first thing he did was to praise and honor the Most, High God of heaven whose dominion is an everlasting dominion and whose kingdom is forever. He also accepted that the inhabitants of the earth, which included himself, are nothing before God. (Daniel 4:34.) This word "understanding" is used to indicate his true awareness of who he was and who God is. Now that he understood the difference, he was able to "see" clearly his true self, and the spirit of God was now able to reside in him also.

Then the king's reason returned unto him, and all his position in his kingdom, note how his views were different from his previous attitude of selfish arrogance and pride, which were symptoms of his fallen nature he had as a carnal man. Then he said, "now I Nebuchadnezzar praise and extol and honor the King of heaven, all whose works are the truth, and his ways judgment: and those that walked pridefully he is able to abase." (Daniel 4: 37.) How could he now say these things, unless both spirits of God and man were now in harmony, in this body of flesh?

This "I" here, tells of the true identity of the king. His acknowledgment of the true and Most High God, reveals that the spirit of the True and Most High God was now in harmony with his spirit. He then knew 'himself'; as part of God in him and understood his relation to the true and living God. The true self of man always acknowledges that the True Most High God is ruler and sustainer of all, including himself.

Now we see that the 'selfish' man does not know 'self' because 'self' and 'selfishness' are opposing entities; they are anonymous. Therefore, selfishness has no place with the true and living God because it does not know the true and living God. Whereas selfishness is a rebellious spirit, and all rebellious spirits are of the devil. However, the self is the spirit of the True Most High God being in you, and being in harmony with your spirit.

Therefore, the man who knows 'self' which comes from the true and living God, will acknowledge the true God, because the spirit of the true and living God is in him, and he knows that he is not his own, but has the self of the true and living God in him. Praise be to the true most high God!!

We also have to remember that man who is just a form. Just like the grass, or the lily of the field, are here today and gone tomorrow. But for the true Most High, a day is like a thousand years. (Psalms 90:4, 2 Peter 3:8.) Nebuchadnezzar here was used to show the frailty of man. We are only a form of something of the earth. The self in us comes from the one Most High God, which occurred when God blew his breath of life into this form of clay call man. (Gen. 2:7.) Therefore, we should remind ourselves that the carnality that we are is what we walk on every day when we go outside our houses: dirt. Without the breath of life in us, we fall back to our cocoon and become one with the earth on which we stand. Therefore again, man is nothing. He does not even have a self, if not for the self of the spirit of God, in him and the spirit of man that is given by the one Most High God, to him.

The carnal self or rebellious nature is owned by the devil if left unchecked. The eternal Most High God owns the spiritual self. Man is just a container that has one or the other of these spiritual 'selves' in it. To prove this unequivocally, you can take a trip to the morgue or a funeral gathering. When you get there, try asking this man in the morgue or at the funeral; that is lying in a box or casket, to boast about just one second in all the days he had lived throughout his life. Ask him how he is doing. If you should be still, and carefully listen to his response, you will hear his loud reply in the stilled absence of his voice. It is a loud shout of silence you can't ignore. This condition is the greatness of man without God: nothing.

Once we understand this, we must now appreciate that every good and perfect thing comes from the Omniscient Most High God. (James 1:17.) So, whatever things we enjoy in this life, including life 'itself,' was given to us by the one Most High God. Not only was it given to us, but we were also given a body to enjoy these gifts through. We were given a mind to appreciate and understand the source and limitations of our existence and functions, respectively. Praise be to the omnipotent Most High God, for our true selves.

Chapter 42

"The time is coming"

He, the messiah, also spoke of the future to the woman; "the time is coming," indicating that there are others who will do the same at another time in the future. The questions are, when did this happen? And how will this happen? How will we know who the true worshipers are?

First, let's look at the "when."

In the book of John, we see the messiah speaking to his disciples in chapters 15:23-27, 16:7-17, telling them about the Father and his spirit, which will be a gift to them. Also, in the book of Acts chapter 1, the account is given bearing witness to the promise of the Spirit of the Most, High God. In Acts chapter 2, we see the outpouring of the Spirit of the true and living God. The fact that these men being filled and anointed with the spirit showed by the way they lived after; they had entire transformed lives. Meaning their minds were changed, from the carnal to the spiritual nature of the one Most High God. So much so that even the way they talked then, was noted by the people around them and the officials. They were able to articulate the truth the same way the messiah had done, with power and with sound minds. (Acts 4:1-4, 13.) It was not the physical looks that spoke of the transformation; it was the power from within, through the indwelling power of the Spirit of the Most; High God. They were also able to perform miracles. These works were not looked on as their own by them, but they gave all the praises and acknowledgment and glory to the only true and living God of all, as the messiah did: "Our Father who art in heaven, holy be thy name, thy kingdom come thy will be done on earth as it is in heaven…." Therefore, these men were true worshipers, who worshiped the Highest God in spirit and truth, because the spirit of the Highest God now dwelt in them. So, there is a pattern here; to be a true worshiper of the true and living God, one has to have the spirit of the Most, High God dwelling within 24/7. If you don't have the spirit of the Highest God in you, you are none of his. There is always a spirit in the heart/mind of man, of good or of ill.

If one is not there, the other is. There is no neutral ground in the heart. You are either for one or the other. The scripture states that "by their fruits, you shall know them." (John 7:15, 16). The reason why we have what we call mixed or conflicting thoughts is that we are having a battle of wills.

A battle between good and evil within our consciousness. The will of the Most, High vs. the will of our fallen nature. This battle is ongoing, though we have the victory already. As long as sin exists, we will have this battle. Only after a total change from mortal to immortality. A new heaven and a new earth where sin no more dwell. Then and only then will this battle ends. (Romans 8:16-23.) One of the most interesting facts is that though the struggle is ongoing, we have been given the victory already. This victory is accepting the precious gift of the Most, High God, and living without sinning, because of the change of our nature in our minds; from carnal to the spiritual nature of God. (Romans 8:23.) It states clearly in verse 23, that our redeemed spirits groan within our bodies, waiting for the redemption or change of our bodies. We are proving again that we have been transformed spiritually only by the renewing of our minds, Romans 12:2. However, we still exist in an unchanged sinful body. This truth must be understood; that while the renewing of our minds transforms us, our bodies remain the same. (Romans 12:2.) Meaning we now have the mind of Christ, 1Cor.2:16, and are sealed for his glory, Rev. 22:12. However, we are still living in a sinful body that will not change until he comes back. (1 Cor.15:51-54.) At that time, a total change will come, however only those with a transformed mind, as that of Christ, will receive a transformed body. From a mortal corrupted body to an immortal, incorruptible body like that of Christ. Even so, come, my lord and savior. (Rev.22:20)

Chapter 43

The outpouring of the spirit

There are many today who have been praying for the outpouring of the spirit of the true and living God. However, they are not preparing themselves, and they don't know-how. They think that by just praying, and still being selfish, they will receive the spirit of the true God. Many assume that if only they pray while backbiting, gossiping, being covetous, lying, stealing, etc., they will still receive the spirit of the true God because they are in an association of so-called believers. However, there is one big problem they are not aware of, and that is, they are already possessed by a spirit that is anti-Christ, which is the spirit of a false god, and their worship experience is one of just formality; being religious. They see nothing wrong with their behavior once their religious leaders and associates support them. Therefore, the spirit of the true and living God doesn't and will not reside in such temples. Whatever sinful condition of yourself, you are aware of, needs to be addressed first. That condition is what prevents us from having that new experience. We have to decide to allow the spirit of God to take over entirely. It's an individual choice, not a group effort. Confessing openly to the church doesn't make a difference. Even the devil believes and trembles. (James 2:19.) What makes the difference is having a transformed mind where the spirit of the Most, High God dwells. Everything righteous will then follow.

Yes, when we were born, we were born with this fallen nature, which is the same sinful nature. (Romans 5:10, Col.1:21-22.) The sinful nature is always at enmity with the true and living God. However, after coming to an age of knowledge and accountability, we will realize we have made choices to please the fallen nature of the flesh. We now have to make counter decisions to turn from that old way of living. Yes, we have to remember, like David, we not only have a choice to make the right decision, but also to acknowledge that we have sinned and to repent of those sins sincerely. Then strive not to do them anymore. If we have to stop talking to some people with bad influence, so be it. We can still pray for them from a distance. If we have to stop hanging out at certain places, so be it. If we have to stop watching, listening, or reading certain materials, so be it. If we have to stop eating certain foods, you never know. Leave certain jobs. Leave a particular church; yes, you read right. You have to carefully look at where you are and what you are doing, and be honest with your questions: Am I better off being here? Have I grown spiritually? Have I learned more about self and the true and living God? Do these environments, activities, and or people help me towards the things of God? If any of these answers are no, then one has to decide to change, shun or relocate from these things, places, and people. (1 Thess. 5: 22-23.) Whatever it takes, we will have to do. Yes, like the woman of Samaria, leave your water pot whatever your water pot is. Whatever you thought your security and sustenance were, you have to rethink. Then the spirit of the Most, High God will be poured out into your life in a fuller measure. And please do not look for a crowd of people, as was in the days of Pentecost, to be with you. You might be the only one in your family, church, or even neighborhood to choose or be chosen. Remember, many are called, but few are (have) chosen. After this, you will know.

Now the real fight will be manifested. Remember, the devil will not give up easily on you. He has many years of investments, and he wants to see a return on his investment. Now he takes off his gloves. Yes, he will fight dirty and nasty. Whatever it takes. Your friends, family, Church, loved ones, bosses will turn on you; whoever is around you, who do not have, or is not seeking the spirit of the true and living God. Those will be used by the devil to come up against you. Now your life is significantly changed. You are no more just existing, but now living. There is now a renewed life from the spirit of the true and living God in you. There is an acknowledgment of a new, consistent, eternal, anointed, and appointed purpose for your life, that will be realized now. The devil is now scared and upset because his kingdom has suffered a BIG blow. You are currently in favor of the Most, High God, with this great experience and power.

When this effort is manifested and multiplied throughout the communities, states, and countries, the world will see the reflection of the image of Christ through us. Then they will see the glory of the Father manifested with such power and clarity. The world will then know the true worshipers. It all starts with a prayerful life, my friends, for the outpouring of the spirit.

Chapter 44

Will worship"

The next expression to follow is "will worship" why will these people worship?

We go back to the purpose of the existence of man. (Eccle.12:13.) The whole duty or the purpose of the life of man is the worship of the only true and living God and the keeping of his commandments. As we had mentioned before, the connection of Adam to the Father was through the spirit of the Most, High God in him, and as such, their relationship was intimate. **The true God only has intimate relationships**. Now, for that to happen with us whom the true God communes, we must first have the spirit of the true God in us; to worship also as the messiah demonstrated. This worship is a spiritual exercise that is only experienced when the Spirit of the true and living God is in harmony with the spirit of the man. The real worship experience is the result of an occurrence of intimate fellowship. Likewise, the disciples individually had to have had the spirit of the true and living God first, to be able to have this close relationship, for the Father seeks such.

Because the spirit of the true and living God knows everything about the Most; High God, even the secret things of the Most; High God. (1 Cor. 2:11.) The spirit knows that God requires true worshipers. However, the spirit does not force us. Besides, the spirit of the true God dwells only in a clear mind that accepts his leading. You see, the spirit while living in us still respects our freedom of choice. We have to choose for the spirit to lead us daily, to do the things of the Highest God. Remember, the true God had made the man with the freedom of choice. If not, Adam could not have sinned, being a perfect man. The spirit is, therefore, there to guide us into all truth; however, we have to choose to accept his guidance and make the right choices. (John 16:13.)

The true God does not force us to do anything, even though his spirit is within us. The nature of the true God is never to force his servants; **we move to his commands from a heart of love**. (John 14:15.) However, while the spirit is within us, in our consciousness, our body will want to please the flesh or the carnal nature, ask Paul.

In Romans 7. Paul clearly describes the battle that rages within the man. When one becomes a renewed son or daughter of the Most, High God, a spiritual fight will and must occur. Remember, everyone who is born of a woman is born into sin, has a sinful nature, and is claimed by the devil. However, the freedom of the "choice act" that was granted to everyone by the only real government of God remains intact. Upon becoming aware of one's condition, you have to decide to serve the true and living God or the devil. That is where the freedom of choice comes in as a weapon for, or against you. You have to decide to serve or not to serve one or the other, as Adam did. Therefore, this war is to establish who you will serve off these two forces. The force of good and the force of evil are now fighting for control of your mind. However, you are in the driver seat and have the right to decide to go left or right. (Matt. 7: 13-15, even though the body is captured by sin already. (Psalms 51:5. Romans 3:23.) Which is described as the carnal nature of man, and is subject to death and will die or be translated; change at the appointed time. In your mind, however, where the fight takes place first and foremost, one has to choose. If we become aware of this truth that our mental ability to choose will determine our outcome. We will realize that the power that is within our minds is there to initiate a change, by making the right choices. However, we will have to make this critical decision to show who is victor, by either result, every day.

Two of the differences in recognizing these opposing forces are; The power of evil is always aggressive and loud, while the strength of good is always gentle and still; when we are talking about the mind. The individual man is made with the ability to make choices, and should be able to distinguish the differences between the two; if his spirit is in harmony with the true and living God's. Even though the individual man is a sinner, he still retains the right to choose. The man, only the man, has this power to decide for himself. The true and living God had given him that morally legal intellectual right to make the final decision. No other being, agency or person in heaven or on earth, has the legal right to take that from the individual man. We make that decision to obey the true eternal God when we ask the spirit of the High eternal God to come in and overrule. We make that decision to follow the devil, when we reject the spirit of the one true God and continue to live in the way, to please the fallen nature. (James 1:13-14.)

This also will take some effort on the part of the spiritual man. Remember, man has a spirit too, as an extension, or part of the spirit of man, which is that reasoning that goes on in our minds that we call consciousness. The consciousness is where everything about the individual is stored. It is not the same as the subconscious; the psychologists talk about; however, the spirit of man the scriptures introduce is the conscious man, this is this man that is spoken of in 1 Samuel 16:7. The heart of man is the consciousness of his conscience, not the heart in the chest, but the one in the brain, the mind. The eternal Father does not judge by the appearance, but the conscience or spirit of man. While man looks on the appearance and makes his judgments, God knows that physical appearance has no substance. (Psalms 8:4-8.) However, his spirit that is in man, making man conscious of who he is, who he is not, and whose he is: is where the substance lies. This arrangement is why the Father judges the heart of man.

The psychologist not having this understanding is baffled whenever a diagnosed schizophrenia or mad person suddenly comes to his senses, as in the case of Nebuchadnezzar. The scientific and medical world is puzzled with situations like this one. They can't explain what has happened, as it is not an ordinary scientific or medical occurrence, but a divine one. Therefore, only those with the holy spirit of the Highest understand these spiritual phenomena.

This same power of the spirit is shown when we are at church, and we are busily involved in 'worship,' and the thought comes to us, reminding us that we need to make it right with someone or to refrain from that which is evil. Talking to those of us from the top, presidents in the offices, pastors in the pulpits, members in the congregations to the janitors cleaning the toilets. The response to that counsel will tell the spirit of the true God to come in or stay out. This is the messiah knocking from the outside, by his spirit, for you to let him in. Rev. 3:20. If, after the spirit comes in, the individual rebels like Adam, that would be rejecting the spirits' leading. Therefore, there will be no true worship in the activities we call worship if we reject the spirit of God. Our so call worship will only be an emotional exercise; to feel good about our fallen selfish nature, and for others to see our appearances. Just a social gathering of singing, talking, and eating. In other words, an indoor or formal outdoor cult or religious picnic!

However, we need to know that this is where true worship happens, in the spirit, within man. Not in the beautiful cathedrals, temples, synagogues, or churches. No! Not in the speaking of tongues: known or unknown. True worship is in spirit and truth, that is within the man, not outside the man. The assembling of the brethren was just that, an assembling of the brethren. Without the Spirit of the true God, there in the midst of them and them, that is in them individually, there will not be any true worship happening. When there is 'true worship' going on, the Spirit of the true God of the universe is always there in the hearts; if not, there is only worship of the devil or what is called "spiritual formality," which is called religion in all its forms.

It does not matter how much we say the word god and pray beautiful long prayers and give many gifts of tithes and offerings, with inspiring sermons and songs. It is still the worship of the devil when the spirit of God is not there in the hearts.

Each person, who is a true worshiper, should have had the spirit of the Most; High God, already within, before going to church to fellowship. When the scripture talks about the spirit being in their midst. (Matt.18:20.) It was not talking about around them, or over them only, but in them. Do not misunderstand the spiritual picture of the spirit descending like a dove over the messiah as the only way the spirit operates. This was done to reveal to John who the messiah truly was, and to indicate an anointment on him by the Father. However, the spirit of the Most; High dwelt inside the messiah all the time and shall dwell in us also, if not already in use, when we allow his spirit to come in and sup with us. (Luke 3:22, Matt. 3:16, John 14:6, 17)

We should not be going to church to worship on the Sabbath, or whatever day we think the Sabbath is because we did not worship during the week. That attitude shows that the spirit of the Most; High is missing in our lives throughout the week. One day "worship" does not cut it. The person who only worships on the Sabbath is not a true worshiper of the true and living God at all. Why? Well, the true worshiper worships the true and living God every day in spirit and truth, wherever he or she is because the spirit of the true God is within at all times. You cannot have the spirit of the true and living God in you and not worship the Most; High God, impossible! This understanding also helps us to be vigilant and keep our shields up. (1 Peter 5:8. Eph. 6: 10-18.) It is a daily living for the real child of the Most; High God. If the spirit of the Most; High is not there, then which spirit is there? If you think you have to go to your church to worship, you have not the spirit of God.

For clarity, let's look again at the story of the Good Samaritan. (Luke 10: 25-37.) On his journey, he came across an injured man who was rob, beaten, and left to die. He helped the man back to life again. However, two others went in the same direction before the Samaritan did. A High priest and a Levite who considered themselves to be worshipers of the true and living God. These men were either on their way to or coming from worship. The high priest position was that of leadership. His responsibility was to represent the people to the true God and the true God to the people. This person was the one that reflected the spirituality of the people, and the Levite was his assistant. In their heads, they were following their traditional teachings, by not defiling themselves with touching a blooded, sick person, or being too close to such a person, similarly to that of touching a Leper. (Lev. 21, 22. Lev. 13, 14.) They thought that avoiding contact with such a person was a part of their ways of worship (religion). They could not stop to help because they were restricted by their traditions of separation from other people by their Levitical laws also, and were not moved by the spirit of the true God that was not in them. They did not know this was an act of true worship, helping others. They would rather be a church on the Sabbath day to lift 'holy hands' to their false god, than allowing the spirit of the true God to use them.

On the other hand, we have this man, a Samaritan going about his daily business, doing what he usually does around this time, coming upon such a scene where help was needed. However, within his usual self, he stopped and administered love to this stranger. He did not have to look into his little red or black book to see if it was ok, with his laws or by-laws to do, he did not have to wait for a board meeting to be held, to work out the details before helping, he did not even have to call for fasting and prayer before. He just did; he worshiped in spirit and truth by his very act.

Yes, that is also true worship, helping one another. And not just those we call brethren. Not for our glory, but the glory of the true and living God. **Anything we do that brings glory to the true God of the universe is true worship**. Therefore, those religious leaders presented themselves as legalistic worshipers. They were very religious, that's all they were, while the Samaritan had the spirit of the true God and was worshiping the true God, in spirit and truth, in the very act of service to his fellow man. Even while he was as an outcast by the 'Jews': the so-called chosen and peculiar people. **Therefore, it is not the outward assembly, but the inward assembly of the spirits within you that will tell whose you are, of which spirit are you? Your action will show**.

It is interesting that in verse 36, of Luke 10, the messiah asked the rich young ruler, which of the three was neighborly unto the man. Remember, the same messiah also said we should love our neighbor as we love ourselves. (Mark 12: 30-31.) Also, the critical question is presented: how can you love God, who you do not see, but hate your brother who you see? (1 John 4:20.)

Now the immediate question to us is, who did the messiah say we should be like of the three? It is evident that true worship is not the assembly of the brethren on the Sabbath or Sunday, but the expression of God's love towards each other every day. Keeping the Sabbath holy by going to church, is only an empty ritual if every day is not kept holy in our lives, by loving those around us during the week. This principle is consistent with keeping or not keeping all the laws by breaking one,

213

which results in breaking them all. Likewise, trying to keep one day holy and living to please the flesh in the others result in not keeping the Sabbath holy at all, whatever day you think the Sabbath is.

Also, we should not think of waiting for others to do the work we can do ourselves. The position of a person should not determine if we should help someone else in need. For example, if a doctor is so busy in his daily work at the hospital or his office, however, is restricted in helping someone on the street who needs help because of the legal arrangement of his contract. I should not judge him. If I am there and can help the person in need, I should help; however, restricted I might be. However, most of us would be very upset at the doctor for not helping, and rightly so, as this is his duty, by profession. Regardless, if he has the spirit of the living God in him, he will do the Godly thing. This also applies to the ministers and their members in the churches. We should not have to wait for a board meeting to occur for us to help. If we have the spirit of God in us, once we see a need for help, we would help without hesitation or judgment.

Imagine if all the Christian folks were working with the Spirit of the true and living God throughout the week. There would be great reports given of the week that was when they gather. There would be no time for covetousness, jealousy, backbiting, lying, greed for other peoples' money, and property, by leaders and other members alike. There would be sharing, caring, esteeming of each other, sincerity in our prayers, caring for the old even though they can't afford to pay tithes. That attitude would be a witness to the world.

Instead, the church, by large, is comfortable being like the world, because the Spirit of the true and living God is not demonstrated there in the lives of the members. So, the opposite righteous living is real. What has been happening in the churches is covetousness, jealousy, backbiting, lying, greed for other people's money, and property, by clergy and members alike. Not only have they found time to engage in such deviant acts, but they have also gone in overtime in doing so. Today we even have armed security within the so-called church of worship, keeping the peace for money, among the so-called brethren.

Now, back in the time of Moses, God commanded Moses to build him a sanctuary, where he would dwell among man. This dwelling with the man was an external experience. The man had to go up to the temple ever so often to offer up sacrifices to the true and living God, to ensure they would not be cut off. Only the high priest was allowed to go into the temple. All others had to stay on the outside in the courtyard. If you were not from these tribes of Israel, you would have to remain in the outer courtyard, not the inner courtyard. How intimate was that? Not intimate at all, but rather inti-mi-dating, to us, just thinking about it now, and not even being there. This old covenant arrangement went on for a very long time too. There were lots of stresses and tensions going on because of this. To think this was the highest point man could ever reach within the old covenant structure was pathetic. Well, only death was an option otherwise.

There was at least one good I must mention though about this arrangement. You see, before the sanctuary existed, there were altars with burnt offerings in the vast open space in various places. With the building of the sanctuary, there was now a specific place where people would gather to worship: a cohesiveness that was, I believe, an improvement. In the sense that the true God seemed to be coming closer to man, and the man coming closer together.

Even so, every high priest had to offer a sacrifice for himself before he could enter this old Sanctuary, not knowing if he would make it out alive or be pulled out with ropes: dead. Even the high priest here had a sense of apprehensive trepidation going into the holy place, let alone the Most Holy. This was what worship was like then. Now we give thanks to the true and living God for his new covenant of grace through his son. He now tabernacles within us. Isn't that great and awesome news?

The promise was made by the true God of mercy to present a new covenant, not like the old one. In Hebrews 8. Verse 2-4, it speaks of a true tabernacle, which the true God pitched and not man.

I particularly like this new covenant because it takes us back to that place of intimacy we had before sin came into the equation. Verse 10 tells us how the new covenant is the putting of the laws of the true eternal God into our minds and the writing of them on our hearts. That is a work only the Spirit of God can do. Only the spirit within can put things into our minds and write them on our hearts. If the spirit of the true God is not in, this will not happen. It's an internal spiritual work. No more an outer sanctuary work, but an inner one, praise the Highest God from whom all blessings flow! We are now the true sanctuary of the true and living God. Just like Adam experienced before the fall. And the messiah did after. In 1 Cor.6:19, 20; 3:16, 17; 2 Cor.6:16-18. We are individual temples of the true and living God. This is the desire of the true and living God towards his people, to dwell in them intimately, through the indwelling presence of his spirit. When this happens, the wickedness and hatred in our hearts will cease, and coming together will be a joy instead of the backbiting, jealousy, covetousness, hatred, and lying we see occurring every time there is a religious "worship" service in the churches. That was not how the messiah worshiped when he was on earth.

Yes, he went to the synagogue and stood up to read and was the custom to do so, even as a child and a young man. However, he did that to expose to them who a true worshiper was. They could not see, because of the blindness by the physical beauty of the temple, and the pomp and religious circumstances of their tradition in those days.

Yes, while gathering with the brethren is good, assembling with the spirit of the true God within each person is what the Father seeks first and foremost. Yes, we should not forsake the assembly of ourselves together; however, each worshiper first has to have a harmonious relationship with the spirit of the Highest God within, with his spirit, then and only then will we see true worship in the churches.

 Most importantly, we noticed that the messiah left the assembly that was not worshiping in Spirit and truth. But he was always in constant communion through prayer and supplication with his father, doing the will of his father and never his own will. This relationship was the result of the presence of the spirit of the Highest God in him. That is what true worship was and still is today. Therefore, we will have to pray, meditate, and fast sincerely, and strive to do the will of the father, the same way he did. We have to purpose in our minds to do the will of the Father while denying the flesh. This 'will' will, indicate to the spirit of the true God that we are genuinely committed to God. Then the spirit of the true God will fill us with more of His presence. These acts of worship will become our first nature, not second. And in many cases for this to happen, we might have to leave the corrupt churches we are members off for many years, just like the messiah did, to be like the messiah and take it to the streets.

Chapter 45

"In spirit and truth."

I know someone might be wondering, does a man really have a spirit that is separate from the spirit of the true God? That is a great question. And the great answer is YES! Really? You ask again, yes! That knowledge might come as a shock to many, but the bible teaches this truth. That is very important to know because the physical can't worship in spirit. Only the spirit or spiritual can worship in spirit. The physical, man, only contains the spirit of man; that's the closes the physical goes to God. Remember, spiritual things can only be discerned and appreciated by the spirit in us. (1 Cor. 2: 14.) The natural man is from the dust, and the spiritual man is from the source we call God, from above.

In 1 Cor. 2:8-14, we see the statement that only the spirit of man knows the things that are deep and intimate of man. Telling us that man indeed has a spirit and that no man knows you more that the spirit that you have within you. Now, what is this spirit, and from where did it come? Well, this spirit, which is in you, which is given to you by the Highest God, comes directly from God. This spirit, which is in you, is the essence of your true self.

 Likewise, the text message continues to say the spirit of the true and living God knows everything of God. Yes, only the spirit knows, even the secret things of the true God. This account tells that God also has a spirit. Now, if spiritual things are spiritually understood, and the true God exists as a spirit. Then, God is not black, white, red, or yellow. God is not any color that you can find anywhere. Remember, God is a spirit and not a physical entity. Then man has to be spiritual, in some way to commune with God and be the image of God. Therefore, Man's spirituality is an essential part of the constitution of man, being the true image of the true God in man. The true God similarly made man for himself as an image or likeness of himself. Consequently, we can only communicate with the true eternal God through the spirits, the spirit of the true God connecting with the spirit of man. Romans 8:16. And only through this means can we truly worship God.

This text message tells us also that the secret things of the true God that he has revealed to us is through the spirit of God in us, from one spirit to the other. Just as having the mind of Christ, who had the spirit of God and man in him, therefore, making us understand the things God has revealed to us through our spiritual being in harmony with the spirit of God, making it possible for God now to communicate with us. That is the reason we know that we have to be transformed by the renewing of our minds, having the mind of Christ. (Phil. 2:5.) The mind is where all the spiritual preparation and communications happen. Then the power of the spirit which is working in us is made manifest in our actions. This in-depth knowledge, the carnal man, will not understand or believe. 1 Cor.2:14. Therefore this unique connection and separation relate to the Highest God, giving the man a spirit of himself as man, as God has a spirit of himself as God. So, the spirit of man is given to man by God, as the spirit of God belongs to God. Remember all good things, cometh of the Highest God. (James 1:17.)

As much as the spirit of man comes from God, they are not the same. If the spirit of man and the spirit of God were the same, God would not need to reveal anything to the man. Man would have known the same time God knows. Then the man would be like God, rather than one with God through the spirit of God. There is a difference. To be like God is to have all the qualities of God. (Isaiah 14:14.) To be one with God is to live according to the will of God, as we see with Christ. (John 17: 20-21.) However, we have to remember that God also puts his spirit, which is the 'spirit of God' into the man. The spirit is what makes a man become one with God (Ezekiel 36:27, John 16:13), which is also him bearing the image of the Highest God. Yes, the spirit of man and the spirit of God are not the same but dwell in the same form of man; one belongs to God, and the other was given to man by God. These acts are the will of God in man. However, God also puts his spirit in man so man can be in harmony with God, while not being like God. These attributes allow us to exercise the power of God, with the knowledge that everything, including us, belongs to God, just as the Messiah did.

To be like God is to have a partnership with God, as was mentioned, is to have equal authority. We have to remember that the true God of eternity has no equal partner, nor can anyone be equal with God in any way. On the other hand, we can be one with God, as in being in harmony with God through his spirit. Meaning we are used by Him, for his purpose. And that is to bring Him glory, by his Spirit dwelling in us, being in harmony with our spirit. (Romans 8:16. John 16:13.)

It's similar to you being hired to work for a company. You are not the owner of the company but the chief executive officer (CEO). Your job is to become one with the company, reflecting the company's ideals, and to facilitate the company's goals. If you perform consistently with the policies within your capacity, you are considered to be one with the company. However, you are not equal with the owners, being in your position, but you are still one with the company. When people know you in your capacity, they see the company you represent. However, you still have to report to the owners, not the other way around. Similarly, as in the relationship with God, we are his servants, and servants obey their masters. Remember, Christ was a servant of God.

Part 8

Here is the power

Everybody wants to be powerful enough to have control over themselves and those around them, at some time or the other. However, the authority granted to us the redeemed is the same power that the Messiah demonstrated while he was here doing the Father's will. We have been given that power again, not to manipulate those around us or exalt the carnal, but to bring glory to the eternal God and King. Only by operating in his will can this power be demonstrated righteously through us. (John 14:12.)

Chapter 46

The two glories

In John 17, we hear the messiah praying to the Father. In his prayer, he asked the Father to glorify him, that he may glorify his Father in return. In verse 2, he talked about the power that the Father gave him over all flesh to give eternal life to as many as was given to him by the Father. Expressing that eternal life is knowing the Father as the true God and his son that he has sent: verse three. Then he revealed that glorifying the Father on the earth was finishing the work the Father gave him to do. Please note that glorifying the Father is: doing his will. Then he asked to be glorified with the Father as he was with the Father before the world was. There is something quite interesting in these first five verses in John 17. These verses speak clearly to the two glories of God. I would like us to note that the messiah also in verse 22, talks about giving the glory that the Father gave to him; while on earth, to his disciples. Very interesting!

Now questions, how was it possible for the messiah to give away glory, while at the same time, he is asking for glory? (John 17: 5,22.) Have you ever thought of that? That is questionable. Therefore, the real questions are; What type of glory did he have? What glory did he give away? And what glory did he ask from his father?

We know by his statement that he had glory with the Father, that only God has, before the world was, John 1:5 exposes that. Is it possible that he could give this glory to his disciples, a glory that only belongs to The Most, High God? Well, let's find out.

You see, there are only two kinds of glories the messiah mentioned. The first glory that he mentioned is in the books of Genesis 1:1-27,31, Psalms 19:1, John 1:1-3, John 17:1, 5, and Revelation 4:11, 5:11-13. The second glory is in Genesis 1:28-30, Psalms 8, John 17: 4, 22, and Heb. 2:6-9. Let's look at these two different glories and see which one he was able to give to us, and which one he had to get from his father.

To understand it better, we will begin with the second, first, the glory that he gave to his disciples and us.

In Gen.1:28-30, after the creation of the earth and its content. We see God giving man blessings and glory, which only God can provide; by giving man dominion over every living thing on earth. This glory given to man was a gift from God: The man being a perfect being. However, in verses 16, and 17, of chapter three, some of the blessings had now been cursed by God because the man had rebelled against God, and this glory was taken away from the man because he had now become imperfect. This curse indicated that the glory that man was given, by God, was taken away from him at this time. Since then, he had been living under such a curse for his entire existence until John 17:22 tells us otherwise. In Psalms 8, we see a summary of God giving the man this glory and honor and setting him over the works of creation; that act of God is corroborated in Hebrews 2:7. It continues in verse 8, to express the extent of the power the Highest God had given the man. However, the last clause in verse eight shows a contradiction of what was previously mentioned. Something had happened: the fall of man and the power and glory was taken from him, as indicated by the expression, "……but now we see not yet all things put under him." To make it clear, verses 6,7 and 8 of Heb. 2, is referring to man and not to Christ.

Notwithstanding all of that, we understand; further, a more beautiful thing was happening. We see the Messiah coming in verse 9, was introduced in the fullness of time, in the same position as a man, being made a little lower than the angels. The messiah also came as a man in the likeness of sinful man. However, he who knew no sin was given back the same glory man had forfeited; so, he could bring man back to this glory through victory in his life, by living, suffering, dying, and resurrecting. (Hebrews 2:9-18.) This glory, the son demonstrated as a man living among cursed men; he was able to heal, multiply, raised the dead, command the sea, winds, and spirits, and many more beautiful things we call miracles.

{*It is very intriguing that this glory given to man is similar in some respect, but not the same. The dominion given to man on the earth over every living thing was and is limited. Man does not receive praise from these creations he has dominion over. (Gen. 1: 2: John 6:1-15, John 11:1-44, Mark 4:39, Luke 4:33-37,8:27-33*}

Christ was demonstrating his glory as a man, because he lived above the curse; while under the curse of man, for man, as a man. Though he was in a body of sin, Romans 8:3, Heb.2:14, this did not impede the power of the glory the Father gave him while he was on earth; because he was obedient to the Father's will. (John 6:38.) This glory here was not the glory of God, but the glory of man that Adam had forfeited in the garden. This same glory was given back to our redeemer, as stated in John 17:2-4. This same glory was given back to us, the redeemed by the redeemer, again by the Father, through the son. (John 14:12, 17:22-23.) Therefore, we have now been given back the true eternal life and knowledge of God and Christ; this grants us that dominion again, over every living thing on this earth realm as before. Yes, we have been given this glory again, because we have been made perfect in Christ. (Heb. 10:14-17, Romans 3:19-31.) This truth, the devil and his angels in the churches, are careful not to make known to the world. However, we know these truths as they are revealed to us by the spirit of the Highest God in us. (1 Cor. 2:4-10.) This truth must be seen again in the world, both in words and deeds. (Matt 24:14)

(Unfortunately, we see the devil's deliberate distortion of this glory given to man, has also been usurped by racist ungodly demon-possessed minds, to dominate others for their own carnal satisfaction.) This glory was the glory of man that the messiah restored, to us the redeemed, who are not racist, ungodly, or wicked in any way.

However, the glory of God: the first glory, is a different matter. This glory, the messiah mentioned he had with the Father before the world, is a glory that only belongs to the true and living God. Let's now look at this glory.

In John 1: 1-3, it states that he was the word that was with God and was God. He made all things, and nothing that was made was made without him. Therefore, this same God is the God of Gen. 1, who made the heavens and the earth. These acts are glorious acts of the only true God, which shows the eternal glory of the Most, High God. (Psalms 19:1.) This same God came into flesh (John 1:14. Phil. 2:6-8.) Remember that the Living God is a spirit, and the word "God" is a title indicating the highest position and power of eternity present, past and future, and of time and eternity. However, God came into man through his spirit: Christ.

And so, here he found himself as a man, having finished the work, he now acknowledges the hour has come for him to be glorified again with the father. This glorification, however, is one not of this earth. If it were, he would not have needed to ask for it, because he had that glory on earth already, while he was here as a man. What he was now asking for was the glory of eternity past, present, and future. (Rev. 4:11, 5:11-13.) And no man can be given this glory. If you remember, he had said 'the glory I had with you'; this meant he stepped out of eternity and that glory, into time to become a man, now having the glory of limited time as a man. (Phil. 2: 6-7, Heb. 2:9.) That also tells us that while on earth, he was not God, and he acknowledges this; hence, his glory was limited and was only of man. After completing his work, he now looks 'back ahead' to eternity. Meaning he was always living in eternity in his mind, spiritually with the Father while being in time in the body of sinful flesh with the man. However, now, the hour had come for him to step out of time back to eternity. (John 17: 1-8.)

However, the Most Eternal Elohim's glory contains blessings, honor, glory, and power total dominion, adoration, and praise, in heaven and the earth, and under the earth and in the sea, of every living thing. To Elohim, the Father and the son, they have all of the glory because they are omnipotent, omniscient, omnipresent, and Omni glorious. (Rev. 4:11, 5:12-14, 21: 6-7, 22-23.)

Remember the ways of God far surpasses the ways and ideals of man. (Romans 11:34, Isaiah 40: 13-14.)

"For who hath known the mind of the Lord? Or who hath been his counselor? Who hath directed the Spirit of the Lord, or being his counselor hath taught him? With who took he counsel, and who instructed him, and taught him in the path of judgment, and taught him knowledge, and shewed to him the way of understanding?"

The graph below depicts the hierarchy of the Elohim

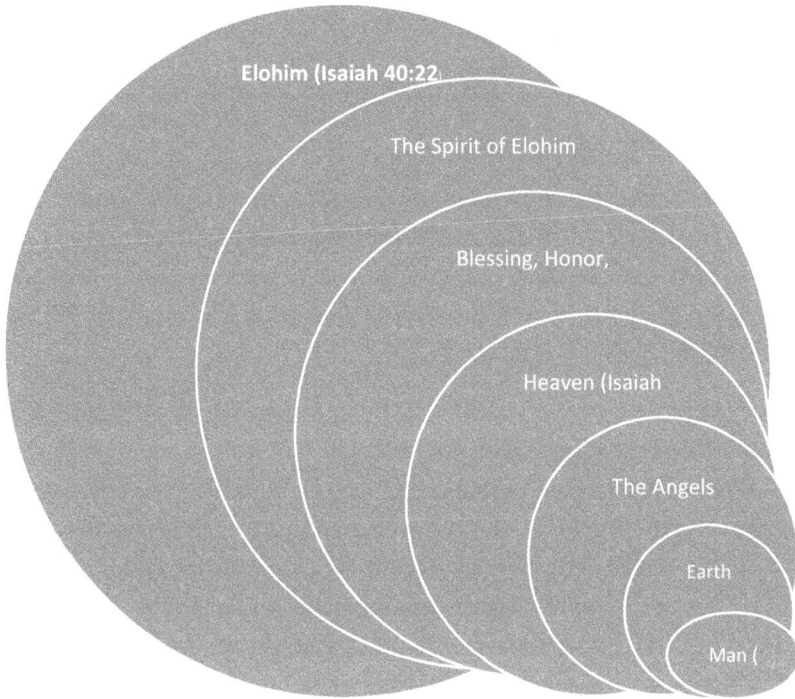

Elohim (Isaiah 40:22

The Spirit of Elohim

Blessing, Honor,

Heaven (Isaiah

The Angels

Earth

Man (

As seen above, the relationship the Most; High Eternal Gods have with their creatures and creation, according to their will and desire.

Man, on the other hand, was made a little lower than the angels, with limited capabilities, hence limited glory. (Heb. 2:7.)

The principle here is simple. We are given a measure of glory because of the measure of our abilities that were given to us. (Matt. 25: 15.) A consistent principle of God.

So, the man was given limited glory within time, but the Highest have eternal glory within eternity: outside of time. However, only the redeemed have been reinstated into that glory that man had before sin. (John 14:12, 17:22-23.) "Verily, verily, I say unto you, He that believeth on me, the works that I do shall he also do: and greater works than these shall he do: because I go unto my Father."

Every act of glory the messiah showed while on earth, we can also demonstrate, if necessary. The glory of man, the messiah illustrated, while he lived on the earth in the flesh, was the glory Adam received after he was created. Now the redeemed can show this same glory again; that the Father gave back to us through his son. (Ephesian 1:7-14. Gal. 3:13-14. Col. 1:2-29.)

An example of this glory is in the account of the demonic. (Matt. 8:28-34.) This account demonstrates the power and glory we have. This power and glory can only be shown by those of us who are exactly like the messiah in our thoughts. These are those who are made one with the Father and Son and have the spirit of Elohim in them. Rev. 12:11 tells how we have this power and glory, and we will demonstrate it. The devil and his angels have no control over those of us who are redeemed. (Acts 5:11-16.) And if we should die, which is just like being asleep, to the spiritual-minded, and we know our death is a matter of God's will, he will allow us to die as witnesses to the world, only if we stand firm on his words. This is a pleasure for us who love the Most, High unto death. (Romans 6.1-18.) "We fear him not; who can kill the body, but only he who can destroy both body and soul." (Matt. 10:28.) This, too, is the demonstration of the power of the Most; High, Amen. Demons have taken over this world in various parts of governments, religions, medicine, science, economics, but only the redeemed of the Most; High can and will stand against the wiles of the devil in all of these areas. (Ephesians 6:11.)

We need to remember that the body or form, man, is a container that the spirit of man and God dwell in, the flesh. (1 Corinth. 2:10-12.) Therefore, when we read that the thoughts of man perish when he dies in Psalms 146:4. It is referring to the carnal flesh of man, not the spirit of man. We also need to see the difference between man, the flesh that goes back to the ground, from whence it came; Psalms 103:15-16, 1 Peter 1:24, and the spirit of man that knows everything about man that leaves him. We notice that the knowledge of the spirit of the saved man does not perish, Rev.6:9-10. But the thoughts and knowledge of man the flesh do, Psalms 146:4.

That is why we are counseled not to fear those who can destroy the body, but him who can destroy both body and soul. (Matt. 10:28, Luke 12:4-5.) You see, this body is a temporary house for the spirit of man to dwell in temporarily. (2 Corinth.

5:1.) Therefore, our true house is in heaven; 2 Corinth. 5:1-9. Also, in verse 3 and 4, we noticed that the spirit of man, that knows everything of man, acknowledges being clothed in this mortal temporary house, but groans to be clothed in the immortal permanent house while acknowledging the investing of the spirit of God in us, verse 5. This shows without any doubt that our true identity is not the house we are in the flesh, but the spirit that is in the house. This knowledge will expose us to the glory we have been given, even now, while in this earthly house on this earth.

To understand how the true glory of the true man works, this, too, is true; the carnal man in the church or outside the church believes that what he sees in the mirror is who he truly is. The carnal man does not know that what he sees in the mirror and what he feels and thinks emotionally are outer shells and surface existence of who he is. The material trappings that comes with that: the Jobs, the positions, the associations, the lands, the houses, the cars, the planes, the food, the clothes, the money, other flesh of people; all this physical world, are all layers of a fake identity that camouflages the essence of the true man. These are possessions that are given to us, the true man, by the true God to be used for his good. These things are not who we are but outward manifestations of the physical world in which we live. Our validation is within us, not outside of us.

That is why it was written: "it is harder for a rich man to enter into heaven than a camel to go through the eye of a needle;" if he thinks that the things he possesses, is who he is. (Matt. 19:22, 24.) The same way the external structures of the various places of worship tell a lie of the true worship and worshipers. The psychological trappings: culture, emotions, norms, fashions, entertainment, false teachings, religion, and politics. Purposely, these trappings of the world tell the perfect lie of the true identity of the true man, which leads to man's total deception and destruction. This tragedy affects not only the rich, but also the poor, from the perspective of thinking, becoming rich will solve all their problems, and make them be who they think they indeed are supposed to be; by gaining more material wealth, or that their unfortunate circumstance is who they are. No, that's not true! Your values are within you, and you are priceless, regardless of your physical circumstances. The true God had put all the values in you before you knew self. (Jer. 1:5.) You are deceived by the devil and his agents when you believe that your worth is reflected by what you have; what you can see in this world: the material trappings. No, your real value is the spirits that God has placed in you of self: both the spirit of God and man. Only by acknowledging and accepting the truth can you then be able to demonstrate that the glory of God has redeemed you through his son.

To explain further how this self-deception works. It's like being very rich, and having the most expensive cars of all time; say cars worth billions of dollars. Sounds ridiculous, might be a little exaggerated, but is intended to make the point. So, you have these cars, and everyone thinks the highest of you. You are the coolest person on the planet. There are news articles and interviews all over the world about you; on the TV and internet, you are the buzz on social media, because of your wealth. People from all over the world tweeting and text messaging about you and wants to see you and your cars. You break the Guinness book of the world record, or you set the record for the most expensive private car owner ever. You are the man or woman of the time. Whenever you drive around, people gather in lines for over hours to get a glimpse of you and your cars. They travel from all over the world to see. Your value is now shown and appreciated by you and the people that value you because of your wealth.

These cars tell of your financial status, how affluent you are, the circle of sophisticated air you breathe, the type of people who hang out with you. This arrangement would say a lot.

However, this is the kicker; nobody knows that you are sick and about to die. Your doctor has diagnosed you with end-stage bone cancer that is very rare and very aggressive.

Let that soak in for a moment, now breathe, ok, let it out.

Now, who are you really, in your mind's reality? Are you a rich billions of dollars luxury car owner, who is on top of the world? Or a chronically sick person who needs a miracle?

In other words, what is important to you now, what people see or what you are experiencing? The world will see you as this wealthy person and still values you from that perspective. But how many of your admirers would trade places with you if they know what you know now about your condition?

So, which of the two are you? Are you what the world sees? Or, are you what you know inwardly to be the truth?

Again, I ask, what is now most important to you? What really matters? The outer material layers or the inward spiritual realities?

The consciousness on the inside that knows all that is going on will remind you every day that you are physically sick and needs a miracle, or the person showing his wealth? How lonely and scared are you, even though you are so wealthy?

It is a shame that there are so many wealthy and rich people in the world, who after acquiring so much wealth, could not pay a friend to take their place or get rid of their diseases and end up dying in a lonely place. There is a better way out yet. You can avoid this lonely transition by giving your heart to God. You might still die of a disease, but you are guaranteed not to die a lonely death. (Rev. 3:20-21.) Besides, what awaits you is far beyond this world's greatest riches and wealth. (Mark 8:36,37.) And guess what! Your death is just a temporary sleep if you are in Christ.

Now, going back to Mark 10:25 and Matt. 19:24. These text messages state that "it is easier for a camel to go through the eye of a needle than for a rich man to go to heaven." Those text messages must be understood within context. Is there a comparison between the rich and the poor here? If we look carefully, we will see it. Also, we should understand that the story of Lazarus and Dives, Luke 16; 19 – 31, has a different application. Lazarus and Dives emphasized the spiritual man, not the temporal, as in the case of the rich man and the camel going through the eye of a needle.

However, we need to understand that our social construct is different today. Back then, most of the rich were look down on by most of the poor as oppressors in that society secretly but admired publicly. Today the rich are put on a very high pedestal by the poor as the ideal position to be, both secretly and openly. Most admired religious leaders are wealthy. Most of the followers of these leaders are poor and want to be just like them, if not in deportment, in wealth. The rich in today's religious world is look on as being closer to God than the poor, and most poor who are religious today think they have to be rich as a sign that they are close to God: materialism. Even by paying tithes, they believe that they will get a bountiful financial return on that investment, apart from securing a place in heaven because they have paid into the treasury of heaven. While the rich then assumed that they had a place in heaven already because they were rich and gave to the treasury. And this is still taught in many churches today. This state of mind is the reason why the lottery has continued generating so much money. And most of the Lottery money is acquired from the poor in our society. Which, by far, is a Christian society. Therefore, if we misunderstand the lesson of the rich man and the camel, we would have lost a lot.

(*What's the difference between the lottery and tithing? Is one voluntary, and the other is by coercion, lies, and trickery, or are they both the same? Just wondering.*)

This text message speaks to what is a priority for whom, within the context of our society today. For the rich man, heaven is not a priority; however, for the Camel getting home is. Likewise, for the poor man, heaven is not a priority; however, getting rich is. So, both the rich and the poor today have the same predicament. The rich will not trade his riches for heaven, while the poor will trade heaven to get rich. (Matt. 19:16-22. 2Kings 5:20-27.) These both have the same problem from different circumstances, because of a lack of true knowledge of self.

Therefore, from the perspective of those poor who are taught that being rich is a sign of being closer to God. They might say they do not think that way. However, their attitudes show exactly that. Their attitude toward money is one of the reasons why they are being taken advantage of by the swindlers in the pulpits. This attitude is indoctrinated in them, to the point that they testify to the notion that as they get closer to God, they will become richer. They call it blessings. So much so that you will find many Christians stealing to attain that status, and have stolen. Throughout history, Christians have proven themselves to be some of the most successful thieves throughout the world. By perfecting the art of stealing in the name of "god." So, the questions for both the rich and the poor, the Christian and the worldly, the sinner, and the saints are: what is it that you need to give up? Or what is your water pot you need to leave, to enter into eternal life? And now that you know have you done the exchange? We all have loads on our backs that prevent us from entering through the "eye of the needle." Those who took the camel to his home knew that the camel could not get into his home with any load on the camel's back. That is the metaphoric comparison here, a load of wanting so much that you steal in the name of religion and a load of having so much that you ignore doing the will of God in the name of greed. These loads need to be rid of, for you to enter into the kingdom of God. (Mark 10:17-27, Acts 3:1-11, Matt.19:16-30, Luke 18:18-30.) And you can't take them off without the true knowledge of self.

 The rich young ruler is a perfect example of the predicament of the rich religious person being unlikely to make it. The rich young ruler had gotten used to his opulence as being his identity. This state of mind sees itself as being rich and nothing else. Therefore, choosing to become poor, for whatever reason, including doing the will of the Highest God and being saved, was out of the question for him. This attitude states that I rather not exist in this life or the next than being poor. There are many among us today with the same mindset. That is the reason we hear or know of many people who have taken their own lives after experiencing a financial setback, even those who call themselves Christian.

Many of these people were rich; however, most are poor who have lost their jobs because of a financial meltdown within their economy. This information can be access by just a click on your computer. Many people, especially men, are measured by and measure themselves and others as someone because of their financial status. Their net worth now values them. This notion belies the true identity of the individual and is used by the deceiver to destroy millions of precious souls, in and outside religion, over an extended time. Though there is nothing wrong with being rich, and there is everything wrong with being poor. We have to remember that the true man is the spirit of the man within. Be it a rich man or a poor man. **Being rich does not disqualify you from heaven; in the same way, being poor does not qualify you for heaven**. This can only be understood by those who are spiritually-minded. When the true God made man, he placed within man the spirit of a man. That is the true essence of the existence of man. In other words, the body of the true man is just a container, as was stated. This container houses the true man. The reality of the true man is his spirit. It does not matter if you are rich or poor. Your true person transcends your condition. **This true man cannot be duplicated or replicated by anything or anyone in this life.**

No computer programmer can reproduce, assimilate, or construct any program, image, or function of the true man. The true man can't be cloned either, as much as they are trying to create a replica of man, in the scientific world. However, they will never be able to replicate the essence of the true man. No amount of wealth and technology will allow them to achieve this goal, not in a billion years. Only reproduction of a manifestation of the physical man, which is physically inferior to the container, can be achieved, nothing more. The artificial intelligence is just that: artificial, no combination, assimilation, or integration of the ideas of man, be it technically advance or otherwise, can match the finished work of the Highest God, period. If we look at the messiah, we could see the true man in action, in John 5:19, 30-31, also, John 14:7.

In John 5:19, 30-31, the messiah acknowledges that the man is subject to the spirit of the Most, High God within him, that is in communion with his own spirit; the true man. Remember, the consciousness of man is co-dependent within the spirits, but he the man has to decide to allow or to seek the will of the spirit of the true God to lead his spirit in the relationship. In Psalm 51: 10, we see David asking the true God to renew the spirit that is within him. Meaning he acknowledges that something is wrong, because of his conscience or consciousness. He, therefore, asked the only one who can fix his brokenness to renew his broken spirit. When our spirit is in rebellion to the spirit of the true God, we are broken. Therefore, David understood this and asked the Father to fix him: the true man who is his spirit. Guess what?

The true eternal God did. In verses 11 and 12, he also speaks of the spirit of the true man that is within him and asked the true God not to take his holy spirit from him. He is here giving notice to the fact that there are two spirits here. The spirit of a man and also the spirit of the true and living God. Both dwelling in him, David. He then asked the true God to restore the joy of his salvation and uphold him with the free spirit of the true God. Only then will he be able to teach sinners the ways of the true God and bring them to the Most, High God. In verse 16, David speaks the truth that only the spirit of the true God could reveal to him. He said the true God does not desire sacrifices, nor does he delight in burnt offerings. The true sacrifice of the true Gods is a broken, humble spirit and a contrite, repentant heart. We realized that David was a rich man, and the Messiah was a poor man. However, the true man was revealed in both of them: the humility of spirit. Yes, we see this been played out many times by the messiah also. Let's look at one such occurrence.

In John 14, the messiah, after conducting the last supper, spoke to his disciples, beautiful words of encouragement, and also wonder. He went on to tell them to love each other. Then he made a statement that shocked and puzzled them all. He said to them he was going away, which was indeed a shock to them. How could he make such a statement? Has he forgotten that we have given up family, friends, jobs, the world even to walk with him? How could he say this now? He must be joking; he doesn't really mean that. We have to remind him that we are committed to his cause. That was the mindset Thomas responded in by asking the messiah to show them the way. Because, where ever Christ was going, they thought we are going with him.

They did not understand the spiritual implications of his statement, but in their minds thought, it was a real place on earth. Then the messiah made it more complicated by telling them that he is the way, and no one comes to the Father except through him. That, I imagine, sounded ridiculous and puzzling to them. However, he preceded in telling them that if they know him, they would know the Father. Philip not understanding these spiritual sayings, now asked Christ to show them the father. This time Christ was more direct and rebuked Philip for not knowing the Father, then made it more puzzling when he then said, "If you hath seen me you have seen the Father, why do you say show us the Father?" The word "see" here means know or to have fellowship.

This would have been confusing to just about anyone of us, including myself. Because the messiah had just said, he was going to the Father when he had said he was going away. Now he says, "if you see me, you see the Father."

If I say to you, "I am going away." That would mean to anyone in their right mind that I am leaving where I am now, to be somewhere else. Then if I say, "I am going to your Father and my Father." That would indicate that the place I am going away to, from where I am now is where our Father is. This is plainly understood. But how can I now say; if you see me, you see the Father, then in the same breath say I am going to the Father? That there is a mind bomb. Well, that would blow anybody's mind. This sounds very confusing and is, if you are looking just on the surface, physically, and trying to go deep, spiritually. No, we have to dissect the thoughts that are express here, to have a clearer understanding. Remember, though; only the redeemed can understand the truth of what is said because we have been reinstated into that glory we once knew, being one with God.

 Now, the truth the messiah was speaking of was not just a physical plane location, but more so a Spiritual place. This only the Spiritual mind can grasp. He spoke of this dual existence, one of the physical, on earth, and the other of the spiritual in heaven.

 The messiah explained the position of the true man. "Believe thou not that I am in the Father, and the Father is in me?" "The words I speak unto you I speak not of myself, but the Father that dwells in me, he doeth the works"; this is both physical and spiritual. On the one hand, the flesh they saw was the physical man, Christ, but the spiritual words and work coming out from within him were from the spirit that dwelt in the physical.

So, the messiah explained that the one who is doing the work that they saw him do was the one in him. Who was the messiah talking about? Who have we found dwelt in him? The spirit of the true and living God, of course, the Father's. The spirit of the true God represented the true God's power and presence in the life of Christ and made things happen; spiritual things, similarly, like the creation of this earth, but now on a lower level. This is why the messiah said if you have seen me, you have seen the Father, that is a spiritual saying. Look at the work that I have done, not me, the physical man, but the one who is in me, not the physical, but the spiritual. In other words, you need not worry and doubt. You need to believe in what I tell you because I represent the Father, and my works manifest this truth. Now to acknowledge the works as of the Father that is within, through his spirit, is total humility and belief. All these teaching came from a poor fellow they called the Rabbi. His poverty, as seen, was not his identity, nor was David's wealth his. Therefore, the body was just a physical container, but the presence of the Father in him was spiritual. The acts through the body demonstrated were physical; however, the initiation and manifestations were spiritual. The space around the body was physical, but the events were spiritual. Hence, if you see me, you see the Father; because the works testify of his presence in me. Also, the first phrase of verse 10 speaks to the harmony of the spirits in the mind of Christ. "I am in the Father, and the Father in me" indicates unity, oneness in vision and purpose. This is why the words that were spoken by Christ were not his words, but the spirit of the Father in him. Similarly, whenever he said the phrase "I am," he was not the one, but the spirit of the Father in him speaking, let's not forget this. Therefore, only those who are spiritually connected could and can understand this statement that the messiah made in John 8:48-59, emphasis on verse 58. The one who spoke was not the body they saw, though the words came out of the mouth of that body; but the spirit that was in the body, which was and is the eternal spirit of the Father; the spirit of the Most, High God, being in harmony with the spirit of the son. Therefore, the flesh had to comply with the power of the spirits that were within; both the Father and the son. Unfortunately, the disciples did not understand this truth while he tabernacle with them; we have no excuse than to pay more attention to him than they did.

This concept of the true self is applied by many who are successful in life at a lower level, without knowing that they are tapping into the power of 'self' that is within, which is the spirit of God being in harmony with the spirit of man. They often say in their testimonies that they believe in themselves, and they knew they would be successful. This shows that the power that comes with the knowledge of self is even available to those who do not profess themselves to be Christians. The rain falls on the just and the unjust. (Matt. 5:45.) Unfortunately, most so-called Christians are not even aware of this power of truth that these types of people, they say, are in the world use. (Luke 16:8.) And let us not assume that the unjust are just people outside of the Christian community. The difference with those of us who know who is doing the work in us and through us is, we give the praises to the Highest eternal true God, and do not take any for 'ourselves' fallen nature in and outside the Christian community; because we know that the true 'self' that is in us, is of and from the true and living God and belongs to the true and living God only. This is the same power that was used by the true and living God to form the earth and the things therein. The same power that the son of the true and living God used to do those miraculous works. The same power is available to us through the spirit of the true and living God in us, as exemplified in David's life and many others, which is a part of the constitution of the true 'self' of man. We are, indeed, fearfully and wonderfully made by God. (Psalm 139:14.)

So, in the body of Christ, the spirit of the true and living God dwelt. However, the Father was still in heaven. Therefore, he was right to say he is going to the Father, and if they see him, they see the Father. Remember that the Most, High God is a spirit, and those who worship him must worship him in spirit and truth. This is referring to the existence of the Most; High, who the messiah said was in heaven. (Luke 18:19.) Then we must also understand that the Highest God has a spirit, 1 Corinth. 2: 11, that was in the son, while the son was on earth, in the flesh, and the Father was in heaven. (Luke 4:16-18.) This is the dual existence of the Father. Similarly, the son expresses his dual presence, when he told his disciples that he was going to the Father, but will come unto them in the spirit, John 16: 28, 17:13-23. Now this dual existence is extended to us being physical, man, which is dust, but having the spirit of the Highest God in us, with the spirit of man. (1 Cor. 2:11, Psalms 51:11.) Yes, dual because the spirits in man are in harmony as one, and also manifested in the physical.

This conversation has so much truth that was hidden from the people because of the 'three cards' religious leaders and their mumbo jumbo theology that have confused the world, but now the truth has come to those who are seeking.

The messiah emphasized the importance of his disciples believing in him, by the evidence of the works that were done by the one who was in him. So, they could be able to do even greater works than he did, because he goes to the Father, whose spirit is in him and will be in them.

This spirit was the image and likeness that is spoken of in Genesis 1:26. An image is a true reflection of the original. However, here we know that God is a spirit, but man is flesh. Therefore, the Spirit has no physical reflections except the works of the spirit demonstrated through the man. Subsequently, to make a man into the image of God is to place the spirit of God inside of man, the same way God has a spirit in himself. (1Cor. 2:11, 12.) Consequently, the image or likeness of God in man is his spirit in man.

(This is the problem some scientists have; they don't know this truth of self.)

The messiah also promised them that if they asked anything in his name, he would do it. He said to keep my commandments: show love to your fellow man, and you would have already loved God, 1 John 4:20. And he will pray to the Father, and he shall give them another comforter, this comforter is the same spirit of the true and living God that was in Adam and was in Christ, so that he may abide with you forever. This spirit is of the Father and the Son. In verse 17, the Messiah speaks of the spirit of **truth**; remember he had told them that he was the "way the **truth** and the life…" now he is saying the spirit of **truth** will abide with them, the world cannot receive, because it sees him not, neither knows him, but you know him; because he dwells with you, present tense; that is Christ and shall be **in you**, future tense; that is the spirit of Christ. Therefore, we know that the Messiah was talking about the spirit of the true God that had made him one with the Father, which was in him presently when he spoke.

Now, who was or is the truth? The messiah said he is the way the truth and the light, no one comes to the Father, but through him. (John 16:4.) Therefore, if the messiah is the truth, then the spirit of truth is the same spirit of the messiah because he is the truth. Then he said, which made it even more explicit, "I will not leave you comfortless: I will come to you." That is so awesome!! He is speaking of his spirit. The spirit of the Father is also the spirit of the son, which is the same spirit that comes within us and leads us in all truth because the spirit is the spirit of truth, the one spirit which is the spirit of the true and living God. (Eph.4:4, 1 Cor. 12:13.) That is the same reason why the messiah could say if you see me you see the Father, and the redeemed can tell by their lives; when you see us, you see the Father and the son by our lives. Then they will be able to manifest the glory given to them on this earth because he will be with us even to the end of this world. (Matt. 28:20)

The messiah was telling his disciples that the man is going away. However, at the same time is trying to let them see beyond the physical. We see this in Matt.1: 1-11. Knowing that though the physical man is gone, he is, as the true man will be with them in a little while, through his spirit, which is one with the Father. "And that day you shall know that I am in the Father, and you in me, and I in you." This is the testament of the truth of his words, the outpouring of the spirit of the true God, on Pentecost. (John 7:39.) This the disciples did not get, and we still will not understand its actual meaning, until the experience occurs with us too. What this means is that the messiah is even closer to us now, than he was with his disciples while he walked with them on this earth, before Pentecost. Think about it; he tells them that he will dwell in them, not outside or among them as he was before. This is the 'another' comforter he speaks of, John 14:16.

God dwelling in him through the spirit of God now dwells in us through the same spirit of Christ. **If I understand this correctly, he was saying he is going to live inside of us the same way the Father lived in him after Adam sinned and in Adam before Adam sinned**. This is also the reason why he did not partake in the sacrificial system. He came to fulfill the moral laws and the prophets but to end the ceremonial laws and ordinances, Matt. 5:17, Col. 2:14, Heb. 7-10. So, we might have life and have it more abundantly. (John 10:10.) This arrangement would make us one with him and the Father. Then we will be doing the same and greater works also that he did, this is the promise that he gave, that we need to acknowledge and accept so that the evidence of his words and actions can be manifested through us.

However, if we reject such great a fulfilled promise, as being an illusion, we then will be left up to our unbelieving hearts, stuck in a cycle of religion, going nowhere, but in a circle of confusion as seen in the many churches today. (John 16:25-28, 17: 14-26.)

Notwithstanding, we, the redeemed, have been given the same glory and power of the Messiah while he walked the earth. Therefore, we must live in, and demonstrate that same glory for the world to know the truth of our redeemed state in Christ.

Chapter 47

Lies told on the spirit, from the pit of hell.

It is imperative to take note of the function of the spirit of the true God. In particular, what the spirit of the true God will not do. In John 16:13-15, the scripture tells us that there is one thing the spirit of the true God will not do. That one thing is to speak of himself.

Now, what does that mean, speaking of oneself?

In John 8, we see the same language, where the Messiah was speaking regarding himself as a man. Telling the people that he speaks not of himself, but does what he was told. Meaning he took no praise for himself, but acknowledge the Father as the source of his existence and functions. Showing that all praises go to the Father. John 8:28 explains verse 12-18, then the messiah said unto them, "when you have lifted up the son of man, then shall you know that I am he and that I do nothing of myself, but as my Father hath taught me, I speak these things." He was making it very clear. He was not taking any praise for himself, and he was sure to let us know that.

The messiah was making the truth plain to his disciples and us, that after they see the works, he is doing and has done, they will lift him up, however, because he knows that he can't take any credit for the works that are done by the spirit of the true God in him. He now explained to them that he does what the Father taught him, and the Father is always within him, and he does everything accordingly to please the Father and nothing of himself. This was to prevent them and us from looking at the messiah, the man, as the one who gets the credits and should be credited with the praises for these mighty works at that time. (John 8:50, 54.)

Likewise, the Spirit of the true God will not take any praises. (John 16: 12 – 15.) Christ is speaking again: "But when the spirit of truth has come, he will guide you into all truth. For he will not speak of himself, but whatever he shall hear, that shall he speak: and he will show you things to come. He shall glorify me: for he shall receive of mine and shall show it unto you. All things that the Father hath are mine: therefore, said I, that he shall take off mine and shall show it unto you."

Now, remember the truth is and was the word that became flesh, which was the Christ. So, when the inspired word said 'the spirit of truth,' what it means is the spirit, which was the word that became flesh as the Christ. Therefore, the same spirit belongs to the word that later came into the flesh. Now that the word that was made flesh has returned to the Father. He has retained his previous position as one with the Father, not just in power and might, but also in glory; he now can receive again the glory and the praise he had with the Father before, which means that the spirit will now show glory to the son through us and inspire us with the things of the son who has retained his title as God (one) with the Father because the spirit is his.

It is interesting that in verse 12, we see the Messiah stating how he has many things to say to his disciples; however they couldn't bear them then, but in verse 13, he continued to state that when the spirit of truth, is come; his spirit, he shall not speak of himself, only what he hears shall he speak, and shall shew you, things to come; completing the promise in verse 12. Verse 14, now confirming the promise that's in verse 12, and given in verse 13. Verse 15, reaffirming, if there is any doubt with what is presented, making it more explicit still that the messiah had retained his position as one with the Father when these things were fulfilled. The statement he made "therefore, said I, 'he shall take of mine, and shall shew it unto you,'" is the verification of him retaining his glory.

So, now we see the same principle that was employed when the messiah was here as a man, him not doing anything of himself, but of the Father; the one he gives all praises to and receives all power from, who is the only true God. Likewise, the spirit of the true God does not speak of himself or taught (showed) anything of himself, but only of the true God, "the word" who became flesh is now again one as God with the Father.

Remember this expression: 'to speak of himself,' means within context: bringing attention to self for praises, adoration, worship, admiration, and glorification. Christ, the son of the true God, as a man, did not take praises for himself, as stated by him in the inspired text messages. (John 5: 19, 30, John 8:28-29.) Neither did or will the spirit of the true God do such things, as stated in the inspired text messages. (John 16:13.) This inspired word is the same word that became flesh. How then can the inspired scriptures contradict the word that became flesh? And how can the spirit of the word, contradict the word, that is now one with the Father as God?

Therefore, those who claim that the spirit of the true God tells them to worship Him, the spirit, as another God, is possessed by a lying spirit from a false god, and not from the spirit of the true and living God. The spirit of the true and living God will never teach such false teaching, ever! There is no place in the inspired word of the true God that anyone can find such commandment or encouragement to worship the spirit of the true God as the third person of the Godhead. It is just not there. Saying that, Peter stated, "if you sin against the spirit of the true God, you sin against the true God." It does not mean that the spirit is another God, but that the spirit is the spirit of the true and living God as plainly stated in the inspired word over and over again. (Job.33:4, Psalm 33:7, Isaiah 40:13, 42:1, Joel 2:28-29, Ezekiel 11:24.) And Peter is not saying we should worship the spirit of God as another God because he is the comforter. No! That is not biblical, scriptural, or inspirational, but a made-up or systematic theology of fallen man. Remember, the same way that God used the messiah to comfort those he comforted, by his spirit in Christ, is as Christ now using his spirit, being shed in us to comfort us. He can do this, as his Father did in him, in us, because he has retained his glory; being now one with the Father again, he the word, can come to us in his spirit, to be the next comforter again, being in us as he told his disciples. (John 16:7-33.) Emphasis on verse 16 of John 16, and verse 9 of John 14. 1 Cor.2:11-14, 2 Cor. 3:3, Phil. 3:3, 1Peter 4:14. Etc.

Similarly, also, when we present the truth to others, if they reject us, they are rejecting God, because we are his servants. We clearly are not Gods, but just his servants. Likewise, the spirit represents God the Father, and the son, but speaks not of himself. Meaning, the spirit takes no praise to himself; in the same breath, the faithful servants of God will take no recognition for themselves, being of Christ.

In Luke 10:16, we see when we are doing the work of the Most, High God, as stated by his Son, whosoever rejects us, rejects God; also, whosoever receives us receives God. Because we do not do the works of man, but of the Most, High God is in us by his spirit. This statement does not mean that we are another set of Gods. But that we represent God. Similarly, the spirit of God is not another God but represents the true and living God.

Now, if you send someone to represent you, whatever is done to that person, by principle, is done to you. Consequently, anything or any attitude shown to the spirit of God is shown to the Most, High God, because the spirit is God's spirit.

If they say the spirit told them to worship him as another God, then this spirit of which they speak must be another spirit; but not the spirit of the true and living God; because that teaching is contrary to the teaching of God, as stated in the scripture. The same way the messiah did not speak of himself as God is the same way the spirit does not reveal, show, taught, teach, or speak off himself to be another God. We as men have no right to assume and teach such figments of our imagination as reality from scripture when it is not there. Such thoughts and teachings are inconsistent with the inspired text messages of the true God and are lies from the pit of hell.

Some say the spirit has a personality and, as such, is another person. What they consistently have overlooked is that the spirit of which they speak is the same spirit of Christ, and as such will have a personality, but does not mean a third person, having the character of Christ. (John 16:13-16, 14:16-20.) This spirit which was in Christ when He walked this earth and was in harmony with the spirit of God; manifesting the power of God, is the same spirit that Christ sent to us; now that he has retained his glorious power of being one with the Father again, manifesting the power of God: the Father and son. (John 16:15.) This way, we have become one in Christ, being one with the Father and Son, through his spirit. (John 17:20-23.) This is why the scripture states, Christ, speaking: "when the spirit of truth comes, he will guide you into all truth, saying this is the way walk in it." which is the same spirit of Christ. (John 16:13.)

 Remember also; only a personality can understand and speak to another personality. Christ's understanding of our feelings and infirmities has now sent his spirit to comfort us with his omnipotent, omniscient, omnipresent anointed power. Praise be to the Most, High God for his graciousness towards us through his son. (Isaiah 53:1-5. Hebrews 4:15.)

You must always remember that you have a spirit, which is not another you but has your personality. Those who can't handle the truth will go crazy just reading this. Yes, in 1 Cor. 2:11, we see the man having a spirit of himself that knows everything of man. Should we then take this spirit of the man like another man, or it this spirit the true essence of the man mentally and intellectually? If you accept the teaching that the spirit of God is another God, then you have to, by principle, agree that the spirit of the man is another man. This will make each man as two men. However, we the redeemed know that that is not true, of the spirit of a man being another man. Likewise, we know that the spirit of God is not another God, but is erroneous teaching by the deceivers. However, the spirit of God is the spirit of God, as the spirit of man is the spirit of man. We pray for the ignorant that the spirit of truth will also come in and sup with them, and lead them into this truth.

Chapter 48

The True Worship of Adam, The messiah and us: The reflective comparative

Now, if we should look to how Adam worshiped the true and living God, it would amaze us that the worship he gave, did not involve all the pompous, flamboyant formalities we see in our churches, synagogues, temples, and meetings houses of the ancients and today. I know there is no record or reflection of Adam worshiping the true God, by looking on our norms and traditions. However, to some, it would appear as strange to think he did not worship in the traditions of the ancients that morphed into the way we do today in the churches. Well, he did not; not before sin, that is, even after sin.

To understand how he worshiped, without seeing any record of him worshipping, we have to look at the messiah and place the messiah in Adam's position. Why? You ask. Well, because Adam, being created perfectly, would have worshiped the Most, High, in a perfect way: in spirit and truth. The only reflection of this would be in the worship of the messiah. We then have to look at the constants and the variables in both their lives to see the way Adam would. I will term this as a reflective comparative.

In a place without sin and where all is peaceful, the messiah would not need to preach, teach, heal, cast out demons, neither would he be tempted of the devil; these are the variables. However, he would be prayerful and thankful and always in constant communion with the Father; allowing the spirit to use him; these are the constants: worshiping in spirit and truth every day. That was the way Adam worshiped before he sinned. The same way the messiah worshiped after sin, excluding the variables, and also except for going to the temple. The same way the true worshiper, the disciples, worshiped yesterday and the true worshipers today, in spirit and truth. **Did you notice that the messiah never offered a sacrifice, or paid a Tithe even after the fall, the same way Adam did not before?** Interesting, isn't it? Think about that for a minute. The offering of sacrifices or paying of Tithe was never, and still, are not a part of true worship. Neither did Adam nor the messiah, or his disciples engaged in those activities before or after the fall. Many of those who are called Christians, are not aware that the messiah never paid a Tithe. He did not pay into that system because it was not only obsolete but became officially obsolete by him: when he died on the cross.

(Hebrews 7, 8, 9, and 10.) This tells us that tithing is not relevant to true worship, from the time the messiah walked this earth. Consequently, true worship does not include those ceremonial activities. Those have been long done away with centuries ago. Those were all forms of a ceremonial system that died with Christ but was never raised with him again. We will look at this truth more in-depth is a separate book.

Chapter 49

The Father

Let's now look at the Father. The messiah in his statement stated that the Father 'would be worshiped in spirit and truth,' for the Father seeks such a one. Who is this, Father?

In the Shema: Hear O Israel, the Lord our God is one God. This was the understanding of the Old Testament thought. From the inception of "Judaism." Deut. 6:4. There was an understanding that there was only one true God. Not two, not three, not four, only one. This understanding continued even to the life of the messiah. It was this messiah who introduced himself as the son of the true God.

 This introduction was very offensive to those who thought they knew better: the high priests, scholars, teachers, and leaders of the day, because of their traditional teachings. Should they be respected by us, because of the stance they took? Remember that the closest person on earth to the true and living God was the high priest. No one else came close. And even the high priest knew his limitations. The high priest had to go within the presence of the true God in the temple, with a rope around him. Knowing he could die at any moment. And he was the one who was chosen by the true God to represent the people to the true God and the true God to the people. Also, to be considered to be a high priest, he had to have been born within a particular tribe: the Levites, which was the only tribe whose descendants could be for such a privileged position in the temple services, but he was not born in that tribe. (Exodus 28.)

 So, the messiah introducing himself or him being introduced as the son of God was very much, way off base by them. (John 1:29, 10:1, 36.) He was not even close. To also consider himself becoming a priest was an absurd thought, let alone a High Priest, but a son!!!

Now, we must remember that the way of thinking within that culture at that time was such that, if one is a son of a King, he is the heir to the throne. After coming to an age of maturity and accountability, the son is considered to be the successor of the King and then at the appropriate time assumes his rightful place as king, having the same bloodline as the son. The story of David and Solomon! (Kings 2:1-4.)

 Also, if a trade or businessman has a son, the son is considered to be the heir to the business or profession. Then after coming to a mature and accountable age, he will graduate from his apprenticeship and then take his position as equal with his father. Well, he can choose not to if he so desires, in some cases. (Matt 21: 33-38.)

 Now, looking from that cultural background, the psychology was if you proclaim yourself to be the son of God, you were telling the world that you are the successor to the King or equal with the King.

Therefore, you have virtually ignored the fact that you had to be at least a priest, who was just a servant, not even a son. Also, for this position of servanthood that you were not qualified for, and it would be considered to be blasphemous for even the thought of it, however, for Christ to have projected himself to be the son of God, how obnoxious can one person ever be? That was the mind of the secular leaders then. (John 8:54, 10:36) This did not go over well with the leaders of the day, and for good reasons, they thought. They, in their way of thinking, had the right to go up against and attack anyone who had the nerve to assume that position. No one had ever thought such crazy thoughts before, let alone articulate it in public as far as they were concerned. Therefore, you must be a mad man and deserve to die for such a blasphemous posture. You must be possessed by deviant spirits to make such a defiant statement. (John 8:12-59.)

So, the messiah was charged with blasphemy and sedition, by both the church and state. (John 11:46-53, Luke 22:66-71; 23:1-24.) He was considered to be the number one suspect and outlaw of the day: the most wanted. Not only was the religious leaders and their subordinates offended by this and wanted his head. But the political leaders on both sides of Israel and Rome were peeved that this uncouth, low breed, uneducated, low class, Nazarite bastard, who would not only challenge traditional norms but would seek to upset the balance of their religious and political powers present. No! No!! No!!! We will not allow this kind of nonsense to go on. Whatever it took, they argued among themselves; we will get rid of this bastard if he doesn't shut up, we will kill him!!! (as my pastor told me that he could have me killed)

 To put insult to injury, "he also went about healing on the Sabbath, working, and encouraging others to work," the religious leaders argued. The man with the withered hand. (Mark 3:1-6.) The man at the pool Bethesda. (John 5: 1-18.)

Braking corn on the Sabbath, with his disciples. (Luke 6:1, 2.) And many more. We indeed shall have his head!!

These religious leader's traditions have been around for thousands of years. They were going back to their father, Abraham. So, to them, this was nonsensical, comical, and embarrassing. Also, he was not even fifty years old yet but spoke of knowing and existing before Abraham. That they knew now prove that the "boy" was not only rude but a nut!! (This was also expressed by another pastor)

However, what the messiah was introducing to them was the only way to know the only true God. But they thought they were still connected to the true God by their traditions, their temple, their degrees, and their ways of worship. (Matt. 21:13.) However, they did not know that they were poor, miserable, blind, naked, and in bondage. (Rev. 3:17.) And their sacrifices and worship were not accepted by the true and living God, but they were only slaves without knowing. (Matt.23:38, Luke 13:35, John 8:32-33.)

He told us that there is only one way to get to know the Father, and that was and is through him. In John 14:6. The scripture says, the messiah speaking, "I am the way the truth and the life, no one comes to the Father, but by me." That tells us that the messiah's coming was also to reveal the Father. He also said to his disciples, "if you see me, you see the Father." That statement was very confusing to them then and still is, to many today. However, the messiah went on to explain that he was not talking about his physical appearance, but the works done were signs of the Father working through him. It was the work of the true and living God. He was only there to carry out the work of the Father. The spirit of the father was in him. These sayings of the messiah were spiritual and could not be understood by the disciples at the time, nor the religious or political leaders of the day, then and now. (Some of these sayings were only said in private to his disciples, for obvious reasons) This truth is illustrated by the scripture that states that heaven declares the glory of the Most, High God, and the firmament shows his handy work. (Psalms 19:1.) The heaven and the firmament are not Gods but show or reveal the Most High's glory to us by the works of his hands. Likewise, the messiah was not God or claimed to be. However, he showed or revealed the Most High's glory to the disciples and us, by the works that were performed through him by the Most, High God.

So, we have to sympathize with the religious leaders, to a point; those who do not know what they are talking about, even today. They should have known better, but they just did not. The disciples who walked close with Christ also had a hard time understanding the teachings of Christ, even though they were not corrupted by the religious system, like the religious leaders of then and now. Interestingly, the messiah did not call any of his disciples from the synagogue or the temple. As we would say today, the church, as they were in a corrupt system as is today. However, they still found it difficult to appreciate his teachings. Notwithstanding, they were willing to learn. The religious leaders by large were not, most were set in their ways of "higher learning" to gain that lifestyle, as they are today.

It is vitally necessary to believe the words of the messiah and to understand what was said then and what is said now about the revelation of the Father. Only the spirit of the true and living God can open our minds to the understanding of such knowledge. (1 Cor.2:12.) There are so many types of distractions today that even those who are elected will struggle. (Matt. 24:24.)

 I want to highlight the three main types of such cunning distracting plots by the devil, plaguing the world and the churches today.

In Matt.27, there is the case of Pilot's encounter with "**The Truth**," that so reflects the times and the way the religious body operates today. (We will continue the revelation of the Father in chapter 51.)

Chapter 50

In Pilot's case for Christ

After all, the chief priest and elders of the people took counsel against the messiah (truth) to put him to death. They had him bounded and led him away and delivered him to Pilot.

And Judas (fake friends) who had betrayed Christ. After he realized what he did, remorsefully 'repented' himself, and brought the thirty pieces of silver again to the chief priest and elders, confessing that he had betrayed innocent blood. He was more remorseful than being repentant. And they responded to him, "what is that to us?" In other words, we don't care; that is your problem now.

As we look at this account, we see that the messiah was hated by those he came to save, those who claimed to have the oracles of the true God. Those who were holy and pure in their own sight hated him. These were the chief priests and leaders then. These are the pastors and institutional leaders of religion today, along with the elders of the people then. These are the elders today who serve these pastors but do not serve the true and living God. Then we have poor old Judas who betrayed his master because of greed. He represents those who were helped and once served, who have decided now to join with the wicked to bring harm to the true believers. Not because of anything terrible the true believers did, but because of the good, the evil ones could not have exploited, done for, and to them, but being unappreciated by their greed, they have and will attack. These are a bunch of sorrowful souls, who are all employed or benefiting from a demonic system that was and is camouflage by the name temple and church or remnant. In some of these institutions today, they have become images of the beast system, in adapting the false teachings of the beast and being managed by the antichrist system. Once you have joined with Babylon, and have adopted its teaching and its false gods, you have become a house of demons and a place for every foul spirit and a cage of every unclean and hateful bird. That is the reason why there is so much hate, deceit, and vice in all the churches today. There is no other way to say it. (Rev.18.) Emphasis on verse 2. The church has taken the place of the corrupt high priest then, in today's world. (Nehemiah 13:4-5, 7-8.) There are so many churches; however, wickedness much more abounds because of the corrupt leadership in the Churches. That is indeed a reflection of the demonic churches. How can you have so many churches in a specific place, or any other area for that matter, then boast of having the most churches per square mile in the world, and at the same time, being close to being the murder capital of the world consistently? That means these churches are corrupted and are synagogues of Satan. (Rev. 3: 14-18.) If the salt has lost its savor, it is fit to throw out.

Now comes, want-to-be innocent or guilty, Pilot.

We should take note that the governor Pilot, was very observant of the messiah not responding to the angry mob of accusers. In verse 18 of Matt. 27, it said that he, Pilot perceived that they were envious of Christ. Even his wife acknowledged that the messiah was just and innocent. So, he (Pilot) tried to retort to diplomacy by introducing Barabbas, but the chief priest and elders would not have any of it and persuaded the multitude that they should ask for Barabbas, and destroy the messiah. Pilot, realizing that the messiah was from Galilee, which was a jurisdiction of Herod, hurriedly sent him to Herod. Herod, having heard of the messiah, wanted to meet him for entertainment purposes to see miracles performed by him.

In Luke 23: 12, Herod and Pilot were made friends. Remember, these men were enemies for some time before, but now, because none of the two wanted to appear to be taking side with the messiah: the outcast, they became friends that same day. There is a saying: An enemy of my enemy is my friend. That is a true statement in the world, however, when this becomes a practice in the church. We know that God's presence is not there.

It is interesting that in verse 14, Pilot found that the accusations were false, and there was no guilt in the messiah. Nor did Herod find him guilty. Three times Pilot attempted to release him, and three times, he met with the opposing cries of the possessed accusers.

In John 19:11-18. The messiah indeed told Pilot that he had no power except that it came from above. So, the messiah acknowledged the power he had. This Pilot did not get or understood. The fact that the Messiah would not talk to anyone else except Pilot tells us that the true eternal God was interested in saving Pilot and his household. His wife also had a dream about Christ. The true God speaks to us in dreams and visions; those he favors. But Pilot was afraid of the things that man could do to him, instead of fearing God, because he did not know the true God of the universe; therefore, the messiah was trying to introduce him to the true God of the world: his father; however, he was distracted by the mob's cry. How often have we known the right things to do for the true and living God, only to be criticized by friends or foes, then neglect to do God's will because of grass man? (1 Peter 1:24, Psalm 8: 4.) That is also the truth to be acknowledged by politicians today. The power you think you have to serve comes from above. All presidents and ministers of government in the world should serve the only true God of the universe, by serving the people in justice and truth.

 The last time Pilot tried to release Christ from false accusations; he was threatened by the priest and leaders through the mob, politically. They stated that if he released him, he was no friend of Caesar, and whoever makes himself a king is not a friend of Caesar. This argument was a double-edged sword used against Pilot. That shows how diplomatic and cunning the leaders were against the messiah, as they are today against his followers. On the one hand, the messiah was presented to be a king, so if any of these two leaders took sides with the messiah, it would be an act of treason. Either by appearing to be promoting the messiah as King or, on the other hand, using the messiah as a ploy to promote self. These notions Pilot could not gamble with; therefore, he had to show that he opposed the messiah or would suffer the faith of his own death on his cross.

That is where the similarity of Pilot and the present religious leaders are strikingly consistent. Here Pilot could not afford to lose the position of being considered a friend with Caesar; it doesn't matter if Caesar did not know him personally. Three things came with being considered a friend of Caesar that he could not afford to lose, even if it cost him his life. And this word 'Caesar' today, is synonymous with the world, as in friend with the world. These are: (1) His position; this has plagued the church to the fullest. Some people will kill and have killed their brothers and sisters in words and deeds, just for a position. Pilot did. Then there is: (2) His association, In some cases, this is only the appearance of being in the company of or known by some so-called dignitaries, because of their position in an institution or their qualifications, over their subordinates. They deny the truth of the true God, to be an associate with a man or an organization. Pilot did. Then we have (3) Money. The scripture tells us that the love of money is the root of all evil. (1 Timothy 6:10.) If you love money so much so that you choose to try and destroy someone's life over it, then you have sold your soul to the devil in exchange for that money. Many have and are doing so today, more so in the church than ever before. Pilot did.

With the increase in joblessness and the more materialistic mindset within the churches, and the world in general today, money has become the god of many both in and out of the churches. Many have been pretending to love others because of money, and many are hated by many because of money. And the worst part about it, if there is such a part. That money and property did or do not belong to them, the haters, but to the ones they hate. I am talking about family members, church members, friends, and so-called loved ones. People who have shown that they do not know the true and living God, who call themselves Christians. They are as Jezebels and Ahabs with their hatred and greed towards Naboth. (1 Kings 21.) Jezebel and Ahab represent these church folks, Christians, in no small degree. Remember, they were religious; they were worshipers of the god Baal, who was a pagan god. We must remember that we act according to the gods we serve. Therefore Jezebel, Ahab, and the elders were religious folks, similar to those, to no small extent in the churches today, who worship false gods. Calling on a god or praying to many gods does not in itself means you are calling on or praying to the right God. Have you checked your gods lately? How you treat and what you teach the people around you will tell which god you are serving. (1 John 4:20-21.) If you are serving Babylonian wine (false doctrine) in your churches, you are indeed a daughter of Babylon and do serve a pagan god; it does not matter if you call yourself the remnant and claim to keep the commandments.

We will not condemn those types but pray for them, that they too will repent and allow the Spirit of the true and living God to tabernacle within them also.

In the account of Jezebel, Ahab, and Naboth, in 1 Kings 21, we see an insidious plot between Jezebel and Ahab to deceive the people. By using official communication from an authoritative source and high position of influence, in today's religious society, we could call this the pastor and the pulpit in the local churches, and in some respect, the conference office. To entrap, sneer, and kill a man of the true and living God for his possession. In Gen. 37:1-4, 11, 18-24. 39: 1-19. This account also speaks to another false accusation of a son of God, by a desperate woman. In the parable of the man who helped his enemies, the woman spoken off is a combination of both of these women in one, that is of Jezebel and Potiphar's wife. The people who conspired with her are like the companies that supported and conspired with these two. These acts still plague the churches and the world today. Some of these evil plotting come from church leaders who think they are entitled to 10% of your money base on an outdated Old Testament law; they refer to in Malachi 3:10. That had nothing to do with the people of old, then, or the people today. (Nehemiah 13 will explain Malachi 3, very clearly. Malachi saw the atrocity that was taken place in God's house and the mismanagement of resources for personal purposes by the high priests. He mentioned a messenger coming. This messenger was no other than Nehemiah, as is shown in Nehemiah 13, which explained what the high priest did. Interestingly, the books of Malachi and Nehemiah were deliberately placed in different and opposite places in the bible, and far apart, to give the impression that they are not connected, and most people who read the bible do not know that they are related. However, if you look carefully, you will note that they are dealing with the same issue of rebuilding Jerusalem and occur within the same epoch of time. They also switched their chronological order to give the impression that they have nothing to do with each other. However, if what is written in Malachi happened after Nehemiah's account, then they would have no connection and are relating to something other. However, if Nehemiah comes after Malachi, then what is in Malachi is exposed in Nehemiah. This deception was deliberately orchestrated by the so call "church Fathers" to deceive the masses, and they have been very effective in doing so. Sorry, I couldn't wait. A word to the wise is sufficient.)

Neither the Messiah nor his disciples adhere to or taught that outdated law. There is nowhere in the scripture that the messiah paid or return a tithe, or taught us to do so. However, these lazy religious leaders today are hell-bent on even persecuting their members psychologically to return something the Most, High eternal God told them nothing about returning. Therefore, this greed they have for easy money, an opulent lifestyle, position, and association like those of old, Pilot as an example, has driven them to plot evil schemes and lie to the people from the pulpit to get what does not belong to them.

Lots of pastors and elders lie to the people today to get a kickback from the various religious, administrative bodies they call offices or conferences. They are lower than the worst scum like politicians. And most poor and ignorant people fall for this trick of the devil because these lying pastors and their associates tell them that they will not go to heaven and will be cursed and become a cost out if they do not obey the command to bring all the tithes into the storehouse. The problem with that is, those laws have long been obsolete, for thousands of years. And that particular scripture was referring to the scum like evil high priests Eliashib and his associates of that time. (Nehemiah 13.)

This is the reason you will not find in the scriptures any of the disciples or the messiah paying or returning a tithe. Paul did not collect any tithes from the brethren, but only offerings. And these were free-willed. Meaning you give because you chose to. However, this practice was brought back by Babylon, and the daughters of the whore had to comply with her dictates then and now. Every church today that teaches this lie is of the whore system of Babylon is a daughter of the whore system. It does not matter what you call yourselves or on which day you claim to worship. The question to the so-called scholars. If the occurrences surrounding the rebuilding of the temple in Jerusalem are the same that is in Nehemiah, Zachariah, and Malachi, why would these books not be together in chronological order and at the right place in the bible?

 It would serve us well to remember spiritual things are spiritually discerned.

So, Pilot refused truth, like many others today, because of the temporary accommodations of this world's offerings. Be careful you do not do the same.

Chapter 51

The Father and Son

The disciples were not converted as yet, and could not understand what the Messiah was saying. They the disciples then and even now; our brothers and sisters outside of Christ. However, the messiah did not forsake them. (John 1:14)

Remember, we are still talking about the Father.

There is a favorite text message of mine that reveals a lot about the relationship of the Father as he relates to the son. In John 1, we see that in the beginning was the word and the word was with God, and the Word was God. It went on to say, and the Word became flesh. We had established before that this flesh was the messiah. Now, if we believe this was so, there is only one conclusion to make, and that is, the word that was with the true God and who was the true God became the Messiah: the flesh, by coming into that flesh. The Father was the true God who the word the messiah, now flesh was with, then the spirit, but the Father remained spirit. That also will show that the Word 'God' is not a proper noun, but an adjective describing a position of supremacy that the two occupied. GOD: the OMNISCIENCE one, GOD: the OMNIPRESENT one, GOD: the OMNIPOTENT one, and GOD the OMNIGLORIFIED one. I am almost sure most of us have never heard of the word **OMNIGLORIFIED**, well if you did not know then, now you know. **This word means all glorified, having all glory.**

 We can also look at Geneses 1, which shows that the two: the true God; the Father and the true God the word; son, made all the world using their one spirit. In John 17, we hear the flesh that the word was in asking the Father for something after he came into flesh; to reinstate him back to the position he had as one with him; the Father, before he came into the flesh.

If you notice he never said 'them' as in to be reinstated with 'them' plural pronoun, but to be reinstated with 'him,' 'thee'; singular pronoun, John 17:5. Therefore we have the word that was with the true God, that was the true God coming into the flesh, and at this time while being flesh prayed to the Father, who is the true God, to be reinstated with 'him,' singular pronoun. That is rudimentary English. Now we will do a first grade, math: 1+1=2, not 3. In another simple expression: The Father + The word = God. Well, we can conclude that the Father and the word are the true God almighty. (John 1:1.)

The expression 'the spirit of God' tells that the spirit belongs to both of them. The word 'God' when used and understood in the proper context means the Father or the son, or BOTH of them, never the Spirit. When the messiah said that 'God' is a spirit, it simply means that the true God; the Father exists as a spirit. The word usage "of" within the context of this text message is a personal possessive preposition, that relates to something being possessed by another or being owned by another. Consequently, the spirit belongs to both the Father and the son. Therefore, he could say he will send the comforter. (John 16: 13-15.)

Interestingly, the messiah describes the oneness of himself and the Father in John 17: 21-26, as between two: The Father and the son. Then he asked the Father that the disciples he gave him, may also become one with them: The Father and the son. The Father and the son work in unison of one spirit.

For example, there were many disciples; however, for simplification purposes, let's say eleven. Now, if we add eleven to two: The Father and the son, that will give us thirteen: 11+2= 13. How can these thirteen become one? This oneness can only become a reality by the indwelling of the one spirit of both the Father and the Son, the spirit of the true God, in the disciples also. This will then result in this oneness that the messiah prayed for. This the Messiah knew would happen because he understood the working of his spirit that belongs to the Father, will now be possessed by the disciples that belonged to him, which will make them all one, and the others he prayed for, including ourselves, just as he was one with Adam before Adam sinned. (John 17:20-26.)

The spirit of the true God is what binds us together to be one with the true God and our fellow brethren. We all are one in the spirit as Adam, and the Messiah was one with the Father in and of the same spirit.

Also, the most recited verse in the scripture: "for God so love the world that he gave his only son …."

If you look carefully at how the word 'God' is used in the singular form, you will see there is only one that gave the son. The singular pronouns 'he' and 'his' tell that God is one being (source), in usage here. If there were more, the rendition would be "they gave their only begotten Son…" we do not see that there.

In Geneses 1, the word says, "In the beginning, God created the heaven and the earth... And God said let us make man in our own image." It is fascinating to note that the word "God" is used in the plural form by the pronoun "us" that is used here, indicating plurality. Well, this plurality needs explanation.

If we look in John 1, we read the inspired word stating that "In the beginning was **the** word (1) and the word was **with** God (2) and **the** Word was God (1). And in verse 14, it states that **the** word (1) became flesh and dwell among us. We notice that there were two (2) beings, and one (1) of the two beings became one (1) man; flesh. Now there was one (1) God left in heaven.

To confirm this, we listen to the direct words of the messiah testifying to this truth. John 17:5 the messiah speaking, "And now Father glorify thou me (1) with thine own self (1) with the glory which I (1) had **with thee** (2) before the world was." This text tells us that both the **Father and the Son** (2) preexisted time; had the glory, and made the heavens and the earth. Also, the word that became flesh (1) had to be glorified by the Father (1), who was in heaven, while the son (1) was on earth. This is the Father of which we speak. The **one (1),** eternal Father who never changes. In whom there is no variableness or shadow of turning. There is nowhere that the spirit is mention here as another God to make them three (3). The concept of three (3) is a human pretense that came out of paganism. The word God is just a title that represents two (2) or one (1), depending on usage, in context. The spirit belongs to the two (2) and also possesses us to make us one (1) with the two (2) to make us all one (1). This oneness speaks to the unity that only the true eternal God can give through their spirit. To understand the spirit usage being applied here, we must first appreciate that both God the Father and God the word are spirits. When the scripture says God is a spirit, it is referring to both the Father and the word, being or existing as spirit; "God is a spirit and they that worship him must worship him in spirit and truth. In the beginning, was the word, and the word was with God, and the Word was God. The same was at the beginning with God. All things were made by him, and without him was not anything made that was made." (John 4:24, 1:1-3.) Then the expression of God having a spirit is referring to how God operates or functions, "and the spirit of God moves upon the face of the deep." (Gen. 1:2.)

  Further corroboration is needed. Therefore, we listen to the messiah again. In the story of the rich young ruler, we notice something exceptional regarding the present subject of controversy. Was it really one God that was in heaven while the messiah was on earth, or were there two? If this is so, this will clearly reveal to us that there is only the Father and the Son as God, and their spirit that is not God, but the spirit of God. This means we have God the Father and God the word, and their spirit, which is described as the spirit of God, the spirit of the two, and not another God. Let's see if the messiah confirms this. To be sure, let's transcribe this text message.

(Matt.19: 16-17.) "And behold one came and said unto him, 'Good master, what good thing shall I do, that I may have eternal life?' And he said unto him, 'why call thou me good? There is none good, but one that is God: but if thou wilt enters into life, keep the commandments."

What! Hold on a minute!!, stop the train!!!, this is huge!!!!

 If we look carefully, we notice that the question is asked of the messiah by the rich young ruler; "what do I need to do to be saved?" He also addressed the messiah as 'good.' Interestingly, the messiah would first take time out to address this misunderstanding of the rich young ruler of his (Christ) true identity as it relates to God. Clearly showing us the necessity of teaching the truth about who he was, even before salvation is introduced by him, which is very important. Therefore, to clarify his position, the messiah first corrected the young man by telling him that there is no reason to call him good. There is only one (1) that is good and that one (1) is God, the Father who is in heaven, and he, the messiah was not God, clearly showing us that there is only one (1) individual God, not two (2), while the messiah (1) was on earth as a man. This position of being God belongs only to that one (1), the Messiah was speaking of at the time. This testimony came straight from the messiah's mouth John12: 44-50. This is not a second-hand testimony of what he said but came straight from his mouth, and the words he spoke were not his words, but the Father's. This he told us through his response to the young man that there is only one being in heaven as God, while the Messiah walked this earth as flesh. **So, where was the spirit,** if there were three Gods? He would have said two in heaven, remember the Father, the spirit, and heaven are spiritual. He did not say "They" but "Him" as in one; therefore, the spirit of God is and was not considered to be a second God with the Father, by the son of God. No! Not God, but as taught by the same spirit, to be the spirit of God, as was described. This teaching is clear, and anyone who refuses this teaching and teach another, clearly has not the spirit of truth, from the true and living God. The teaching of three gods does not fit and is not consistent or congruent with the teaching of the Messiah, as seen in the biblical texts, but is of a pagan cult religious order from hell. Only the truth will set us free, by the spirit of truth. The rich young ruler refused to accept the truth and went away empty, just as many do today. If you noticed, the revelation of the Father could not be explained without the son because only through the son, the spirit of the Father came to introduce us to the Father. Anyone who tries to teach about the Father without the son is creating or introducing another God because there is no other way to know the Father, but through the son.

Chapter 52

"Is Coming"

This phrase "is coming" denotes the future. However, within the context of its usage, it expresses a twofold application. How do we know this? Well, in the prayer the messiah gave, he prayed for two sets of peoples: the disciples, and for those who will believe in him through his words and their testimonies, (John 17:20.) First, the immediate future, meaning the persons who were living in the time of the Messiah; namely, the disciples will experience this "is coming" when they will have that awakening of the new birth experience — resulting in them becoming true worshipers. That tells us that at the time they were with the messiah, they were not true worshipers. However, the messiah did not reject them. Instead, he prayed for them to have this new birth experience. (Luke 22:31-32.) We, who are one with God in the spirit, must pray for those who are on the outside of this experience. This experience happened for the disciples on the day of Pentecost after he had left, Acts 2. It states that while they were together in one accord, meaning they had decided to make their 'wrongs, right' by forgiving each other, helping each other, sharing, praying for each other, sincerely. They were just real with each other. Because the messiah had promised the spirit of the true God, and the disciples were ready to receive. The spirit of the true God came in like a mighty rushing wind and filled the house. And it came upon them and filled them. This was the start of their new beginning, the new birth they were now experiencing. The life of the disciples and those around them soon took a different turn. They became selfless; Their selfish ambitions were no more; their only desire now was to please their Lord and Father, resulting in an explosion of the fire of truth throughout their world.

Many souls changed as a result. Just on that one occasion, thousands were transformed and became true worshipers. This experience continued throughout the life of the disciples.

The others the messiah prayed for, are those who came after. We are a part of that group; those who came after the disciples, and have received the true testimonies of the disciple's account of the messiah and the messiah's account of his Father, throughout the centuries. This group today is not of a religious denominational institutional order that follows the traditions of man as the 'Jews,' or the Samaritan did in the messiah's days. Nor anyone who is living today, in any religious affiliation, who rejects the Father and the living word of God as his son. The Lamb of God, which taketh away the sins of the world. They simply do so because there is no light in them, meaning the spirit of the true God is not within them. However, the true followers of Christ are a spiritual group that is made up of the servants of God, who believe not in the traditions of religions, but in the truth in every aspect of our existence.

Therefore, by process of elimination, some will not be a part of this experience of true worshipers. And most of the religious world today is not true worshipers because most are deceived into believing religious lies and myths.

Firstly, if you do not know and understand "self," you have not the spirit of the Most, High God. If you worship anything other than the true and only living God, you do not have the spirit of the true and living God in you and is not a true worshiper. The spirit of the true God will not lead you to worship anyone or anything other than the true and living God. Consequently, if you worship a man or any created things by man, or created things of the true God, or anything of God that is not God, you are not a true worshiper of the true and living God, and cannot be.

If you teach any tradition of man or any theology that conflicts with the basic truths of the inspired words from the true God, you are not a true worshiper and cannot be.

If you support any organization that persecutes or opposes the true gospel of the true and living God, you are not of the true God and cannot be.

If your main reason for preaching is the money you get and having a comfortable living, you are of Caesar, but are not of the true God and cannot be.

If you join yourself to a people you think are of the true God, just for the association, you are not of the true God and cannot be.

If you attend these various religious schools, colleges, universities, and seminaries, just for a position and employment you will receive upon graduation, you are not of the true God and cannot be.

If you worship the spirit of the true and living God, as another God, you are not of the true and living God and have been deceived in doing so. Therefore, you are not of the true God and cannot be. The messiah did not say we should worship the spirit, **but** we should worship **in** spirit and truth. John 4:24. If you follow those that teach these errors, you are also not of the true and living God and cannot be.

The above descriptions will eliminate the majority of those who call themselves Christian as false worshipers.

So, who are the true worshipers?

The true worshipers are those who are a part of this invisible organization, which is organized by the spirit of the true and living God, in and outside of these religious bodies.

Those who seek to know who the true and living God is diligent. Just go back and look at the disciples and what they did and how they did it. We have to go back and look carefully on the testimonies of the disciples and more so on the words and life (testimonies) of the messiah, not the words of the religious leader of the day. It does not matter which religious body you belong to or affiliated with. **You have to know the truth for yourself**. The scripture explicitly states: you shall know the **truth,** and the **truth** shall set you free. It is the spirit of the Messiah and the Father in us. This is the **truth** of which we speak. It did **not** say your leaders: pastor, bishop, pope, speaker, president, or anyone else, shall know the truth, nor your leader, pastor, bishop, pope, speaker, president, or anyone else, shall set you free. It when on to state, the messiah speaking, "I am the way the **truth** and the life, no man comes to the Father, but through, or by me. It did **not** say your leader, pastor, bishop, pope, speaker, president or anyone else, is the way the truth and the life, no one comes to the Father, but through him, her or them. If anyone doesn't apply these two scriptural principles in his life, he is not and cannot be a true worshiper of the true God. No one can represent the messiah to you. Only the spirit that was sent to bear witness of the messiah (truth). Anyone who tells you he or she is representing the messiah to you, lies, and the spirit of the true and living God is not in him, and he is of the devil.

Those who have the Spirit of the true God in their lives, the spirit will lead. These people will not run around proclaiming that they are Christian, their work, which is of the spirit, speaks for them.

You do not need to say you are a vessel of the lord. If you are, then the spirit of the true and living God will be manifested in and through you, so all who need to see will see and know the works that are done in and through you.

The true worshipers are gracious, calm, consistent in well-doing. They seek not their own. Rejoice not in evil, but the truth. They are patient, kind, and longsuffering. Speaks no evil of others, but the truth. Loves their enemies, but do not trust them. They above all is dead to self; he; the 'carnal self' dies daily for the Most, High God to use them; the true self of the believers. Consequently, they fear not. Death is but a sleep to them. The threat of death is like music to their ears because it tells that they are not of this world. Therefore, the world hates them, and they know this. The same way it hated their master. (1 Corinth. 13.)

Now, the coming of this time is anticipated by those who know the true and living God. Similarly, to the statement, the messiah made in regards to his time while he was on this earth. In John 7: 1-7, we notice the messiah addressing the desire of those around him to show himself to the world. They, not knowing that this was a spiritual operation, and the messiah was not in charge of it. Similarly, in our time, this time will come, and we will not be in charge of the spiritual operations, as we are not now, but must be prepared by the spirit of God, to be used by the spirit of God for such a time as this.

Chapter 53

The truth about the sins of the church in Sodom and Gomorrah, and Nineveh

I think the expression of '**loving your enemies**' will be explained within the proper context here.

First and foremost, if you are obedient to the will of the Most, High God, you will have enemies. Being in harmony with the Father and the son, through their spirit, is the qualification for having a host of enemies, in and outside the so-called churches. (Acts 7: 51-52, John 15: 18-25, Matt. 5: 10-12.) This truth must be understood. Now the scripture state that those that are to be loved are the ones that persecute you for his namesake. Meaning they hate you because you represent him the true and living God, who they do not know, and can't see. These types are hostile toward God, but they can only see us as his representatives. Therefore, they will naturally persecute us. These are ungodly, but these are the ones we love because God is love. And as we love them, they will continue to see the Most, High through us. That does not mean you should expose yourself to their attacks, or that they necessarily will receive God. No! That would be absurd. However, if an opportunity presents itself for you to help, then, by all means, do so. Yes, we should be witnesses to the ungodly, both in and outside the churches. Matt. 5: 43-48, and Luke 6:27-36, have to be balanced with Proverbs 3: 27. After being witnesses, then the end will come.

However, on the other hand, some are not just your enemies but representatives of Satan, the arch-enemy of the true God. These are two different breeds and set of issues. These types are not ignorant of the Highest God but are indifferent towards the Highest God and his people. These types consist of the ones who have signed a pact with the devil and reject God. While the others reject God because of the pleasure of pleasing their carnal nature, above pleasing God, they do not hate because they are deceived, but hate because they have become hateful of God, the things and people of God by their own will or choices. Being children of the devil and enjoy being such. (John 8:42-44.) These are the wicked. Two stories depict these three different types.

First, we will look at those who are hateful and ungodly because they are deceived and do not know better. In the story of Nineveh, Jonah/church was sent by the Highest and compassionate God, twice, to proclaim against Nineveh for their wickedness that came up before him. You can read this in Jonah 1: 1-2, 3: 1-2. However, the people heeded the words of God, though they were ungodly in their ways because of ignorance, and the Most Compassionate God of heaven and earth had mercy and spared their lives. (Jonah 3: 4-10. Acts 17:30-31.)

Secondly, those who are hateful, ungodly, and wicked, because they by nature seek to do evil, and are not taught the truth. Notwithstanding, there is also a twist in the story of Sodom and Gomorrah, of which most Christians are ignorant, or they pretend it is not there and think that will make it go away.

In that account, God wanted to hear praises from his people; however, he listened to the cry of the wicked the rebellious sinners instead. Similar to Adam not giving the praise God required, therefore God had to come looking for his people to implement measures to correct the situation.

In Gen. 18, we see the Lord and two angels visiting Abraham. In verse 16, we see the interest is directed toward Sodom. We realize that God has come down in response to the sinful evil cry of Sodom and Gomorrah. God tells Abraham what he is going to do because God knows that Abraham can be trusted. Abraham being a friend, tried to plea for the righteous (Christian) in the city. Note carefully, both Abraham and the Lord expected that there were righteous honest people (church) in the cities. These were Church folks today who claim the position of righteousness. He was able to ask God to extend his mercy on the cities if ten righteous or Christian were found there, starting from fifty. God, the Highest agreed.

How are you, as a Christian righteous in your living? Are you trying to introduce righteousness in truth to those around you who need to see? Or do you think that just being branded as a Christian is enough?

The twist is that God wanted to save Sodom and Gomorrah if only he could find fifty righteous Christians (church) folks, he even went down to ten, because of Abraham's love towards the people. Abraham being familiar with these Christians (church), realized that they do a lot of talking, but no living, so he tried to negotiate with the All-Knowing One. Some of these Christians might not have been involved directly with the sexual immoralities within the cities, but they were sure greedy for the temporal wealth coming from it, and would suppress the truth of preaching (living) against sin, because of fear of not getting, or losing the

264

government checks and exemption status they so eagerly enjoyed. They value these benefits more than the precious souls of these people in sin. They were sent to do a work of exposing the truth to these doomed souls, but failed and became doomed themselves. Is it also possible that they walk around with the name "church member" or "remnant" but might have been so jealous, covetous, hateful, and deceived by gains, to the point of becoming comfortable or greedy for what they saw around them? Lot's wife is an indication of those whose minds are so captivated by the offerings of this life; they can't live without it. Therefore, they try to blend in with the crowd, which is the religious churches of the world then, and now, their nature has not changed.

What about those who act like Christian only when they are in church on Sabbaths or Sundays? There were probably those hating the others involved, but not living a righteous life themselves. Similar to the Pharisee accusing the publican, but not living for God. Luke 18: 10, see also Ephesian 5:1-12, Rev. 21:8. These are the enemies of God that we are warned against. Those who refuse to present the truth because of temporal benefits are wolves in sheep's cloning. Matt.7:15. Not the ungodly, the ungodly are true to their ways; they are not hypocritical; they not only tell but live their unrighteous lives knowingly and unknowingly of the consequences. However, these so-called Christians or righteous today who are ready to condemn others, while they are living contrary to righteousness, are worst, compared to the ones they condemn and shall be judge first, by the same judgment they administered. (Matt. 7:2.) They are also considered wicked by God, and are the wolves in sheep cloning we are warned against. These wicked know of God but live a lie. The ungodly do not know God and are true to their nature.

Think about God as an investor, investing in a place like Sodom and Gomorrah. Religious Christians would say God would not dare do such a thing, that thought would be preposterous. Guess what? That is, believe it or not, what God did because he wanted to save these wicked cities. (Gen. 18: 26.) God invested fifty into Sodom and Gomorrah, which is forty-nine more than what was invested in Nineveh; Ninety-Nine percent. This tells how interested God was in the salvation of these wicked cities. This fifty is considered a hundred percent by investors. Therefore, when God asked Abraham for the fifty, he was only asking for the capital he invested to save the cities, not the interest. If only those of Lot's house (Christians) remained faithful, he would have saved these wicked cities.

If we were to think this through, anyone who invests in any business is looking, usually for a return on investment: capital plus interest. If we know that there will not be a return, we will not invest in such. Therefore, after the maturity date has passed, we are almost hoping there is a profit. Now, if we should ask for our investment and are told that out of the fifty, there might be just ten left, what would you do? You might blow a fuse, considering that ten of fifty is only twenty percent, which is an eighty percent loss. That is a failed investment in our minds. However, God invested in them anyway. This tells that God would have saved Sodom and Gomorrah even on an eighty percent loss on his investment. Meaning God was willing to lose all of these of his people to save the cities of Sodom and Gomorrah. That is what real love is, and everyone needs to experience this love.

Now the kicker, however, is, that those he was relying on as salt to this part of the earth, lost their savor because not even fifty percent of the ten was found, which is a mere one-tenth of the total. So, if the salt lost its' zest, then what do you think will happen? Consequently, there is only one thing to do with such salt. (Matt 5:13.) And if the salt does not stand a chance, then what of the others? Christian be warned; do not judge, but live because God's moral laws and principles do not change and will not change for anyone.

Another demonstration of God's principles is demonstrated in the parable of the three servants receiving their gifts. The servant who received one represents the wicked servants who pretend to be on God's side but is slothful and wicked. Knowing the will of God, but refused to be obedient to God. They shall perish with the ungodly who remain in their ways. (Matt. 25:14-30.) The man at the wedding also depicts this group without the wedding garment. Matt.22:1-13. This tells us that having access to the kingdom of God, and thinking we can attain it by our own self-righteousness is a defeated effort already.

Interestingly, the three servants were doing an excellent job of being servants of the master while he was present. So much so that the master would even think of blessing them with not just more responsibilities, but gave them free rein to use these gifts as they see fit. That tells us that they all were proficient in their jobs as servants. Therefore, taking care of our basic needs is like being a servant, which is comparable to our nine to five job, situation, or whatever arrangement we have to make a living. However, the extra time we have on our hands, what do we do with that time? This time is relatable to the time the servants got to use these gifts.

Consequently, what you do with your extra time will determine which of the servants you are. Are you using your gifts during those times, or are you sitting on them? I want us to notice that each was given more, as his abilities were able to manage. Therefore, there was no excuse to be inconsistent with their work. Their performance now was not dependent on what they were taught as servants, as their natural talents would show, but their spiritual God-given gifts. Many of us have been given many gifts, and some probably just one, but no one has an excuse not to use these gifts. The master who gives these gifts is expecting a return on these gifts when he comes back. Have you been using, or sitting on your gifts? By the way, going to church to worship is not a gift here, within the context of usage. These gifts are natural and spiritual abilities and blessings, apart from our necessary provisions and needs met. So, what have you done and are doing with the master's gifts that you have?

The cursing of the Fig tree, in Mark 11: 12-15, was a literal act with a symbolic meaning, also a warning to us the servants. The fig tree appeared to be of fruit, and the messiah being hungry sought to be refreshed by eating a fig. However, the tree had no fruit and proved to be worthless. Consequently, the messiah cursed the tree, by saying, "No man will eat of this tree anymore." Shortly after, they entered into Jerusalem, the messiah went into the temple and began to cast them out that sold in the temple with the money changers. And would not allow any man to carry any vessel through the temple. Then he began to teach, saying, "Is it not written," he said to them, "My house shall be called of all nations the house of prayer, but you have made it a den of thieves?" Now those who allowed these commercial activities, the scribes and the Pharisees, heard what he had done and sought how they might destroy him. (Matt. 7: 28.) Interestingly, the condition of the tree and the temple displeased the messiah. They both appeared to have something to refresh, and they should; however, upon closer inspection, they fail miserably in their functions.

Remember also the messiah telling the disciples that he was refreshed because of sharing the living world with the woman at the well. (John 4:31-34.) Likewise, the temple was supposed to be a house where weary souls could be able to come and be refreshed of the living word through testimonies, praising, and prayer. Rather, like today, the churches are places of commercial activities, and the weary souls are left unrefreshed and have become worse than when they came in. (Matt. 23: 13-17.) These churches are the wicked ones who pretend to be what they are not. You see, the house of God should not be a place of personal business achievements for anyone or an organization, but a place of prayer and praise for all, to the Most, High eternal God. Neither should the servant be a person of idleness, slothfulness, or laziness, but of productivity and growth both physically and spiritually for God's purposes.

Similarly, Sodom and Gomorrah should have become a place of prayer, praises, and admiration to the Most, High God, by those who called themselves Christians, living there as witnesses. At least ten should have been there doing so if not fifty, then the praises of the righteous should have been heard by God, and not the cry of the wicked.

 What of America, and the world?

The failure of those who were to represent God was the main reason for the destruction of Sodom and Gomorrah. Those who claimed to be of the household of the Most, High God, failed in their purpose to reflect the image of God to their neighbors. If you are the salt of the earth and you have lost your savor, then how will the earth be salted? And how can you be light if this light is not seen? (Matt. 5:13-16.) Remember, we are not called to condemn, but to represent God's righteous ways to a sin-sick world. Most so-called Christians are eager to condemn, while not serving through living the gospel themselves.

Note also the parable of the three servants. (Matt. 25: 14-30.) In this parable, these servants were given the master's goods as their abilities were able to manage. One got five, one got two, and the other got one. Then the master went away for a long time, given them enough time to established and apply their talents as best as possible. After coming back from his trip, each servant came and presented what he had done with the master's goods. The first brought an additional five talents to the five he got. The second brought a further two with the two he got. However, it is most interesting how the third responded to the master. He came back complaining to the master about the master! Are you kidding me!!! The gall he had!!! Saying that his master is a hard man reaping where he had not sown and gathered from where he had not invested. This was indeed a strange way to make an excuse for being slothful and lazy. It is rather pleasant to see the response of the master to this servant's stupidity and wickedness. He used the same judgment; the wicked servant had used against him, toward the servant. Therefore, he was stripped of the gift and was cast out into utter darkness.

This parable also has significant application to the condition of Sodom and Gomorrah. In that, God does not look for a return on something that he has not first invested in. God had invested the household of Lot into Sodom and Gomorrah and knew there should be a return of fifty and by extension of mercy, at least ten. It is then evident that Sodom and Gomorrah did not use the gift that God had given them through Lot and his family, or the family failed in representing God to them. Now the big question: Did God destroyed the cities of

Sodom and Gomorrah, because of the sins within, or because of the failure of those who professed to know him, not sharing the truth of him with their neighbors through their lives as testimonies in the cities?

I contend that the latter is the case. The scripture states that those who know the truth and refuse to do the truth are worst, yes, then the unbeliever. (James 4:17, 1 Tim. 5:8.) Meaning that those who came to Sodom and Gomorrah, from the family of Abraham, the spiritual church father, had a responsibility to present the gospel of that day to these people. However, they did not; therefore, both the wicked and the ungodly all perished together, as they were now considered to be just like them, if not worst.

How do we know that God invested in these wicked cities?

Well, in Gen. 13, we saw the separation of Abraham and Lot, his nephew. They separated because they were both blessed with great substance, workers, and family. Therefore, when Lot left and pitched his tent toward Sodom, he took his content and workers with him: a blessing from God. We can, therefore, deduce that there were many people with Lot when he moved, at least more than his family members. So, the questions are: Did the culture around them assimilate them? Did they give up the God they knew? Did they become more progressive, modern, educated, liberal-minded in their thinking, or conservative in their ways towards God? Why were they not able to influence the heathen, but instead was influenced by the pagans? And what of the so-called Christians today, living in modern-day Sodom and Gomorrah?

Now, in Genesis 19, we see the two angels entering Sodom at even. Lot, while sitting in the gate of Sodom, sees them and greeted them as Abraham did. The fact that Lot was sitting at the entrance indicates he had influence in the city or even possibly a part of the government. He invited them to stay at his place for the night and then leave early in the morning, but they refused to do so and stated that they would remain in the streets. Lot, knowing of the evil that permeates the city pleaded with them. They finally heeded and when into his house, and had a feast. However, before they could lay down to sleep, all the men of the city summon Lot to let the men out, so they can rape them. At this, Lot went outside and shut the door behind him so that he could reason with those demon-possessed men. (Men who rape women are also demon-possessed) He tried to pass his daughters to them, who were virgins, but they attacked Lot accusing him of playing a judge while being a sojourner, foreigner, or immigrant.

They then came upon the door as they pushed lot aside; however, the angels inside Lot's house put forth their hands and pull lot into the house and shut the door, then cause blindness to fall on the men outside. At this time, Lot is told by these angels to gather all his family and leave at once, as the city will be destroyed. Because the noise or sins of the wicked city has waxen great before the Lord, and he has sent them to destroy it.

Those who professed to be of God should not allow the roar of the wicked to be above the cry of the righteous.

This was the downfall of Sodom and Gomorrah, the "Fake Christian" was not living for God and crying to God enough, but were rather busy prospering and having a good time, under pretense.

(I know there were no so-called Christian there at the time; however, most Christian today fall right there in that position as Lot and his family, especially those from other countries, who should know better, who are now living in modern Sodom and Gomorrah. When you were in your country living for God, the relationship with him was great, but you were drawn away to the pleasant land that looked like it was flowing with milk and honey, as was Lot. However, now that you are here, you have forgotten about having that close relationship with God but have become assimilated to the customs and culture of your new church and government. And now you are just living it up, with no cares in the world, just doing your thing and accepting the wickedness done by your church and government. Still going to church, but the relationship with God is dead.)

In this case, was it that the wicked were destroyed because they did not know better, but because their nature had become so perverted to the point, where they have literally refused to have anything to do with the God of mercy they knew not, as their minds had become seared as with a hot iron? (1 Timothy 4: 1, 2.) Or was It that the righteous Christians' (Lot's household) were responsible for having interceded and witness to the people of the city without judging, had failed miserably? Our righteous love (Agape) is the only spiritual antidote that can only restrain the wicked, and God is unable to draw them by his mercy and this love if we have not shown the gospel in love, for that to happen. (Love here does not mean condoning with, but teaching the truth and allowing change. Similar to the cases of the woman at the well and Jonah.

However, those who professed to have known God, and would call themselves Christians or followers today, should have been righteous enough so that God could have extended his mercy to the wicked city, because of his presence in his people there. Unfortunately, there were not enough righteous Christian to stay the judgment of the Most, High God on Sodom and Gomorrah. Will it be the same today, when the Most, High God revisits this earth? (2 Timothy 3. Rev.21:8.) Are you a homophobic Christian, who is also afraid of liars, fornicators, murders, backbiters, adulterers, etc. Did you not know that fear is of the devil and is a fruit of that same tree? Or are you a son of God endowed with the gospel power of truth, without fear or favor of anyone or circumstance; who spread the Agape love to all by obedience to God. That, there, is truth and righteousness, without compromise. (2 Tim. 1:7, 1 John 4:18.)

In 2nd Timothy 3, Romans 1, Galatians 5. we can visualize in our minds these two trees that bear all manner of fruits unique to their own kind. The first tree is rooted in sin, and carries these fruits: lovers of their own self, covetous, boasters, proud, blasphemers, disobedient to parents, unthankful, unholy, without natural affection, trucebreaker, fierce, despisers of those that are good, traitors, heady, high minded, lovers of pleasure more than lovers of God, having a form of godliness, but denying the truth, ever-learning, but knows not truth, foolish, changing the truth of God into a lie, worshiping the creature than the creator, leaving the natural use of a woman and lusting after another man, taking God out of their knowledge to do evil, filled with fornication, wickedness, maliciousness; full of envy, murder, debate, deceit, malignity; whisperers, backbiters, haters of God, despiteful, inventors of evil things, without understanding, covenant-breakers, implacable, unmerciful, adultery, uncleanness, lasciviousness, witchcraft, variance, emulations, wrath, strife, seditions, heresies, drunkenness, reveling, etc.

The other tree is rooted in righteousness and bears all manner of fruit unique to is kind, such as: knowing the scripture through experience, by the faith of Christ, love, joy, peace, longsuffering, gentleness, goodness, faith, meekness, temperance, etc. Of which root are you, the fruit of your actions will show.

We can't hide the fact that the entire household of Lot perished with the evil city, except for his two daughters and himself. This tells us the rest of his house suffered the same fate as that of the wicked cities. Neither can we ignore the fact that the ultimate reason for the destruction of the wicked cities was not just the wickedness that was in the cities, but mainly the absence of righteous fruit in the lives of those who claimed to be virtuous; who were in the cities, that God depended on to represent him. Those who claimed to be God's representatives showed themselves not to be a part of the solution, but of the problem, which simply meant they were also a part of the wickedness in the cities. Christians, be careful you do not compromise the truth, for the love of money, the things of this world, and its association.

We are not here to judge anyone as we are not the judges of anyone, as the messiah showed us by example in act and speech; he did not judge. (John 8: 15-16, Matt. 7:1-5.) However, we are entrusted with the word of the Highest God to present the truth of his word, to this sin-cursed world, and ourselves as a living sacrifice to God, holy and acceptable unto him. Being a living sacrifice for the highest God includes representing the truth of the gospel through our lives without condemning others, even if the world does not like it. We live to please God rather than man. The laws of man do not have the same high standard as the laws of the Most, High God, and should not be considered as equal. Civilian laws are laws that are created by men for his limited civil capacity to rule over himself within his limited jurisdiction. However, Moral laws are laws that are created by God and is verified by his creation in the principles of the universe, and of man in all of his ways, in every place, he is found. Therefore, the civil laws of men are subjugated to the righteous moral laws of God, with no exceptions.

The problem with Martin Luther's attempt for equal rights for the blacks was, it appealed to the limited capacity of the constitutional civil laws that were instituted for those who drafted them; for themselves and their offspring, which by the way was not civil in its constitution to all, but barbaric to most whereas the basis of his premise should have been on the transcendental moral laws of the Most, High God. Therefore, the movement that the real church of God will engage in is the moral rights movement that has no political affiliations and will not be looking for a handout from the government.

The racist natural selection bigots might have also looked at the bible text messages in Heb. 2:6-8, and Psalms 8:4-7, and then concluded that the natural man is not a total man, but a fraction of a man, liken to a beast of burden not fully developed. By this demonic perspective, they were able to construct a racist structure that lingers still today, resulting in problems such as immigration issues, treating other people as animals without human rights, and stealing others' resources with their neo-colonialism strategies. By practicing this demonic behavior, they the racist think they are the owner of the world while imagining themselves as better, but we know better than.

The constitutional attempt to express the above text messages was abused by those possessed by demons but should have been corrected by the church, which has failed miserably again, because of its alliance to this demonic racist system of government, which makes the church a political-religious institution, and not of God.

It is interesting to note that all those in Sodom and Gomorrah, the evildoers, those who profess to be Christians but were not living witnesses, and those who lived in open rebellion towards God both perished because of their hatred towards God. I hope you notice that only three of Lot's family (Christians) were saved, including himself, out of a household of at least fifty, which is only six percent. And now we see how desperate his daughters had become. In Genesis 19: 31-38. If you notice, their thought pattern was not after the manner of the world they knew. To them, men refused to go in unto them and lay with them because of the rebellious nature that existed toward God. (Romans 1:18-32.) , they were taught and knew was not the norm on the earth, verse 31; however, they also became weakened by the environment and association they were in, which led them to defile the law of God by laying with their dad. Lev. 18. Another distortion of God's natural laws, moving from one extreme to the next.

It would be an insult to God if the earth that Christians dwell on today should now think that these abominations have become acceptable to God. They, the Christians, would also have to be destroyed by God, because of the absence of righteousness in their lives and not just the presence of wickedness around them. If those who call themselves Christian, and, or followers of the Most, High God refuse to present the truth in love, even if it goes against man's civil laws, they also are guilty of rebellion towards God and will suffer damnation. I believe that the civil laws that are enacted to protect every right of the citizenry should be applauded; however, it is the responsibility of the righteous to present the gospel truth in love to all, regardless, while respecting the freedom of all.

Now the gospel is the life of Christ being replicated in us. We have to remember also that the gospel was and is the life of Christ. In the Old Testament, the introduction of the gospel was given through the sacrificial system of teaching and obedience to the laws of God, including the ceremonial laws. In our present time, the introduction to the gospel is through the sacrifice of Christ for the sins of the world, a transition from the ceremonial back to the moral through our lives, living the way Christ lived.

We saw in the Old Testament, the sacrificial system, the gospel in symbolism in the rituals, leading to Christ. While in the New Testament, we see the actual sacrifice of Christ, which points to his life as the gospel of salvation through actualism in us. John was the forerunner of the gospel, John 1:2-34, bearing witness to this gospel, not just in words but in his living. We are the forerunners of

Christ returning as King, bearing witness in our lives as holy royal and peculiar righteous citizens of the kingdom of God, bearing witness to the gospel. However, Christ did not condemn anyone, and we should not, either, but our lives should show the difference.

In Rev.3: 14-19, this text speaks to the three categories of people's relationships towards God. First the cold, which are the ungodly, then the hot, which are the righteous, and lastly the lukewarm, which are the wicked servants; he who knows to do right, but do not; to him, it is a sin, regardless of how he thinks his relationship is with God. The same servant who got his one talent and did nothing with it is likened to the wicked servant who went to the wedding feast without the proper garment and was cast out.

The above arguments only apply to those who believe that there is a real God, and these were real places and people that were judged for their sins, referring to Sodom and Gomorrah. If you do not believe there was a righteous God, and a wicked Sodom and Gomorrah that existed then and exist today, that was destroyed then and will be destroyed again, because of their immorality, ungodliness, wickedness, and perversions, this might not apply to you. Only the Highest God can be the judge of that. Those of you with this inclination will have to have a personal encounter with the Highest God, and we pray that God might have mercy on your precious souls.

A question to the Christians who think they hold the keys to heaven: In Luke 23: 39-43, we see two persons hanging on their crosses on both sides of Christ. If they were both from Sodom and Gomorrah and were charged for the sins of those cities, speaking the same words to Christ as the thieves did, what would Christ say to each, would he say the same things he said to those thieves?

Chapter 54

"Is Spirit"

This expression is off times misunderstood and taught wrong because of the traditional false teaching of man. The conventional school of thought in the religious world is this expression speaks to the third person of the godhead. Most people who believe this erroneous school of thought will attempt to tell others that "the Holy Spirit" is another God, and as such, this text message proves to them that there is another God, which would make them into three Gods. We will investigate this subject further in another book.

However, what We will be doing here is explaining the correct understanding and usage of this expression in this text message. The text message states, "the time is coming and now is that the true worshiper will worship in spirit and truth. Because; God seeks such to worship him. God **is a spirit,** and they that worship him must worship him in spirit and truth. "

We have established before that the term "God" is a title that refers to the ultimate position of supremacy. This term can be ascribed to any and everything we want to attribute it to. We make that determination by 'worshiping' that thing, person, or persons. God has given the man that right. However, this right should encourage man to have a desire to worship the true and living God alone. To Worship is to give total credence and homage to something or someone alone. However, that pronouncement has certain limitations. Meaning that whatever we make as gods other than God, can only do so much and no more; they're limited. These objects of our devotions are ultimately powerless and can't help us at all. Our religion and emotions will tell us that these gods are helping us; however, as soon as our emotion changes, our gods also change if we are giving homage to the wrong God. Therefore, these are the projected gods of our own imaginary making. There is only one true God, who is spirit. If we do not ascribe this position of supremacy, to the one and only true God, then we are not of his. (The terms "his" and "them" are used interchangeably, meaning the same; "his" referring to the title: God, and "them" referring to the beings; the ancient of Days that sat on his throne, and the word that became the lamb) (Daniel 7:9, Rev.4:1-11, 5:6. John 1:1-3, 14, 4-5.)

We can go back to the book of Exodus, where Israel was rebuked by the one and only true God, because of their open rebellion against God. They were not to have any other gods before "him." (Exodus 20: 1-7.) This tells us that there can be other gods. If the one and only true Gods acknowledge this, who are we to deny it?

There were many gods in Egypt that the children of the true God were exposed to. They started worshiping many of these gods. (Exodus 32: 1-6. 1 King 11: 4. 12: 27-33.) These acts were abominable toward the one true God of Israel. (Ezekiel 8:14.) In 1 John 5: 21, we are clearly instructed by the servant of the Most, High God, to stay clear of other Gods, all idols included. The holy word tells us why we should. In 1 Cor.10: 19-20, it explains that though the Idols are nothing, no life in them, and the services are meaningless; however, by participating in these acts, you do fellowship with the devil. Therefore, wherever: Homes, Synagogues, Churches, temples, or Mosques, you see an Idol, and you worship it; you are paying homage to the devil. Even to those statues, they call Christ and Mary. (1 Chron. 16:26.)

These blasphemous acts of worshiping of these false gods, all had several things in common. First, they have to be made by man or perceived and conceptualized from a storyline by demon-possessed minds. Meaning again, they are limited. There is no life in them, and they can't look after themselves, if not attended to, they would fade away into nothingness. They were and are lifeless. This act is also a total defiance of God's law not to have any other gods or graven images before him. (Ex. 20:3-5.)

However, limited they are, there are enough evil influences behind them to distract the people from the true and living God and captivate the minds. The one thing that stands out most about these gods is they all have to be made or conceptualize into something to be seen by sinful men. But the true and living God cannot be seen by sinful man. Because God is Spirit and only Spirit can 'see' spirit. Meaning only a spiritual man can be able to look through a spiritual eye to "see" the true and living God, who is spirit. This word "see" here means to understand and appreciate. (1 Cor. 2: 9, 10.)

Now we need to know the difference between the spirit of the true and living God and what is called a ghost. The spirit of the true God belongs to the true God of the universe. The messiah comes walking on water towards his disciples. They, the disciples, because of their ignorance impregnated with superstitions, thought he was a ghost. The messiah corrected them by declaring that he was not. (Matt. 14: 22-27.)

Ghosts are the antics of the devil, or what we call an apparition. He uses his evil spirits to impersonate the dead and the living. The disciples seemed to be aware of this Spiritism. By the declaration of the Messiah, that he was not a spirit or ghost, tells us that he also acknowledges that evil spirits do exist.

In the account of King Saul and the witch of Endor. (Samuel 28: 3-25.) In this account, many people genuinely believe this was actually Samuel; unfortunately, even Christians do; however, that is not so. The messiah testified to this at his death. Just as he died, he committed his spirit to God. Therefore, all spirits of man go back the God from which they came, upon death as we see in the death of the messiah. (Luke 23:46.)

Two spiritual things happen within, upon the time of death, because there are two spirits within a holy man; the spirit of man and the spirit of God. (1 Cor. 2:11, Romans 8:16. 2 Cor. 4:16-18.) First, the spirit of God leaves the man. There is no more need to be in this container of flesh: man. When the messiah cried out the first time, "my God, My God, why has thou forsaken me?" this was about the spirit of God that had left him. (Psalm 22, Matt. 27:46-50.) Then he cried again, the second time "into thy hand I commit my spirit" Luke 23: 44-46, he was now talking about the spirit of the man, his spirit, which he had in him. He recognized that the body was retiring back to its lifeless state, nonfunctional form. With the absence of the spirit of God, there is no need to live there anymore. Why stay? So, Christ understood this. It was more than Christ just dying of a broken heart, as some would have you think. No! He understood that the absence of the spirit of God in him renders his body useless, except as a sacrifice for sin, as demanded by the law, and he gave it up willingly. That is a truth that cuts to the core of my being, just thinking about it. We are nothing without the spirit of God in us, but because of the love he gave us through his son, we are worthy to be called children of the Most, High God. When we understand this, we would rather die than live without the spirit of the Highest God in us also. He knew he had to give his life for our redemption. He volunteered to give his life. As he was hanging on the cross, his human life source was leaving his body: the blood from his side. The spirit of God had left him. While still being consciously aware of his state, what else could he do but commend his spirit, the spirit of the man, to the one who is the giver and keeper of the spirits of life? (2 Cor. 4:16-18. Eccl. 12:7.) That was the best way to go. If we notice that there is a "thy spirit" and a "my spirit," acknowledging that there is a difference between the two, one belongs to God, and the other was given to the man Christ, as is given to every man by God. Therefore, both spirits dwelt in Christ as in every son of God. We see Stephen testifying to this truth also in Acts 7:59.

Remember, only spirits can exist in the spiritual realms. That is where the true and living God dwells. That is where some call heaven. Therefore, the true and living God is a spirit, meaning he exist as a spirit, while man exists as flesh, but the true God exists as the spirit within man also, while man has a spirit of himself which was given by God. (Romans 8:16, 1 Cor. 2:11-16.)

In heaven, the Ancient of days did sit on his throne. What is the true God? He is a spirit. The Lamb of God, who was able to broke the seals, stood in his presence. He also is a spirit, being in the presence of the Ancient of Days in heaven, who is spirit. Also, for John to have witnessed this great revelation, he had to have been caught up in the spirit to appreciate these spiritual things in this spiritual place. (Rev. 1:10, 4:2.) Meaning that the spirit of the man John was caught up in heaven to witness these spiritual things.

Now, if we were to follow human logic, there would be three spirits, counting the spirits of the three Gods, one spirit for each God. Then there would be six gods. Then the human logics would not stop there, because each spirit would be another God that would result in many spirits with more gods that would continue to increase exponentially. But this is not so; there is only one spirit that belongs to the two Gods: The Father and the son. This spirit is also given to us to become one with the two, through the same one spirit, having the mind of Christ. (1 Cor. 2: 9-16. John 17: 1-26.)

We have to remember also that the word states: that there are only one spirit and one lord. (Eph. 4:4, 5.) This is why the word had to have come into flesh to dwell as a man, with man; to make man one with the Father again. Therefore, the word which was a spirit, which was one with God, as God is a spirit, before coming into the man. Please remember that the term "God" here is used as a title.

The same way the word was spirit before coming into the man is the same way the true God the Father "is a spirit" but has never changed. There is no change or variableness in him. The same yesterday, today, and forever. (James 1:17.)

That is why we must worship him in spirit because he "is a spirit." And Spiritual things can only be spiritually discerned. To worship the true and living God who is Spirit. The worshipers have to be spiritual, by the indwelling spirit of the true God, being in them also. By having the indwelling Spirit of God in us, we are taught of the living God. By these teachings, we are now able through the spirit to approach the true God in reverence and truthfulness of heart. Then and only then can we start to worship in spirit and truth. Any other teaching on worship is fake and will not be accepted by the Most Eternal Father and true God of all, because he is a spirit, and this is the desire of the true and living God towards us. The living God wants to be one with us again, and can only be one with us in spirit. The way he intended before. Then we will be able to worship in spirit and truth. (John 16:32.)

When we experience this sweet fellowship with the true and living God, as Christ did, there will be nothing in the universe to replace that throughout eternity. That is when heaven lights up earth, and the glory of the living God is seen through us. Then the true gospel of truth will be lived out in our lives as a faithful witness to all the earth, then and only then shall the end come. Even so, come Most High and Holy One. (Matt. 24:14.)

Chapter 55

The sweet summary.

As we have seen, there are two spirits in every man. The conscious essence of man is his spirit, and the conscious essence of the presence of God is his spirit. (Gen. 2:7, 1 Cori 2:11, 1 Cori. 3:16. Romans 8: 14, 16)

Similarly, there are two Gods, in the universe and one spirit of these Gods, as taught by the inspired scripture. (John 1:1, John 17:5, John 14:16-20, Romans 8:9.) The spirit of God and the spirit of Christ is the same one spirit that dwells in us, who are called by him, that make us one. (John 16:13-15, 17: 17-26.)

The expression "God is a spirit" speaks to the existence of God in his true essence. How he exists. (John 1:1, 14, John 4:24.)

The expression "God has a spirit" speaks to the functions of God, how God operates. Through what medium. (Gen. 1:2, 1 Cor. 2:9-16.)

Similarly, man being flesh speaks to his existence of being flesh. (Gen. 2:23.) And he also functions in the flesh, by his true essence, which is spirit. As a man, the spirit of man functions in the limited capacity of his body; similarly, the spirit of God functions in the vastness of the universe and beyond.

Also, the expression of "man has a spirit," 1 Cor. 2:11, speaks to the movement or function of man by the spirit that is within man. The spirit of man functioning in the flesh. (1 John 4:1-4.) His spirit is also working in harmony with the spirit of God in him. (Romans 8:16.)

The word "God" is a title; this title is ascribed to the Father and the word, as stated in the scripture, but never to the spirit. This title is attributed to the Father at all times, but not to the son by the Father or the son after he was now in the likeness of fallen flesh. Romans 8:3. However, having been reinstated to the Father as one with the Father, not anymore like a fallen man. He is now once again with the Father as God. (Exodus 20: 3-7, Romans 14:11, Mark 10:18. Rev. 5:13, John 16:27, 28) However, the spirit of God is never referred to as God the spirit, but the spirit of God.

Remember also that man is flesh in existence. (Gen. 2:7, 23.)

However, the redeemed man functions with two spirits within; the spirit of God and the spirit of man, working in harmony. (1 Cor. 2:11. Romans 8:16.)

When the spirit of man is in harmony with the spirit of God, man has become one with God. (Romans 8: 1-16.)

The Father and the Son are one because they possess the same spirit. (John 14: 6-20. 16: 15, 21, 23.)

The Father, the Son, and the redeemed are one because we all possess the same spirit. (John 16: 7-15, 17:17.)

The son of God came, lived, and died to bring rebellious man back into harmony with God, in oneness by the indwelling Spirit of God in man. (Romans 8: 8-11. John 17: 20-22.)

Therefore, to worship "in Spirit" is to be of one mind with the Eternal God, as we live from day to day, having the mind of Christ. 1Cor. 2: 16.

The giver of life is Spirit

God the Father is spirit   +   God the word is a spirit

The son of God was flesh

There is one spirit of both the 'Father' and the 'son.'

Which is the spirit of God

The spirit is available to his true followers

This

makes us, "One." With God: the ancient of days and the word

Epilogue

"Seeks" equals "Love."

There are three times that the word, "seeks" is used in the text message here, to indicate the importance in action by the true and living God towards man, and man towards the true and living God.

We have established before that the word 'God' is a title that belongs to both the Ancient of days and the word. The interesting thing is, both the Father and the son have something that they seek. Also, man has something that the father seeks.

We see in the conversation that the messiah told the woman that the Father "seeks" something from the man, which is true worship, that we have been emphasizing: which is worship that is in Spirit and truth, which is the most essential thing in the relationship from the true and living God to man.

We also see the messiah as a man, sought to do the will of the Father. (John 4:34.) The most important thing in their relationship; from the son to the Father. Doing the will of the Father was the delight of the son. He was always in readiness to heed the Father's voice. David captures this eloquently when he stated, "I delight to do thy will, o my God: yea, thy law is within my heart." (Psalm 40:8)

This would indicate that the law of God has to be in the heart (mind) of man before he can do the will of the Father. Hence, the transforming of the mind; having the mind of Christ, 1 Cor. 2: 16 is a spiritual work of God through the spirit, by the son. (John 16:13-14.)

In the relationship from a man to the true and living God, the most critical element is a man "seeking first the kingdom of the true and living God and his righteousness and all things shall be added to him." For the man to do so, he has to know himself, first, from man to the true God. (Matt. 6:33.) This knowing also includes man fearing God and giving glory to him.

Interestingly, all these things that are promised to man now were given to him in the beginning before he sinned.

Therefore, if the man had everything because of the relationship he had with the true and living God then, it goes to prove how important that intimacy; worship is between the true and living God and the man now. This is the only way for man to have everything that was made for him again. Man will never come to his full potential or enjoy everything that was prepared for him, without first having that relationship with the true and living God, while on earth, let alone heaven. So, seeking to do the will of the kingdom of the living God is man's priority. And what is the true God's kingdom will? The same will that man started with before sin. And that is worshiping the true and living God in spirit and truth. This is the ultimate will of the Father in his relationship with the man. This worship is not a religious exercise but a daily living reflection of the intimate relationship between man and God.

Now to seek something shows that there is a need, and the true God needs this kind of intimate relationship for man to reflect his image. If we were to say the true and living God has a need, this would be the only need that the living God has towards us. Not that God cannot exist without man, but rather that man can't exist without God, and God made man so he can exist with him.

This can only be demonstrated by using a love relationship between a man and a woman who both love each other.

For that relationship to thrive and all the benefits realized, some essential elements have to be woven into the fabric of that relationship.

Let's take a look at a number of these:

There is a need for *companionship*; we need to be with each other. When you are in love, you have this need to be with the person you love. Even if it is to be in the same room.

There is a need for *affection.* It will show that we still value being with each other. There is never too much affection that can be given or received in such a relationship.

There is a need for *respect*. That shows we value the person as an individual. It tells that neither will take the other for granted.

Honesty is an indication that both are comfortable with each other, to the point of being vulnerable. It is something that many people, if not most people, have a problem with. I was one such person and still have some reservations with being vulnerable. However, I must say I am not where I used to be and hope to move further along, but it is a work in progress.

Freedom is enormous in a love relationship. Freedom encompasses all the other values. That is where one is free to make his or her own decisions, but chooses to involve the other. Freedom will diagnose any relationship correctly every time. If one wants not to allow the other to make his or her own decision independently, that person does not love. God shows his love by giving man the freedom to choose.

The other side will also show if the person demonstrates their freedom by making a decision contrary to the stability of the relationship. Adam chose to disobey the true and living God and rejected God's love, which brought instability to the relationship. However, with God, there is no variableness. His love is constant. Likewise, like Adam, when we abuse our freedom; we bring instability to our relationship, and destroy this gift of freedom. Some would say he traded his freedom by giving Eve the freedom to choose for him.

In the case above, neither person will be faithful, who chose not to accept their readiness for such a committed relationship. Therefore, *Maturity* is an essential element in such a relationship.

These are some of the same principles by which our relationship with the true and living God is measured on a deeper spiritual level. The living God needs somethings from us to maintain the health of this relationship. Likewise, we need somethings from God to continue this arrangement. However, the difference with the relationship between human to human, compared with human and the living God is; it takes both man and woman to take equal effort for the human relationship to be sustainable, and work. However, a relationship with the true and living God is the best, because he is the sustainer of all things. He does the initiation, the calling, and the sustaining. The only thing man takes into this relationship is his willingness to worship the Most, High in spirit and truth, doing the will of God. That is the best relationship we can ever have. There is nothing else to compare with such love. The man did not have to pay, nor does the true and living God expects the man to play an equal part. That can't be, as the eternal God did not make the man an equal partner in this relationship. Also, the man did not play an equal part before or after his redemption: he did not have to die. The Father sent his Son to die for man. "Greater love has no one than this: that a man should die for his friends" (Romans 5:10, Col. 1:21, John 15:13.) This is a love that transcends all boundaries, a love we will be studying, as we live throughout eternity.

THE TRUE GOSPEL

This is the love of the Messiah texts and tweets again.

Anyone who has read this book in its entirety is now qualified to ask me any question related to the various subjects spoken off in this book.

THE BIGGER QUESTION

After reading all of that, where do I start?

Simply by prayer and meditation each day at a specific time and place. Preferably alone with no distractions. That's where you start. The spirit will come into your heart, and lead you into all truth. All your other questions will be answered.

God Bless.

About the Author

I was born in the beautiful island of sunny Kingston, Jamaica, WI. I was born a thinker, one of curious intellect. Always wanting to find out about the who, when, why, where, what, and how of everything that interests me. As a normal boy like the others, I liked playing soccer and listening to cricket commentators, which were two of my favorite pastime activities.

My first school was Mrs. Shirly Basic School on Shortwood Rd, in Kingston, Jamaica. Then off to Marverly All-Age School. Secondary School was at Edith Dalton James and high school at Tivoli Comprehensive High School. I did some classes at Mico Teacher College Extension and Jamaica School of Music.

The arts were my first experience. As a child, I would always think outside the box of new things to draw and songs to sing. Then I became interested in numbers, so math was next in line. Accounting was another interest to follow. Civics was also on my favorite list. I worked as a payroll accountant and artist, at "Creative Endeavors" in Kingston, also as an accountant and farm supervisor at Agro-flora Ja, St. Catherine.

The writing was never, and still not, one of my favorite activities, however, I knew I had to adapt because of my fourth and fifth interests; Bible Studies and History. I became interested in bible studies while in All-Age School and was further propelled by my elders at the Shortwood Church, in particular, elder Jackson, which I became a part of during my teen years. My interest in History started in secondary school, where I was a member of the Four H Club. In High School, I was also a member of the debate club, the science club, the vice president of ISCF (Inter-School Christian Fellowship), and the unofficial chess club.

The notion of writing came about because of the many religious and biblical questions I have been processing over these many years. Unfortunately, in my experience, the churches that I thought had the answers, have either failed or refused to give honest answers to these questions, in my quest for truth.

I still believe the righteous in these churches have a moral responsibility to tell the truth to the people; however, they have failed miserably by holding in these truths that have been given to be revealed. Instead, they have become obsessed and distracted by the temporal gains of this world: the monies, associations, possessions, and positions of this world. As a result of this chronic condition, these churches have become spiritually constipated to the point of being religiously bloated and unable to function in or teach the word of truth in its body without compromising truth. (Matt. 5:13.)

That said, however, should not prevent the truth from been presented by others who have been blessed by and with it. It is, therefore, one of my many purposes to present these questions in a forum, and on a platform that can reveal the truth to the people, on these questions and concerns, without fear, favor or objection of anyone. Hence this book: "The Messiah's Tweets, and Text messages."

THANK YOU

www.ingramcontent.com/pod-product-compliance
Lightning Source LLC
Chambersburg PA
CBHW021219090426
42740CB00006B/284